CRIME ANALYSIS
and
CRIME MAPPING

CRIME ANALYSIS
·······*and*·······
CRIME MAPPING

Rachel Boba
Florida Atlantic University

SAGE Publications
Thousand Oaks ▪ London ▪ New Delhi

For information:

Sage Publications, Inc.
2455 Teller Road
Thousand Oaks, California 91320
E-mail: order@sagepub.com

Sage Publications Ltd.
1 Oliver's Yard
55 City Road
London EC1Y 1SP
United Kingdom

Sage Publications India Pvt. Ltd.
B-42, Panchsheel Enclave
Post Box 4109
New Delhi 110 017 India

Printed in the United States of America

Library of Congress Cataloging-in-Publication Data

Boba, Rachel.
Crime analysis and crime mapping / Rachel Boba.
         p. cm.
Includes bibliographical references and index.
ISBN 0-7619-3092-2 (pbk.)
    1. Crime analysis—United States. 2. Crime analysis—United States—Data processing.
3. Digital mapping—United States. 4. Geographic information systems—United States.
I. Title.
HV7936.C88B63 2006
363.25'0973—dc22   2005006693

This book is printed on acid-free paper.

05   06   07   08   09   10 9 8 7 6 5 4 3 2 1

Acquisitions Editor:	Jerry Westby
Editorial Assistant:	Laura Shigemitsu
Production Editor:	Denise Santoyo
Copy Editor:	Judy Selhorst
Typesetter:	C&M Digitals (P) Ltd.
Cover Designer:	Glen Vogel

Contents _____

Acknowledgments____

I have been eager to write this book since I was a crime analyst years ago. It has been with the assistance and support of both individuals and organizations that I have finally been able to achieve that aim. I would like to thank current and past members of the Tempe, Arizona, Police Department for taking a chance on a naive graduate student and providing me with the practical experience that has served as the foundation for all that I do today. I would also like to thank the Police Foundation for providing me a forum to work with crime analysts and police officers from around the United States and the world. Specifically, I would like to express my gratitude to Mary Velasco for her hard work and friendship and to David Weisburd for mentoring me and encouraging me to pursue this goal.

To Sean Bair, I give a special thanks for being a good friend, teaching me the basics of crime analysis, challenging me, and being a part of this book by donating his software. My thanks go as well to Erin Lane, for taking the time to review the final draft, and to Jerry Westby, Sage editor, for believing in this book and helping me through the reviews and publishing process. I would also like to thank the professionals who assisted Sage in reviewing the book in its various stages.

I would like to acknowledge my family (Bob, Jerre, Becky, Jed, Jim, and Joey) for their support and encouragement as I was writing this book. And finally, I look forward to the conversations over glasses of red wine that will inspire me to achieve even more.

PART I

Introduction to Crime Analysis and Crime Mapping

1

Introduction and Overview

Crime analysis is a field of study and practice in criminal justice that utilizes systematic research methods and data, supports the mission of police agencies, and provides information to a range of audiences. Crime mapping is a subset of crime analysis that focuses on understanding the geographic nature of crime and other activity. Crime analysis is a new topic in criminal justice education, and this book is one of the first to bring crime analysis and crime mapping to an undergraduate audience. A class in crime analysis provides students with opportunities to apply theory, research methods, and statistics learned in other courses as well as presents information on a viable career path for criminal justice majors.

My purpose in this book is to provide an introduction to crime analysis and crime mapping through discussion of the concepts, theories, practices, data, and analysis techniques associated with these fields of study. The software on the CD-ROM that accompanies this text provides students with the means to conduct crime analysis techniques themselves through exercises. In the chapters that follow, I provide examples from my own experience as a crime analyst as well as from discussions and associations I have had with analysts and police officers around the United States and internationally. Although much of the information contained in this book is currently available in a variety of other works, a significant portion of what is included here is new material—that is, the techniques described have only been practiced; information about them has not been published before.

The book is divided into five parts: Part I covers the definitions, process, and state of the fields as well as criminological theory relevant for crime analysis and crime mapping; Part II addresses the data and technology used in crime analysis; Part III covers the methods and techniques of tactical crime analysis; Part IV looks at the methods and techniques of strategic crime analysis; and Part V covers the methods and techniques of administrative crime analysis. The chapters in Part I lay the foundation for the rest of the book. Following this introductory chapter, Chapter 2 presents the definition of crime analysis and discusses the crime analysis process and the different types of crime analysis. Chapter 3 presents a discussion of the history of crime analysis practice and the current state of the field; it also includes information on crime analysis career opportunities. Chapter 4 provides an introduction to crime mapping, including definitions of crime mapping and geographic information systems and discussions of types of geographic features, types of maps, and geocoding. It also includes material on the history of crime mapping, the current state of the field, and crime mapping career opportunities. Chapter 5 provides an overview of the criminological theories that help to guide the practice of crime analysis.

The two chapters that make up Part II are devoted to the topic of the data and technology used in crime analysis. Chapter 6 provides a review of key terms, a discussion of the kinds of databases commonly used in crime analysis (e.g., crime, arrests, calls for service, and accidents databases), and information on what analysts must consider when using different kinds of data for analysis. Chapter 7 presents an overview of the types of hardware and software commonly used in crime analysis for data collection, data storage, analysis, and dissemination of analysis results.

The chapters in Part III describe the data, methodologies, techniques, and products of tactical crime analysis. Chapter 8 contains details of data collected specifically for tactical crime analysis and the methodologies analysts employ in identifying and finalizing patterns. Chapter 9 highlights specific analytic, temporal, and spatial techniques that analysts use to identify and understand crime patterns. The chapter closes with some general guidelines for creating tactical crime analysis products, along with some examples.

The chapters in Part IV concentrate on the techniques that analysts use in analyzing crime and disorder problems. Chapter 10 discusses the definition of a problem (in contrast to the definition of an incident or a pattern), the importance of understanding the context in which a problem occurs, and the use of statistics and available data to understand the current nature of a problem. Chapter 11 addresses the techniques that analysts use to understand the temporal nature of a problem, provides some material on victims and repeat victimization, and discusses the technique of collecting primary data to enhance the analysis of a problem. Chapter 12 describes a range of techniques that analysts use to conduct spatial analysis of problems, including the classifications they employ in mapping tabular data and methodologies for determining and classifying areas of high activity (known as *hot spots*). Chapter 13 discusses the types of strategic crime analysis products and provides guidelines for the substantive and format development of such products.

The single chapter in Part V is concerned with administrative crime analysis. Chapter 14 discusses the factors that analysts need to consider in presenting crime analysis information to different audiences. The chapter uses a hypothetical scenario to clarify the guidelines presented for administrative crime analysis and ends by highlighting a popular dissemination medium for administrative crime analysis information, the Internet.

By no means does this book cover all facets of crime analysis; however, it does lay a solid foundation for students' understanding of the conceptual nature and practice of crime analysis. It provides an in-depth description of this emerging field, guidelines for the practice of crime analysis that are based on both previously available and new information, and opportunities for students to explore possible future careers, with the ultimate goal of creating knowledge to enhance modern policing.

2

Crime
Analysis Defined

This chapter provides an overview of the key definitions and concepts in the field of crime analysis. It begins with the definition of crime analysis and then describes the crime analysis process, covering the various types of crime analysis as they are practiced in police agencies around the world.

Definition of Crime Analysis

Over the past 20 years, many scholars have developed definitions of **crime analysis.** These include the following:

> Crime analysis refers to the set of systematic, analytical processes that provide timely, pertinent information about crime patterns and crime trend correlations. It is primarily a tactical tool. Patrol reports and crime records furnish data about crime scenes, weapons, modus operandi, stolen or getaway vehicles, and suspects. Analyzing and comparing data on file with those on current cases can give patrol officers important information on activities in their beat areas. This includes developing crime patterns, stolen property descriptions, and suspect identities. Using this information, patrols can better deploy resources. (Emig, Heck, & Kravitz, 1980, p. v)

> [Crime Analysis is a] set of systematic, analytical processes directed at providing timely and pertinent information relative to crime patterns and trend correlations to assist the operational and administrative personnel in planning the deployment of resources for the prevention and suppression of criminal activities, aiding the investigative process, and increasing apprehensions and the clearance of cases. Within this context, Crime Analysis supports a number of department functions including patrol deployment, special operations, and tactical units, investigations, planning and research, crime prevention, and administrative services (budgeting and program planning). (Gottlieb, Arenberg, & Singh, 1994, p. 13)

Crime analysis is a detail-oriented discipline wherein the analyst endeavors to seek the truth of a given situation utilizing methods and the right information to confirm the truth so that an effective plan can be formulated. (Vellani & Nahoun, 2001, p. 8)

Although these definitions differ in specifics, they share several common components: All agree that crime analysis supports the mission of the police agency, utilizes systematic methods and information, and provides information to a range of audiences. The following definition, which will be used for the purposes of this book, distills these elements into a simpler form:

Crime analysis is the systematic study of crime and disorder problems as well as other police-related issues—including sociodemographic, spatial, and temporal factors—to assist the police in criminal apprehension, crime and disorder reduction, crime prevention, and evaluation.

Clarification of each aspect of this definition helps to demonstrate the various elements of crime analysis. Generally, *to study* means to inquire into, investigate, examine closely, and/or scrutinize information. Crime analysis, then, is the focused and systematic examination of crime and disorder problems as well as other police-related issues. Crime analysis is not haphazard or anecdotal; rather, it involves the application of social science data collection procedures, analytic methods, and statistical techniques.

More specifically, crime analysis employs both qualitative and quantitative data and methods. Crime analysts use **qualitative data and methods** when they examine nonnumerical data for the purpose of discovering underlying meanings and patterns of relationships. The qualitative methods specific to crime analysis include field research (such as observing characteristics of locations) and content analysis (such as examining police report narratives). Crime analysts use **quantitative data and methods** when they conduct statistical analysis of numerical or categorical data. Although much of the work in crime analysis is quantitative, crime analysts utilize simple statistical methods, such as frequencies, percentages, means, and rates.

The central focus of crime analysis is the study of crime and disorder (e.g., noise complaints, burglary alarms, suspicious activity), problems and information related to the nature of incidents, offenders, and victims or targets of crime (targets are inanimate objects, such as buildings or property). Crime analysts also study other police-related issues, such as staffing needs and areas of police service. Even though this discipline is called *crime* analysis, it actually includes much more than just the examination of crime incidents.

Although many different characteristics of crime and disorder are relevant in crime analysis, the three most important kinds of information that crime analysts use are sociodemographic, spatial, and temporal. **Sociodemographic information** consists of the personal characteristics of individuals and groups, such as sex, race, income, age, and education. On an individual level, crime analysts use sociodemographic information to search for and identify crime suspects. On a broader level, they use such information to determine the characteristics of groups and how they relate to crime. For example, analysts may use sociodemographic information to answer the question, "Is there a white male, 30–35 years of age, with brown hair and brown eyes, suspect to link to a particular robbery?" or "Can demographic characteristics explain why the people in one group are victimized more often than people in another group in a particular area?"

The *spatial* nature of crime and other police-related issues is central to an understanding of the nature of a problem. In recent years, improvements in computer technology and the availability of electronic data have facilitated a larger role for spatial analysis in crime analysis. Visual displays of crime locations and their relationship to other events and geographic features are essential to our understanding of the nature of crime and disorder. (For in-depth discussion of this type of analysis, called *crime mapping*, see Chapter 4.) Recent developments in criminological theory have encouraged crime analysts to focus on geographic patterns of crime, examining situations in which victims and offenders come together in time and space. (For discussion of the importance of place in the analysis of crime, see Chapter 5.)

Finally, the *temporal* nature of crime, disorder, and other police-related issues is a major component of crime analysis. Crime analysts conduct several levels of temporal analysis, including (a) examination of long-term patterns in crime trends over several years, the seasonal nature of crime, and patterns by month; (b) examination of midlength patterns, such as patterns by day of week and time of day; and (c) examination of short-term patterns, such as patterns by days of the week, time of day, or time between incidents within a particular crime series. Throughout this book, I present discussion of specific analysis techniques used to examine the temporal nature of crime.

The final part of the above definition—"to assist the police in criminal apprehension, crime and disorder reduction, crime prevention, and evaluation"— generally summarizes the goals of crime analysis. The first goal of crime analysis is to support the operations of a police department. Without police, there would be no crime analysis as it is defined here. It follows, then, that the second goal of crime analysis is to assist in criminal apprehension, given that this is a fundamental goal of the police. For instance, a detective may be investigating a robbery incident in which the perpetrator used a particular modus operandi (i.e., method of the crime). A crime analyst might assist the detective by searching a database of previous robberies for similar cases.

Another primary goal of the police is to prevent crime through methods other than apprehension. Crime analysis assists with the identification and analysis of crime and disorder problems as well as the development of crime prevention responses to those problems. For example, members of a police department may wish to conduct a residential burglary prevention campaign and would like to target their resources in areas that have the largest residential burglary problem. A crime analyst can assist them by conducting a spatial analysis of residential burglary, examining how, when, and where the burglaries occurred, and analyzing what items were stolen. The analyst can then use this information to develop crime prevention suggestions (such as closing and locking garage doors) for specific areas.

Many of the problems that police deal with or are asked to solve are not criminal in nature; rather, they have more to do with quality of life and disorder. Some

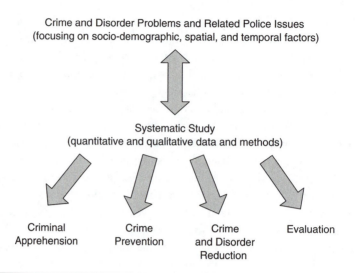

Crime and Disorder Problems and Related Police Issues
(focusing on socio-demographic, spatial, and temporal factors)

Systematic Study
(quantitative and qualitative data and methods)

Criminal   Crime   Crime   Evaluation
Apprehension   Prevention   and Disorder
                                 Reduction

Figure 2.1   The Definition of Crime Analysis

examples include false burglary alarms, loud noise complaints, traffic control, and neighbor disputes. Thus addressing and reducing disorder has become a police objective and, by extension, a subject of crime analysis. Crime analysts can assist police with these efforts by conducting research and analysis of disorder problems such as traffic accidents, noise complaints, code violations, and trespass warnings to provide officers with information they can use to address these issues before they become more serious criminal problems.

The final goal of crime analysis is to assist with the evaluation of police efforts. Such evaluation concerns two main areas: (a) the level of success of programs and initiatives implemented to control and prevent crime and disorder, and (b) how effectively police organizations are run. In recent years, local police agencies have become increasingly interested in determining whether various crime control and prevention programs and initiatives they undertake are effective. For example, an evaluation might could be conducted to determine the effectiveness of a 2-month burglary surveillance or of a crime prevention program that has sought to implement "**crime prevention through environmental design**" (**CPTED**) principles within several apartment communities. Crime analysts also assist police departments in evaluating internal organizational procedures, such as resource allocation (i.e., how officers are assigned to patrol areas), realignment of geographic boundaries, the forecasting of staffing needs, and the development of performance measures. Police agencies keep such procedures under constant scrutiny in order to ensure that the agencies are running effectively.

The flowchart presented in Figure 2.1 clarifies the various components of the definition of crime analysis used throughout this book. Crime analysis examines crime and disorder problems as they occur as well as ongoing police-related issues in order to assist police in criminal apprehension, crime prevention, crime and disorder reduction, and evaluation.

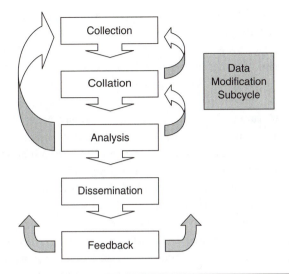

Figure 2.2.   The Crime Analysis Process

The Crime Analysis Process

Figure 2.2 illustrates the **crime analysis process,** or the general way in which crime analysis is practiced. The steps involved in this process are data collection, data collation, analysis, dissemination of results, and incorporation of feedback from users of the information (Gottlieb et al., 1994). The crime analysis process begins with observations (data). Data come from many sources, including, in most cases, from outside crime analysis. That is, crime analysts examine data observed and collected by others, such as police officers, call-for-service dispatchers, community service officers, census workers, and geographers.

Collection

The first step in the crime analysis process is the collection of data; this step is closely connected to data storage. As noted above, this step occurs outside the direct control of the crime analysis function. In most police agencies, officers and/or civilian employees enter crime reports and other data into a computer system. Officers may write reports in longhand that are then entered into the computer system by data entry clerks, officers may input incident reports directly into a computer system, or police dispatchers may write reports directly into the computer system. The policies dictating data entry procedures, as well as the care taken by the individuals who execute the procedures, are crucial to crime analysis because they affect both the quantity and the quality of the data and subsequent analysis.

Some of the data collected in police departments are not relevant for crime analysis, so subsets of information are compiled for analysis purposes. For example, police officers draw diagrams of car accidents for purposes of insurance claims and other legal concerns. Crime analysts are generally not concerned with the exact circumstances of each car accident; rather, they are concerned with compiling data on the dates, times, locations, and nature of all accidents, as this information can help them to understand this type of activity more generally.

In addition, the manner in which data are stored and the amount of data stored are important in crime analysis. Data must be in an electronic format, collected regularly (e.g., on a daily or weekly basis), and collected for a significant amount of time to be useful for crime analysis. Paper copies of reports and other information are not useful to crime analysts because data in this form are too time-consuming and cumbersome to analyze. Information has to be coded into an electronic database to be useful for crime analysis.

The time that elapses between the observation, or data collection, and the availability of data needs to be reasonably short if the data are to be useful for crime analysis. For example, electronic crime report data that are not available until 6 months after reports are written are not useful. The amount of data stored also needs to be adequate (e.g., multiple years) for crime analysts to have enough information to conduct satisfactory analyses. For example, 2 months' worth of data cannot provide a comprehensive picture of a burglary problem. Finally, it is also important for crime analysts to have access to raw data. Many police computer systems only allow retrieval of individual records and/or the creation of statistical reports on paper. Crime analysts must be able to download electronic data into myriad software programs to conduct analyses using the various techniques discussed in this book.

To summarize, the crime analysis data collection process requires the following:

1. The data must be collected accurately and consistently.

2. Only data appropriate for crime analysis should be compiled (i.e., some characteristics important to crime analysis may not be collected because they are not relevant for official or legal purposes).

3. The data must be collected in a timely manner (e.g., not 6 months after the observations).

4. The data must be stored for an adequate amount of time to allow for satisfactory analysis.

5. The data must be accessible in raw form to be queried and downloaded.

These requirements apply to any data used in crime analysis, including data obtained from outside the police agency (e.g., geographic data and census information).

Collation

The main sources of the data (e.g., crime and calls for service) used in crime analysis are general police data collection systems. These systems are generally designed to capture and store data, but not necessarily to facilitate analysis. Because of this, crime analysts often find it necessary to change the data purposefully before they can use them for analysis. This can include selecting subsets of data, reformatting and creating new variables, and performing quality control. Data collation entails a number of different tasks, but it generally takes three forms:

1. *Cleaning*: the process of correcting mistakes and inconsistencies in the data

2. *Geocoding*: the process of bringing crime analysis data together with geographic data so that they can be analyzed spatially (discussed in depth in Chapter 6)

3. *Creation of new variables*: the process of recoding or computing new variables from existing variables for more effective analysis (e.g., response time and categories of crime)

Analysis

Analysis, which takes place after data are collected and prepared, includes the use of many different statistical and visualization techniques, all of which are described at length in Parts III, IV, and V of this book. Unfortunately, it is often the case that a crime analyst is unaware of problems with the data (e.g., they do not measure what needs to be studied or they have not been collected correctly) until the analysis begins. When this occurs, the analyst must often return to the collection and collation steps to improve and/or change the way data are collected, stored, or collated. This practice, which is called the **data modification subcycle**, is intrinsic to the crime analysis process.

Data Modification Subcycle

The arrows in Figure 2.2 illustrate how the data modification subcycle operates. In this subprocess of crime analysis, data collection and collation are changed based on the crime analysis process itself. The crime analysis process is not linear; it moves from collection to collation to analysis, but what the analyst finds is that each of these steps can inform the next step. For example, in cleaning the data during the collation process, the analyst may gain insight into new ways data can be collected; the requirements of the analysis may cause the analyst to make changes in both collection and collation. The following are some specific examples of this interplay:

- An examination of the nature of loud parties in a particular area reveals that call-for-service data contain only a "loud noise" call type, so the analyst cannot distinguish reports of loud parties from reports of general loud noises. The analyst must go back to the data collection step and create a new call type labeled "loud party" for police officers and dispatchers to use.
- The chief of police requests that an analyst examine crime data for the past 10 years, but the data have been stored for only 5 years. The analyst conducts an examination of the existing 5 years of crime data and recommends the

adoption of new policies for data storage that will allow for the preservation of 10 years of data.

- Through analysis, a crime analyst determines that there are inconsistencies in the crime location variable (e.g., addresses are assigned to incorrect police beats); this leads to the development of a more comprehensive data cleaning process.

Although issues such as those described above may not appear in every analysis situation, an undeniable aspect of crime analysis is that analysts should never take the data at face value, because unanticipated complications often arise and data on new aspects of crime, disorder, and policing have not yet been collected. (For more detailed discussion of a variety of these issues, see Chapter 6.) The data modification subcycle is a key component of the crime analysis process; crime analysts spend a significant amount of their time and resources addressing such issues.

Dissemination

Once the data analysis is completed, the crime analyst needs to communicate the results to various types of audiences. The methods of disseminating crime analysis results include paper reports and maps, presentations, e-mails, Internet documents, and phone calls. The audiences for crime analysis information include police officers, police management, citizens, students, other analysts, and the news media.

Analysts need to keep two important considerations in mind when communicating crime analysis results. First, the presentation should be tailored to the knowledge of the particular audience. For example, for an audience of citizens, analysts might need to clarify the definitions of various types of crimes (e.g., robbery vs. burglary) before presenting analysis results. Second, the presentation of results should convey only the most necessary information. Much of the work of crime analysis takes place behind the scenes (e.g., collation of data), and the presentation of results need not include information on all that work. In disseminating their findings, crime analysts should include only information that is relevant to the topic or issue at hand. For example, it is not necessary for an analyst to present every detail of an analysis project when the project's findings can easily be communicated through one or two key points. Although it is important that analysts document their data collection, collation, and analysis methods, in disseminating their results they should present only the content most appropriate for their particular audiences.

In addition to assisting police departments, crime analysts can contribute to the creation of knowledge about crime, disorder issues, and general police practices through the dissemination of their analysis results to other analysts, researchers, and police practitioners. Such results can inform police practices (e.g., enforcement or prevention efforts) and crime analysis practices (e.g., duplication of successful data collection methods and analytic techniques) as well as add to the general knowledge about crime and other police-related issues (e.g., the nature of prostitution in rural areas). This is not to say that one report from one crime analyst is likely to create all the knowledge about a given topic; rather, the dissemination of crime analysis results from numerous police agencies over time can begin to form a body of knowledge, which is the goal of any social science.

Feedback

After disseminating the results of their analyses, crime analysts receive feedback from the individuals to whom they provided the information. As in the data modification subcycle, feedback from the use of the products of an analysis can help to inform the entire process further. Analysts may receive feedback about the quality of particular analyses or reports, about the nature of the data analyzed, or about the usefulness of their analyses for decision making.

Summary

To reiterate: The crime analysis process is not linear; it is cyclical in that each step in the process can inform subsequent steps as the analyst gains insight and receives feedback. Crime analysts spend much time and energy on the subcycle of data modification; however, with improved policies, technologies, databases, training, and examples of effective analysis, the process is constantly evolving. In each of the types of crime analysis discussed in the next section, crime analysts follow the basic process described above, although the specific data, methods, and purposes of their analyses may differ.

Types of Crime Analysis

The term *crime analysis* refers to a general concept and to a discipline practiced in the policing community. This discipline is further broken down into subsets of crime analysis that differ in purpose, scope, data, and analysis techniques. These subsets range from data-rich, investigation-focused types of crime analysis to more general and research-focused types, as described below.

Intelligence Analysis

The purposes of **intelligence analysis** are to identify networks of offenders and criminal activity as well as to assist the police in apprehending those violators of the law (Petersen, 1994). These networks are typically related to organized crime ("the Mafia"), gangs, drug traffickers, prostitution rings, financial fraud rings, or combinations of these criminal enterprises. Intelligence analysis is conducted within police departments and is centrally concerned with criminal activity occurring within specific jurisdictions (e.g., city, county, or state borders); however, police departments often work with neighboring jurisdictions and national officials concerning criminal activity in their local areas.

Much of the data examined in intelligence analysis is gathered by police through surveillance, wiretapping, informants, and participant observation (i.e., undercover work). The type of information examined is not limited to criminal information; it may include the telephone conversations, travel information, financial/tax information, and family and business relationships of those under investigation. By analyzing these data, intelligence analysts seek to link information together, prioritize information, identify relationships, and distinguish areas for further investigation. Intelligence analysts work closely with police officers and are often officers themselves.

Criminal Investigative Analysis

In the 1970s and 1980s, what is now known as **criminal investigative analysis** was usually referred to as *criminal profiling*. The frequent misuse of the term *profiling* in the popular media since that time has led practitioners to change the term to *criminal investigative analysis*. This type of analysis entails the process of constructing "profiles" of offenders who have committed serious crimes. Criminal investigative analysts use the elements of the crimes these offenders have committed to infer certain things about the offenders, including characteristics such as personality type, social habits, and work habits. For example, a crime scene that is very bloody and messy implies a different type of offender than does a crime scene where the offender has cleaned up all the blood.

The primary purpose of criminal investigative analysis is to help criminal investigators identify and prioritize suspects by inferring the personal characteristics of likely offenders. This very specific type of crime analysis is done primarily on the national police level, as the crime patterns associated with serious crimes frequently cross jurisdictional boundaries.

A subset of criminal investigative analysis is **geographic profiling.** In this type of analysis, the geographic locations of an offender's crimes (such as body dump sites or encounter sites) are used to identify and prioritize areas where the offender is likely to live (Rossmo, 2000). Once again, the goal is to identify and capture the offender.

Although intelligence analysis and criminal investigative analysis are both types of crime analysis, the analytic techniques, products, and purposes associated with them differ significantly from those associated with the three types discussed below. In practice, intelligence analysis and criminal investigative analysis are seen almost as separate disciplines; thus I have included the above information on these two types of crime analysis for background purposes only. The remainder of this book focuses on the three types described below: tactical, strategic, and administrative crime analysis.

Tactical Crime Analysis

Tactical crime analysis (TCA) may be defined as follows:

Tactical crime analysis is the study of recent criminal incidents and potential criminal activity through the examination of characteristics such as how, when, and where the activity has occurred to assist in pattern development, investigative lead and suspect identification, and case clearance. (adapted from Boba, 2001)

TCA focuses on recent crimes and on specific information about the methods of the crimes as well as the individuals and vehicles involved. The data analyzed come from formal police reports, which include information on the characteristics of crimes, such as method of entry, point of entry, suspect's actions, type of victim, and type of weapon used, as well as date, time, location, and type of location. The types of crimes typically examined in TCA are those in which the offender does not know the victim and those for which adequate information about the crime (method of the crime) is available for analysis. These include, but are not limited to, commercial and residential burglary, robbery, and sexual crime (e.g., rape, public sexual indecency, and indecent exposure). TCA also examines field information collected by patrol officers regarding potential criminal activity, such as suspicious activity calls for service and criminal trespass warnings, along with information on scars, tattoos, or other marks that police officers report about their contacts in the field.

TCA has three goals: (a) to link crimes and thus identify patterns, (b) to identify potential suspects of crimes or crime patterns, and (c) to link solved crimes to open cases and thus help to clear or close cases. Because detectives and police officers spend most of their time investigating individual cases, they often do not have time to take a step back to identify patterns. TCA is the process of taking this step back; by examining many crimes together, tactical crime analysts can identify patterns as well as assist with linking patterns to potential offenders.

Strategic Crime Analysis

Strategic crime analysis (SCA) may be defined as follows:

Strategic crime analysis is the study of crime problems and other police-related issues to determine long-term patterns of activity as well as to evaluate police responses and organizational procedures. (adapted from Boba, 2001)

Because the scope of SCA involves long-term patterns of activity, the data and analysis methods employed in this kind of analysis are primarily quantitative (although in-depth analyses may also make use of qualitative data and methods). That is, strategic crime analysts use various statistical methods to examine electronic databases containing hundreds, thousands, and tens of thousands of records. These analysts deal with variables such as date, time, location, and type of incident instead of with qualitative data such as narrative descriptions of incidents.

The two primary purposes of SCA are (a) to assist in the identification and examination of long-term crime problems and (b) to evaluate police responses to problems and the organizational procedures of police agencies. Examination of problems may include the analysis of crime rates, repeat victimization, hot spots, and environmental characteristics that affect opportunities and incidents of crime. The findings of strategic crime analysts' research and evaluation of police responses to crime problems assist police agencies in assessing their effectiveness. The examination of such police procedures as deployment and staffing or redistricting of beats or precincts is also called **operational analysis** because it deals with the operations of police agencies and not the nature of crime problems and patterns.[1]

Administrative Crime Analysis

Administrative crime analysis (ACA) may be defined as follows:

> Administrative crime analysis is the presentation of interesting findings of crime research and analysis based on legal, political, and practical concerns to inform audiences within police administration, city government/council, and citizens. (adapted from Boba, 2001)

ACA is different from tactical and strategic crime analysis in that it is concerned with the *presentation* of findings rather than with pattern identification, statistical analysis, or research. ACA is the process of selecting interesting and important findings from previously conducted analyses and formatting that information appropriately for specific audiences. Often the type of information presented represents only the "tip of the iceberg" of the complete analysis and research. The purpose of the analysis and the audience for its findings largely determine what is presented; in addition, the crime analyst must take into account legal (e.g., privacy and confidentiality), political (e.g., union issues, election concerns), and practical (e.g., complexity and length of the information) concerns.

The primary purpose of ACA is to inform audiences. As the audiences for crime analysis information vary from one situation to the next, the type and quantity of information selected for presentation also vary. Unlike tactical and strategic crime analysis, the audience for which is usually line officers and line supervisors, ACA is primarily intended for administrators and command staff, city government officials, news media, and citizens. The use of the Internet to disseminate information on crime analysis provides an example of ACA. The audience for a police Internet site includes citizens, police personnel, business owners, victims, criminals, and news media outlets—essentially everyone—thus the type of information published on such a site is selected and formatted with a wide array of consumers in mind.

Summary Points

This chapter has defined crime analysis, described the crime analysis process, and described five different types of crime analysis. The following are the key points addressed in this chapter:

- Scholars have defined crime analysis in many ways, but all of their definitions share these elements: Crime analysis utilizes systematic methods and information, supports the mission of the police agency, and provides information to a wide range of audiences.

- Crime analysis is the systematic study of crime and disorder problems as well as other police-related issues—including sociodemographic, spatial, and temporal factors—to assist the police in criminal apprehension, crime and disorder reduction, crime prevention, and evaluation.
- Crime analysis is not haphazard or anecdotal; rather, it involves the application of data collection procedures, analytic methods, and statistical techniques.
- Crime analysis entails more than the study of criminal incidents; it includes the examination of other information that is of concern to police, including disorder activity and police operational information.
- Temporal, spatial (crime mapping), and sociodemographic factors are key areas of focus in crime analysts' examinations of crime, disorder, and other police-related issues.
- The goals of crime analysis are to assist police in criminal apprehension, crime and disorder reduction, crime prevention, and evaluation.
- The crime analysis process—that is, the general way in which crime analysis is practiced—includes the steps of data collection, data collation, analysis, dissemination of results, and the receipt of feedback from users of the information.
- The data modification subcycle is a subprocess within the crime analysis process in which the analyst makes changes in data collection and collation procedures based on insights gained during the analysis.
- The term *crime analysis* refers to a general concept and to a discipline practiced in the policing community. The five major types of crime analysis—intelligence analysis, criminal investigative analysis, tactical crime analysis, strategic crime analysis, and administrative crime analysis—differ from one another in purpose, scope, data, and analysis techniques.
- Tactical crime analysis is the study of recent criminal incidents and potential criminal activity through the examination of characteristics such as how, when, and where the activity has occurred to assist in pattern development, investigative lead and suspect identification, and case clearance.
- Strategic crime analysis is the study of crime problems and other police-related issues to determine long-term patterns of activity as well as to evaluate police responses and organizational procedures.
- Administrative crime analysis is the presentation of interesting findings of crime research and analysis based on legal, political, and practical concerns to inform audiences within police administration, city government/council, and citizens.

Exercises

Exercise 2.1

How is the crime analysis process (data collection, data collation, analysis, dissemination, feedback) different from the scientific process (theory, hypothesis, observation, empirical generalizations)? What might explain the differences between the two?

Exercise 2.2

Compare and contrast how the five different types of crime analysis (intelligence analysis, criminal investigative analysis, tactical crime analysis, strategic crime analysis, and administrative crime analysis) can contribute to the field of policing in general and to policing's effectiveness in addressing crime and disorder.

Note

1. In the past few years, crime analysis conducted as part of problem-oriented policing has been distinguished from strategic crime analysis, with the former often referred to as *problem analysis*. Problem analysis may be defined as "an approach/method/process conducted within the police agency in which formal criminal justice theory, research methods, and comprehensive data collection and analysis procedures are used in a systematic way to conduct in-depth examination of, develop informed responses to, and evaluate crime and disorder problems" (Boba, 2003, p. 2). Problem analysis is distinguished from strategic crime analysis by its specific focus on identifying and understanding particular problems, assisting police responses to the problems, and evaluating those police responses.

3

The Crime Analysis Profession

This chapter provides an overview of the crime analysis profession in the United States, including the profession's history, its current status, and descriptions of potential career paths for crime analysts. As I noted in Chapter 2, the histories and practices of intelligence analysis and criminal investigative analysis are distinct from those of tactical, strategic, and administrative crime analysis, and the remainder of this book concentrates on these latter three types. I include here only a brief discussion of international crime analysis practices, highlighting how they have influenced crime analysis in the United States.

History of Crime Analysis

Human beings have analyzed crime and criminal behavior throughout history. That is, humans have always made observations about crime events (i.e., collected data) and developed ideas about patterns based on those observations (i.e., conducted analysis). For example, in the old American West, a rancher may have noticed that he was losing one or two head of cattle from his grazing land every week. He also may have noticed that the cattle went missing only at night and only from a certain field. These observations and analysis may have led him to respond either by sitting and watching the cattle in that field overnight or by moving the cattle to another field. The rancher's thoughts and actions constitute a simple form of crime analysis. Historically, police officers have conducted crime analysis by using memory to link key suspects and property to specific patterns of crime.

The present-day discipline of crime analysis represents an evolution of the kinds of crime analysis illustrated by these examples. It is a systematic process in which data about crime and other related factors are collected and stored for long periods of time. Where earlier "crime analysts" relied mostly on their own observations and their own memories of crime incidents, modern crime analysts utilize complex computer systems to apply various analytic techniques, ranging from simple pattern analysis to complex statistical analysis.

Beginnings of Crime Analysis

The history of the analysis of crime is long, but the history of crime analysis as a discipline begins with the first modern police force, which was created in London in the early 19th century. This makes sense, given that the main objective of crime analysis is to assist the police. Through the Metropolitan Police Act, passed in the 1820s, England organized about a thousand men to form a London police force. In 1842, this force created a detective bureau, which was given the responsibility of identifying crime patterns to help solve crimes. According to London's Metropolitan Police Service (2004), by 1844 the detective bureau's officers were collecting, collating, and analyzing police information. For example:

> Richard Mayne, Commissioner, called to give evidence to the Select Committee on Dogs. He stated that in the Metropolis there were a rising number of lost or stolen dogs. In the preceding year over 600 dogs were lost and 60 stolen. He declared the law to be in a very unsatisfactory state as people paid money for restoration of dogs. "People pay monies to parties whom they have reason to believe have either stolen or enticed them away in order to get the reward. . . ." Mayne believed it to be organised crime.

Additionally, the Metropolitan Police Service notes that aggregate crime statistics were available for the city of London as early as 1847: "Statistics for the year were; 14,091 robberies; 62,181 people taken in charge, 24,689 of these were summarily dealt with; 5,920 stood trial and 4,551 were convicted and sentenced; 31,572 people were discharged by the magistrates."

United States: 1900–1970

Although many large cities in the United States began to create police departments in the mid-1850s, corruption within these departments as well as a lack of organization and technology prevented them from conducting crime analysis systematically. The first indication of an instance of formal crime analysis in the United States is found in the early 1900s. August Vollmer, the most famous police reformer, in addition to instituting the innovations of vehicle patrol, radio communication, and fingerprinting, encouraged the use of pin mapping, the regular review of police reports, and the formation of patrol districts based on crime volume (Grassie, Waymire, Burrows, Anderson, & Wallace, 1977).

O. W. Wilson, who worked with Vollmer and created an advanced training program for officers, was the first to mention and define the term *crime analysis*, in the first edition of his book *Police Administration* in 1963. In the fourth edition of that book, Wilson and McLaren (1977) distinguish between "operations" analysis and "crime" analysis, asserting that crime analysis is the "process of the identification of crime trends and patterns through statistical treatment of information and through examination of actual investigative reports" (p. 175).

From Wilson's writings, it appears that crime analysis was being conducted in (or at least was recommended to) police departments in the 1950s and 1960s; however, no evidence of crime analysis products is available from that period. In his lesser-known book *Police Planning,* which was first published in 1952, Wilson discusses crime mapping and crime analysis, although he does not use those terms. In the second edition of that volume, he outlines the structure of police planning to include a "cartography unit," which, among other things, "provides technical advice . . . in depicting crime trends or occurrences . . . in located places of arrest," and a "statistics unit," which includes many of the functions of crime analysis that are still practiced today (Wilson, 1957, p. 10):

1. Interpreting and disseminating crime statistics and other related material to be used as aids for more effective and efficient operation of the department

2. Preparing and distributing periodical statistical reports

3. Preparing special surveys and reports relative to crime trends, modus operandi, and special problems

4. Preparing statistical charts, graphs, and artwork as needed by other department units

5. Assisting other agencies in the analysis of statistical information

6. Maintaining and operating the modus operandi files

7. Processing and preparing crime reports for keypunch and tabulating operations.

8. Interpreting and disseminating crime statistics and other related matter

United States: 1970 to Present

The 1968 Omnibus Crime Control and Safe Streets Act brought about increased awareness of the use of analysis and evaluation in policing throughout the 1970s. The act allowed the allocation of federal grants to assist state and local police agencies with any purpose associated with reducing crime. The U.S. Bureau of Justice Administration, established by the act for the general purpose of supporting police agencies, provided extensive assistance, helping police departments establish evaluation programs and providing training, technical assistance, and information to support the work funded by the grants (Pomrenke, 1969; U.S. Congress, 1990).

As a result, publications from the 1970s about crime analysis techniques as well as evaluations of crime analysis functions indicate that police departments had begun to take Vollmer's and Wilson's advice to formalize crime analysis. In an annotated bibliography prepared for the National Institute of Justice, Emig, Heck, and Kravitz (1980) provide information on crime analysis publications and products of the 1970s. The bibliography includes entries for many handbooks and articles devoted to the techniques of tactical and strategic crime analysis that were produced by various nonprofit organizations and funded by the U.S. government, such as the following:

- *Police Crime Analysis Unit Handbook* (Austin et al., 1973)
- *Application of Pattern Recognition Techniques to Crime Analysis* (Bender, Cox, & Chappell, 1976)
- "Crime Analysis and Manpower Allocation Through Computer Pattern Recognition" (Cox, Kolender, Bender, & McQueeney, 1977)
- *Integrated Criminal Apprehension Program: Crime Analysis Executive Manual* (Grassie et al., 1977)
- *Application of Time Series Methodology to Crime Analysis* (Marshall, 1977)
- "Management Function of a Crime Analysis Unit" (Booth, 1979)
- *Crime Analysis System Support: Descriptive Report of Manual and Automated Crime Analysis Functions* (Chang, Simms, Makres, & Bodnar, 1979)

During the 1970s, the U.S. government held several symposia on crime analysis and brought academics and practitioners together to work on specific technical assistance projects aimed at increasing the crime analysis capabilities of police agencies. These included agencies in Omaha, Nebraska; Dallas, Texas; Mount Prospect, Illinois; Simi Valley, California; Kansas City, Missouri; Austin, Texas; Boston, Massachusetts; and Norfolk, Virginia (Emig et al., 1980). Popular media sources also provide evidence that formal crime analysis units existed during this period. For example, two *New York Times* articles published in 1972 mention crime analysis:

Crime analysts at NYC Police Hq say on July 21 that record 57 homicides in 7 day period that ended at midnight July 20 is attributed partly to hot weather in met area. (July 22, 1972, p. 1)

New tactical patrol unit will be sent into Warren County, NJ, with specially trained traffic and crime analysts, on Oct 19 to help area cope with rapidly rising crime rate. (October 19, 1972, p. 98)

In the mid- to late 1970s, a small group of academics began to emphasize the importance of the characteristics of criminal events, where they take place (locations), and the geographic analysis of crime (discussed in Chapter 4) (Brantingham & Brantingham, 1981). Also in the late 1970s, Herman Goldstein (1979) suggested another focus, which he called **problem-oriented policing**. This shifted the focus of the police from administrative and political concerns to an emphasis on addressing crime and disorder problems. Ideal problem solving, a systematic process within problem-oriented policing, involves the use of formal analysis to provide a comprehensive understanding of crime problems and to develop baseline measures and methodology to enable the evaluation of police responses to problems (Scott, 2000). Goldstein and other scholars who were working with police agencies began to demonstrate the analysis of crime and disorder problems.

Growing recognition of crime analysis in the police practitioner community around this time is evidenced by the creation of the **Commission on Accreditation** for Law Enforcement Agencies (CALEA) in 1979.[1] To receive CALEA accreditation, police agencies were required to have crime analysis capabilities. This meant that agencies began to assign personnel to crime analysis and created new positions to meet the CALEA standards.

Crime analysis practitioners began to organize in the 1980s and early 1990s. The Colorado Crime Analysis Association, the first state association on record, was formed in 1982. It consisted of an active group of professionals who benefited from the sharing of tools and techniques, according to Dale Harris (personal communication, September 12, 2003), a founding member of the association and its first president. In 1989, the California Crime Analysis Association was founded; it is currently the largest state crime analysis organization in the United States, with more than 330 members. The **International Association of Crime Analysts (IACA)** was created in 1991. Dale Harris (personal communication, 2003), who became the IACA's first full-term president, recalls its creation:

> By 1989, we [Colorado crime analysts] were wondering why there was not a national or international organization for crime analysts, and we began talking about forming one on our own. I was invited to speak at the California association meeting in that year, though that association was just being formed at that time. I found they had the same issues that we had in Colorado, even though they had many more analysts. After I returned from the meeting, members of the Colorado association began to get serious about forming a group. In mid-1990, we got in touch with others who had recently attended the International Association of Chiefs of Police crime analysis course and were looking for a professional association to continue the networking. The group from the IACP class set up a meeting in Kansas City in November 1990. There were about 15 of us from Colorado, Texas, Oklahoma, Georgia, Ontario, Canada, and Missouri. We spent two days discussing the concept, creating a set of bylaws, electing officers and planning the first conference. It was held in Aurora, Colorado, in August 1991 and included about 50 attendees.

In the early to mid-1990s, the discipline of crime analysis grew slowly in the United States. In his 1990 book *Problem-Oriented Policing*, Herman Goldstein further specified the role of crime analysis he had described in his 1979 article, outlining the importance of police agencies' using data and research to identify problems, understand their underlying causes, and evaluate crime prevention programs.

A number of other events that occurred in the mid-1990s fostered the expansion of crime analysis. The philosophy of community policing, which was being adopted by departments across the country, emphasized communication between police departments and the citizens they serve; in many cases, such communication involved crime analysis and statistics. The 1994 Violent Crime Control and Safe Streets Act, which amended the 1968 Omnibus Crime Control and Safe Streets Act, provided significant funding for new police officers ("100,000 new cops on the street") and created the Office of Community Oriented Policing Services (known as the COPS Office) to administer the police officer hirings. A significant amount of federal funding also went toward crime analysis in addition to the adoption of a new analysis tool, computerized crime mapping.

In 1997, the COPS Office included crime analysis and crime mapping in its focus, with grants aimed at providing substantive as well as technological support of crime analysis and community policing (for details about these technology grants, see Chapter 4). Finally, in 1994 the New York City Police Department's conception and implementation of **Compstat,** a data- and mapping-driven police management strategy also used in other departments in subsequent years, increased both awareness of crime analysis and its incorporation into the everyday functions of the police (Weisburd, Mastrofski, McNally, Greenspan, & Willis, 2003).

Coinciding with and facilitating the events described above were vast improvements in computer technology. In the 1990s, enormous increases were seen in the speed and memory of computers, and the creation of the Windows operating system had a significant impact on crime analysis practices. These changes made it much easier for analysts to examine large amounts of data using desktop statistical programs and crime mapping software, to clean data, and to generate reports.

In the 1980s and early 1990s, practitioners focused on strategic crime analysis and on providing police agencies with statistical information about long-term trends as well as recommendations for organizational procedures stemming from the work of policing planning units. Although tactical crime analysis was conducted throughout this time, the identification of short-term crime trends and patterns became more widespread in medium- to small-sized agencies during the mid-1990s. This was in part a result of the decentralization of crime analysis units (i.e., the shift toward having individual crime analysts operate in police precincts out in the field rather than together at headquarters), the teaching of specific techniques in crime analysis training at the time, and a renewed emphasis on the police goal of apprehending criminals.[2]

Current State of Crime Analysis

Today, the discipline of crime analysis is recognized as important by both the policing and the academic communities. However, it is still being developed (e.g., crime analysis scholars and practitioners are creating a body of literature, testing and retesting analytic techniques, providing training and education), and many police agencies, particularly smaller ones, remain skeptical about the usefulness of crime analysis practices and have not adopted them. Most medium to large police departments in the United States, however, do have a crime analysis function; that is, they employ individuals, either police officers or specially trained analysts, specifically to conduct at least one type of crime analysis. National surveys of police departments conducted in the late 1990s found that between 58% and 86% were using technology for crime analysis or crime mapping (Mamalian & La Vigne, 1999; U.S. Bureau of Justice Statistics, 1999).

More recent evidence about the state of crime analysis practice in the United States comes from a systematic study conducted in 2000 by the University of South

Alabama's Center for Public Policy. The researchers examined the data collected in two national surveys, one of all U.S. police agencies with more than 100 sworn personnel and another of a random stratified sample (by size and region) of 800 agencies with fewer than 100 sworn personnel, and conducted site visits of large agencies that were specifically selected for the quality of their crime analysis operations. They found that most crime analysts were being asked by the agencies in which they worked to focus on criminal apprehension or on identifying areas with high crime levels. These findings suggest that crime analysts as well as police managers place high value on tactical analysis, which supports short-range planning and is primarily interested in activities aimed at crime control. They seem less interested in strategic analysis, which supports long-range planning and is primarily interested in more complex organizational issues (such as departmental strengths, weaknesses, opportunities, and threats), or even problem analysis, which supports the identification of and response to persistent community problems (O'Shea & Nicholls, 2003).

Although these findings may not be surprising, given that short-term pattern analysis and real-time data analysis support a core function of police agencies, they indicate that most U.S. police agencies are not using crime analysis to its full potential. Crime analysts and police managers alike are directing crime analysis efforts toward short-term pattern and hot spot identification instead of toward long-term, in-depth analysis of crime and disorder problems to seek solutions for these problems. In short, analysts and police are focusing on "catching the bad guys" rather than on understanding the larger crime and disorder problems that affect their communities.

Why is crime analysis being used more often for investigative purposes than for research? There are many possible reasons, as I have noted elsewhere:

> The first is that the investigative process is the traditional and most established process of law enforcement. It is most relevant to street level officers who make up the highest number of potential customers for crime analysis. The investigative process focuses on linking recent incidents together in hopes of identifying and/or apprehending the suspect; that is, "catching the bad guy." Thus, conducting investigative analysis elicits more recognition and support for crime analysis and mapping from police officers and management. In contrast, problem solving, research, and evaluation are newer concepts to law enforcement, and there may be less knowledge or support of the concept throughout a particular agency because, unlike tactical crime analysis, its benefits may not be immediately apparent. In addition, problem solving attempts to get at the root of a problem in order to develop a solution which oftentimes is a much more ambiguous and difficult process than identifying and "catching the bad guy."

> Time may be another significant reason for the emphasis on investigative analysis in crime analysis. Law enforcement has been traditionally reactive to issues and problems and has been required by a community, even our entire society, to react quickly. The investigative process, compared to the research or the problem solving process, occurs very rapidly. The investigative information is compiled and analyzed daily to produce patterns that can be acted upon

as soon as they are identified and disseminated. Task forces seem to be created and disbanded in the time it would take to conduct the first step of the problem solving process. On the other hand, problem solving, research, and evaluation all require time—time to determine the problem at hand, time to analyze the problem, time to respond, and time to evaluate the response. Oftentimes, this takes a year or more which could be considered an eternity in the culture of police response and action.

Another reason is that the skills of the analysts are oftentimes more suited to conducting investigative analysis. Many analysts have been or are officers or have worked in the law enforcement setting, particularly in patrol and investigations, for a long period of time. They often do not have formal research methodology, program evaluation, or statistical backgrounds that would enable them to conduct research and evaluation more effectively. Additionally, analysts are often required to conduct data entry and create lists of incidents or simple reports, which, in reality, is not analysis at all. (Boba & Price, 2002, pp. 79–80)

The concerns of crime analysts themselves provide some insight into the current state of crime analysis. In general, crime analysts today are concerned about the following:[3]

- The availability of relevant training and education
- The effectiveness of the use of their findings
- The need for police officers and managers to take crime analysis seriously
- The availability of data that are adequate in both quantity and quality
- The ability to communicate with other crime analysts in neighboring jurisdictions
- The availability of adequate time to conduct their analyses

Whereas in past decades crime analysts' concerns might have centered on the need for adequate technology, today the technology for conducting analysis is available but may not be used to its full potential, and analysts may not have adequate data, time, training, or management support to allow them to conduct useful analyses.

The International Association of Crime Analysts is currently working to establish crime analysis further as a profession. It has established national certification and training programs, and it has developed a handbook for crime analysis that includes definitions, descriptions of concepts and techniques, and examples. Based on a survey of IACA members, the association has defined a skill set on which it focuses in the certification and training of crime analysts. The elements of this skill set include, but are not limited to, knowledge of crime analysis basics, ability to evaluate the integrity of information, knowledge of criminal behavior, understanding of descriptive and inferential statistics, and ability to perform spatial analysis (for a description of the entire skill set, see the IACA Web site at http://www.iaca.net).

Another part of the effort to establish crime analysis as a profession is the development of a body of crime analysis literature. Academic journals such as *Police Practice and Research* and *Policing: An International Journal of Police Strategies and*

Management and practitioner-focused newsletters such as the Police Foundation's *Crime Mapping News* and the IACA's *Forecaster* include articles about crime analysis written by practitioners and researchers. Increasing numbers of books about crime analysis are being published, and formal communication networks for crime analysts, such as Listservs, have been established.[4] College courses that introduce students to the discipline and provide instruction in crime analysis techniques are also being established at both undergraduate and graduate levels to encourage the pursuit of the profession of crime analysis. Although some crime analysts working today do not have college degrees, it is becoming standard for police agencies to require college degrees for crime analyst positions (O'Shea & Nicholls, 2003), and individuals with master's degrees and even doctoral degrees are becoming crime analysts.

In the past few years, the term **problem analysis** has been used increasingly to refer to a specific type of analysis conducted during the problem-solving process. Even though analysis has always been part of problem solving, the current use of the term *problem analysis* came out of a forum that was conducted in February 2002 in which leading crime analysis scholars and practitioners discussed analysis in the context of problem solving and made recommendations for the widespread adoption of such analysis in policing. The Police Foundation published the findings and recommendations that resulted from this forum in a document titled *Problem Analysis in Policing* (Boba, 2003).

Another effort to further the profession of crime analysis is the establishment of the Center for Problem-Oriented Policing (known as the POP Center), a Web-based organization whose stated mission is "to advance the concept and practice of problem-oriented policing in open and democratic societies. It does so by making readily accessible information about ways in which police can more effectively address specific crime and disorder problems" (Center for Problem-Oriented Policing, 2004). Although the center's focus is broader than just analysis, the numerous resources, guidebooks, and learning tools it has made available have contributed significantly to knowledge about and analysis of crime problems.

If we look outside the borders of the United States into the international policing community, we find evidence that the profession of crime analysis is also growing in other countries. Most European countries have formal crime analysis functions within their national or state police agencies, as do Japan, Australia, Brazil, South Africa, and other nations. In 2003, at a conference titled "Crime Analysis and Strategic Planning" put on by the College of European Police (CEPOL), analysts from more than 12 European countries came together to discuss the nature of crime analysis and its role in strategic planning. Most of the discussion at the conference centered on issues similar to those noted above as important to crime analysts in the United States: the need for standards, training, and recognition by police management.[5]

Police agencies in the United Kingdom have also seen a significant push for crime analysis, both within the problem-solving process and tactically. The concerns of crime analysts in the United Kingdom mirror those of their counterparts in the United States, revolving around issues of data integrity, effectiveness of techniques, usefulness of crime analysis products, and staffing and resources. Recently, the United Kingdom's National Criminal Intelligence Service (2000) has developed and implemented the national intelligence model (NIM) of policing, which centers on keeping police informed through the use of a set of standardized crime analysis techniques and products.

To summarize: The discipline of crime analysis is fairly young, even internationally, and is still being incorporated into police practice. By developing training programs, providing education, creating a body of literature, testing analytic techniques, and evaluating their effectiveness, scholars and practitioners help to promote and institutionalize the profession of crime analysis. As a dynamic and growing profession, crime analysis offers significant opportunities to individuals who enter the field.

Crime Analysis as a Career Track

Opinions differ somewhat concerning what makes a "good" crime analyst, and usually the opinions that people hold on this subject mirror their own experiences. That is, a crime analyst who is a police officer is likely to believe that all crime analysts should be police officers, and a crime analyst with an advanced degree is likely to feel that all crime analysts should have such degrees. Although this a simplification, debate continues about what experience and education crime analysts need in order to do their jobs. Is it necessary for a crime analyst to have been an officer, so that he or she knows the ins and outs of a police department, or is an advanced degree in statistics more valuable? In addition, because so much of modern crime analysis relies on computers and software technology, some argue that crime analysts should be computer experts as well.

Ideally, a crime analyst should have police knowledge, research skills, and technological capabilities. One person is not likely to have all of these qualifications at the beginning of a career in crime analysis; rather, he or she may have a particular strength in one of these areas and need to cultivate the others over time. Figure 3.1 illustrates how a crime analyst's capabilities should represent a balance of knowledge and skills in these three areas. One individual may have a relatively academic slant but be able to relate to the everyday work of policing and effectively explain crime analysis information. Another person who is lacking in formal education may have a street-level knowledge of crime and police activity as well as skills in technology and statistical analysis.

The current trend in police agencies is to hire civilian crime analysts. Officers tend to change positions every few years, and agencies do not want to risk losing the investment that intensive crime analysis training represents when officers move. In addition, civilians are less expensive than officers (in terms of salary and retirement benefits) for police agencies to employ. Although this makes the position of crime analyst a good entry-level job, the position also lacks opportunity for career track advancement. In many police agencies, especially small to medium-sized police departments, crime analyst is one of only a few professional support positions, and the only way an analyst can advance is to go to a larger department or move to a different position in the city government.

Figure 3.1   Capabilities of a Crime Analyst

That being said, police agencies vary greatly in how they fill crime analyst positions with both civilians and officers. Generally, a successful analyst is an expert in data collection, data manipulation, statistics, theory, and research methods. The analyst is the authority in examination, research, and assisting other police personnel in doing their jobs more effectively. A successful crime analyst also has knowledge about policing in general, about police culture, and about the characteristics of the community in which he or she works. Each crime analyst has his or her own style of dealing with people, but to be successful, an analyst must be able to explain complex ideas clearly to many different types of individuals (e.g., police officers, managers, city officials, citizens) in a way that is not condescending. In addition, a crime analyst must be able to relate to police officers (even if he or she has never been one), work within police culture, think clearly under pressure, defend his or her views on important issues, and keep a sense of humor.

Crime Analyst Qualifications and Job Descriptions

Police departments have many different types of crime analysis positions. Some employ only one crime analyst, whereas others have several who function in what is typically called a **crime analysis unit**, or **CAU**. Below, I provide general descriptions of several crime analysis–related positions and their roles within CAUs to show the range of levels and activities in the profession of crime analysis as well as the qualifications necessary for employment at various levels.

Interns/Volunteers

Police agencies have used volunteers to conduct crime analysis for many years. During the 1970s and 1980s, many police departments employed volunteers for this purpose because few crime analysis professionals were available or because they lacked the resources to hire professionals. Today, police departments typically use volunteers and interns to support and/or enhance their crime analysis resources and productivity. **Volunteers** are people who work for the police department without pay; they tend to be students or retired persons. **Interns** are undergraduate or graduate students who work in a police department to obtain practical work experience and college credit. An internship can often serve as a proverbial foot in the door, gaining the intern access to future career opportunities.

Internship programs can be extremely beneficial to both police departments and their interns. Interns not only help departments by performing crime analysis duties, they learn the skills they need to become crime analysts and gain practical experience. Police departments recruit student interns from many disciplines, including criminal justice, sociology, political science, geography, English, psychology, and computer science, depending on the needs of their crime analysis units and the availability of students. For example, a police department that is instituting a geographic information system might recruit geography students, whereas a department looking to conduct tactical analysis might recruit students majoring in criminal justice.

Individual academic programs typically administer the internship programs through which student interns are placed. These programs usually require that a student work as an intern for a minimum of one semester (the number of hours per week varies with the number of course credits given), document his or her experiences through field notes, and write a final paper for a grade. Internships can be paid or unpaid, depending on the resources of the police agency. Volunteers and interns handle many different tasks within CAUs, including tactical data entry, data analysis, production of monthly strategic reports, and the writing of requests to participate in complex analysis projects.

One note of caution about internships: Even though student interns are not becoming police officers, police departments often put applicants for internships through the same screening process as that used for applicants for police officer training (e.g., lie detector test, extensive background checks, drug testing) because interns have the same access officers have to department areas and records. Students applying for police department internships should be aware that any illegal behavior in which they have taken part might have a significant impact on their being accepted and, subsequently, on their ability to work in a police agency at all.

Crime Analysis Assistant/Technician

A **crime analysis assistant or technician** is an administrative support person who answers the phone, conducts data entry, makes copies, keeps files, produces simple standardized reports, and does anything else that arises administratively in the CAU. This position normally requires a high school diploma and 1 to 2 years of secretarial/data entry experience. It is typically filled by someone who has been a secretary or by an individual just beginning in the profession of crime analysis (e.g., a student). In some cases, crime analysis assistants are able to move up in the CAU as they obtain additional education and experience.

Entry-Level Crime Analyst

When a police agency has multiple levels of crime analysis positions, one of these is often described as **entry-level crime analyst.** An analyst in this position usually conducts relatively routine crime analysis duties, as he or she is likely to be new to the field and has had limited experience. Typically, this position requires an undergraduate degree in criminal justice, political science, sociology, or a related field that includes statistics and research methodology in its curriculum and 1 year of analytic experience, although not necessarily crime analysis experience (a master's degree is often seen as the equivalent of a year of experience). Some police departments require that applicants for the position of entry-level crime analyst have crime analysis certification (offered in several states) when they are hired or that they obtain such certification within a specific period after they begin working in the position.

Experienced Crime Analyst

An **experienced crime analyst** may be part of the structure of a CAU or may be a solo practitioner of crime analysis in a police agency. In departments that employ a number of analysts, this level exists to create career advancement opportunities for analysts. Compared with the entry-level crime analyst, the experienced crime analyst holds more responsibility and is expected to conduct more advanced analyses. An individual in this position may also have the duty of supervising lower-level personnel, such as crime analysis assistants/technicians, volunteers, and interns. Typically, the position of experienced crime analyst requires at minimum a bachelor's degree in criminal justice, political science, sociology, or other related field that includes statistics and research methodology in its curriculum and 2 years of crime analysis experience.

Specialty Crime Analyst

A **specialty crime analyst** is an analyst who is hired to conduct a particular type of crime analysis. An agency with a relatively large CAU may prefer to employ crime analysts who are specialists (i.e., who have their own individual sets of specialized skills and knowledge) rather than generalists (i.e., who are cross-trained so that all members of the unit have similar skills and knowledge). In some cases, agencies may receive grant funding that requires crime analysts to analyze particular types of crime or other activity. For police agencies, the advantage of having specialty crime analysts available is that these individuals have substantial skills and knowledge in their particular areas of crime analysis; the disadvantage is that their work cannot be shared easily with other analysts, so if a specialty analyst resigns no one else can conduct the work until another analyst with the same specialty is hired.

There are numerous types of specialty crime analysts, and the education and experience required for these positions varies by specialty. In general, however, the position of specialty crime analyst is typically considered to be equivalent to the experienced crime analyst level, as both positions require proficiencies in particular areas. The following are some examples of types of specialty crime analysts:

- *Tactical crime analyst:* This type of analyst conducts only tactical crime analysis and does not produce long-term reports or statistics.
- *Problem analyst:* This type of analyst conducts analysis within the context of problem solving only.
- *Sex crime analyst:* This type of analyst conducts tactical, strategic, and administrative crime analysis having to do with sex crimes and is likely to work closely with detectives. The position of sex crime analyst might exist in a large agency that has developed a long-term task force to address sex crimes. (Other types of crime analysts also specialize in particular kinds of crime, such as violent crime analysts, property crime analysts, and robbery crime analysts.)
- *School safety analyst:* This type of analyst conducts analysis on the safety in and around schools, working directly with school administrators and school resource officers.
- *Geographic information systems analyst:* This type of analyst specializes in the use of geographic information systems and conducts spatial analysis of crime and various types of police activity.

Crime Analysis Supervisor

The **crime analysis supervisor** is a person with substantial crime analysis knowledge and experience who supervises a crime analysis unit. This job title is not applied to police managers (sworn personnel) who supervise the crime analysis function as part of their other duties. The position of crime analysis supervisor is considered to be a "working" position in that it involves hands-on crime analysis work. The key responsibilities of a crime analysis supervisor are to represent the interests of the CAU at high-level organizational meetings (such as command staff and patrol or investigations operations meetings), to lead the development of CAU goals and objectives, and to be knowledgeable about the crime analysis discipline regionally, nationally, and internationally. Typically, this position requires a master's degree in criminal justice, political science, sociology, or other related field, 2 years of crime analysis experience, and at least 1 year of supervisory experience.

CAU Organizational Chart

Figure 3.2 depicts a hypothetical CAU organizational chart, including the positions discussed above and their minimum requirements. The arrows in the figure indicate potential routes for career advancement.

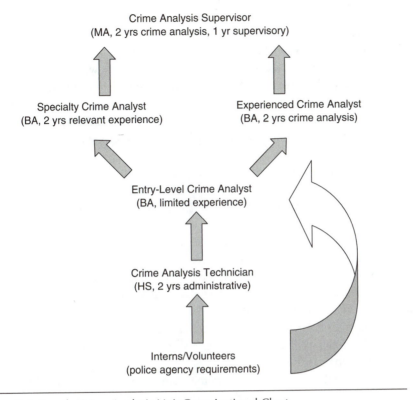

Figure 3.2. Sample Crime Analysis Unit Organizational Chart

Summary Points

This chapter has provided an overview of the crime analysis profession in the United States, including its history, its current status, and the career paths within the profession. The following are the key points addressed in this chapter:

- Citizens and police have conducted informal crime analysis throughout history, but formal crime analysis did not begin until the first formal police department was established in England in the early 19th century.
- Crime analysis did not begin to develop in the United States until the 20th century.
- In the early 1900s, August Vollmer, the most famous police reformer, was the first police practitioner to write about crime analysis and the mapping of police reports in the United States.
- O. W. Wilson, a student of Vollmer, developed recommendations for analysis and "crime mapping" units in police departments in the 1950s and 1960s.
- The 1968 Omnibus Crime Control and Safe Streets Act helped to fund police agencies' crime analysis endeavors throughout the 1970s.
- A number of publications—including manuals, media articles, and conference proceedings—provide evidence of the use of crime analysis in police agencies in the 1970s.

- Scholars' focus on the geographic analysis of crime and problem-oriented policing increased attention to crime analysis in the 1970s and 1980s.
- The first professional associations concerned with crime analysis were established in the 1980s, and an international association was formed in 1990.
- In the mid-1990s, the U.S. government's emphasis on community policing and problem solving led to the availability of federal grants that enabled police agencies to implement crime analysis. In addition, improvements in computer technology encouraged the use of crime mapping and crime analysis in everyday policing.
- Crime analysis is now a recognized profession within the policing community. As a profession, it is still in the process of being developed (e.g., scholars and practitioners are creating a body of literature, testing and retesting analytic techniques, and providing training and education).
- Most large and many medium-sized police agencies in the United States conduct some form of crime analysis.
- Most crime analysts today focus on tactical crime analysis and/or on providing statistical information directly to police management.
- Recent efforts by the International Association of Crime Analysts, crime analysis scholars, and police practitioners have addressed the development of crime analysis literature as well as research, training, and practical assistance for crime analysts.
- Anecdotal information from crime analysts in countries around the world indicates that they share the same concerns about development, training, data, and management support issues as crime analysts in the United States.
- The role of the crime analyst is to serve as the police agency's expert in the use of data, research methods, and statistical techniques in analyzing crime and related police activity as well as to provide explanations for and ideas about how to study crime and disorder problems.
- Ideally, a crime analyst should have police knowledge, research skills, and technological capabilities. One person is not likely to have all of these qualifications at the beginning of a career in crime analysis; rather, he or she may have a particular strength in one of these areas and need to cultivate the others over time.
- Although many police agencies employ only one or two crime analysts, the crime analysis discipline includes a range of potential careers, from assistant positions to specialty and supervisory positions.
- Students who are interested in pursuing careers in crime analysis may gain a "foot in the door" through internships or volunteer positions.

Exercises

Exercise 3.1

Review the crime analysis information available on the Web sites listed below. Compare and contrast the content of the sites run by various agencies, government programs, organizations, and private companies to get a better understanding of the field.

- Tempe (Arizona) Police Department, Crime Analysis Unit: http://www.tempe
  .gov/cau (local police agency)
- Redding (California) Police Department, Crime Analysis Unit: http://www
  .reddingpolice.org/rpdcau.html (local police agency)
- Watsonville (California) Police Department, Crime Analysis Department:
  http://www.ci.watsonville.ca.us/crimestats (local police agency)
- National Institute of Justice, National Law Enforcement and Corrections
  Technology Center, Crime Mapping and Analysis Program: http://www.nlectc
  .org/cmap/ (federal government program)
- International Association of Crime Analysts: http://www.iaca.net (international professional association)
- Massachusetts Association of Crime Analysts: http://www.macrimeanalysts
  .com/index.html (state-level professional association)
- Crime Analysis Center: http://crimeanalysiscenter.tripod.com (private
  company)
- Alpha Group Center for Crime and Intelligence Analysis Training: http://
  www.alphagroupcenter.com (private company)

Using an Internet search engine, conduct your own search for "crime analysis"
to find and compare other types of sites that include crime analysis–related information on academics (class information and books), training providers, and police
agencies, as well as informal personal thoughts on crime analysis.

Exercise 3.2

Find four different crime analysis (or related) job descriptions or job announcements (i.e., announcements posted by agencies advertising for new hires) on the
Internet, in newspapers, or from other sources (e.g., direct contact with police agencies) and examine them to get an understanding of current job opportunities in the
field. (Try to obtain an original of each job description or announcement rather
than use a secondhand source.) Compare and contrast the following information on
your four examples:

- Agency (city, state, and type of police department)
- Title of the position
- Salary range
- Minimum requirements (education and experience)
- Roles and responsibilities (summarize)

Notes

1.   CALEA is an independent accrediting authority whose purpose is "to improve delivery
of law enforcement service by offering a body of standards, developed by law enforcement
practitioners, covering a wide range of up-to-date law enforcement topics" (CALEA, 2004).

Chapter 15 of CALEA's *Standards for Law Enforcement Agencies* specifies requirements for police agencies concerning crime analysis; this information has been included in every edition of that manual since it was first published in August 1983.

2. These conclusions are based on my own experience, as no study has been conducted to date concerning the evolution of crime analysis in the 1990s.

3. This list of concerns is based on my own experience as well as discussions I have had with crime analysts around the United States and on information gathered from a practitioner forum held at the Police Foundation (see "Practitioner Recommendations," 2003).

4. The three main Listservs used by practitioners, researchers, and software developers interested in crime analysis and crime mapping (internationally) are the "leanalyst," "crimemap," and "IACA" Listservs.

5. This conclusion is based on my own observations as an attendee at the CEPOL conference.

4

Introduction to Crime Mapping

Ever since maps have been available that depict the geographic features of communities, such as streets and city boundaries, police departments have used such maps to determine patrol areas and emergency routes as well as to assist patrol officers in finding specific addresses. Police departments have also mapped crime, a process that, until recently, involved the manual placement of pins on hand-drawn wall maps. This chapter discusses the emergence of computerized crime mapping as a tool for conducting crime analysis. It begins with an introduction to key terms and then describes basic concepts before presenting a history of crime mapping and information on the field's current status and career paths.

Definitions: GIS and Crime Mapping

A **geographic information system (GIS)** is a powerful software tool that allows the user to create any kind of geographic representation, from a simple point map to a three-dimensional visualization of spatial or temporal data. For the purposes of this book, the definition of a GIS is as follows:

A GIS is a set of computer-based tools that allows the user to modify, visualize, query, and analyze geographic and tabular data.

A GIS is similar to a spreadsheet or word processing program in that the software provides a framework and templates for data collection, collation, and analysis, and it is up to the user to decide what parts of the system to use and how to use them. A GIS does more than enable the user to produce paper maps; it also allows him or her to view the data behind geographic features, combine various features, manipulate the data and maps, and perform statistical functions.

Crime mapping is a term used in policing to refer to the process of conducting spatial analysis within crime analysis. For the purposes of this book, the definition of crime mapping is as follows:

Crime mapping is the process of using a geographic information system to conduct spatial analysis of crime problems and other police-related issues.

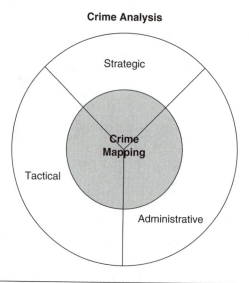

Crime Analysis

Figure 4.1   Relationship of Crime Mapping to Crime Analysis

Clarifying where different types of crime and other incidents occur is one of the many important functions of crime analysis. Because of the unique nature of the software used and the prominence of geographic data in crime mapping, this type of analysis is often discussed as though it is distinct from crime analysis; in reality, however, crime mapping is a subdiscipline of crime analysis. Crime mapping serves three main functions within crime analysis:

1. It facilitates visual and statistical analyses of the spatial nature of crime and other types of events.

2. It allows analysts to link unlike data sources together based on common geographic variables (e.g., linking census information, school information, and crime data for a common area).

3. It provides maps that help to communicate analysis results.

Crime mapping is complementary to all forms of crime analysis in that it plays an important part in almost every analysis. As Figure 4.1 illustrates, crime mapping does not stand alone; rather, it is a process that occurs within the larger process of crime analysis. The following are some examples of how crime mapping is used within the three types of crime analysis that are the focus of this book:

- In *tactical crime analysis,* crime mapping is used to identify immediate patterns for crimes such as residential and commercial burglary, auto theft, and theft from vehicles. For example, spatial analysis of auto theft incidents may reveal clusters of activity at specific locations that might indicate a crime pattern.

- In *strategic crime analysis,* crime mapping is utilized in long-term applications to analyze the relationship between criminal activity and indicators of disorder, such as a high volume of vacant property or disorder calls for service; to assist in geographic and temporal allocation of resources, such as patrol officer scheduling and determination of patrol areas; to examine patterns of crime at or around specific locations, such as schools, bars, or drug treatment centers; to calculate crime rate information, such as numbers of residential burglaries per household; and to incorporate crime data with qualitative geographic information, such as information on teenage hangouts, student pathways to school, or drug and prostitution markets.
- In *administrative crime analysis,* crime mapping is a valuable tool used by police, researchers, and media organizations to convey criminal activity information to the public. Web sites operated by police departments and news organization routinely post maps that depict areas of crime, along with corresponding tables and definitions. For example, a police agency can reduce citizen requests for neighborhood crime information by placing monthly or weekly crime maps on a Web site that members of the public can access using computers in their homes or at the local library.

Geographic Features

A geographic information system translates physical elements in the real world—such as roads, buildings, lakes, and mountains—into forms that can be displayed, manipulated, and analyzed along with police information such as crime, arrest, and traffic accident data. A GIS uses four types of features to represent objects and locations in the real world; these are referred to as point, line, polygon, and image features (for a discussion of the attribute data behind these features, see Chapter 6).

Point Features

A **point feature** is a discrete location that is usually depicted on a GIS-generated map by a symbol or label. A point feature is analogous to a pin placed on a paper wall map. A GIS uses different symbols to depict the locations of data relevant to the analysis, such as crimes, motor vehicle accidents, traffic signs, buildings, police beat stations, and cell phone towers. Figure 4.2 shows circles on the map that could represent any of these types of locations.

Line Features

A **line feature** is a real-world element that can be represented on a map by a line or set of lines. The lines in Figure 4.2, for example, represent streets. Other types of line features include rivers, streams, power lines, and bus routes.

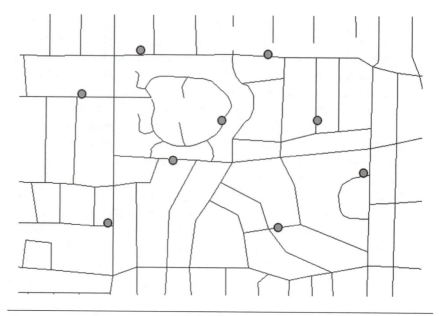

Figure 4.2   Point and Line Feature Example

Polygon Features

A **polygon feature** is a geographic area represented on a map by a multisided figure with a closed set of lines. Polygons can represent areas as large as continents or as small as buildings; in GIS-generated maps they may be used to depict county boundaries, city boundaries, parks, school campuses, or police districts. The five polygons in Figure 4.3 might represent police districts in a city.

Image Features

An **image feature** on a GIS-generated map is a vertical photograph taken from a satellite or an airplane that is digitized and placed within the appropriate coordinates. Such photos, which may appear in black and white or color, show the details of streets, buildings, parking lots, and environmental features (landscaping). Figure 4.4 is an example of an image feature, an aerial photograph of a residential neighborhood.

Types of Crime Mapping

Several types of mapping are used routinely in crime analysis. This section provides a brief introduction to the various types of crime mapping to set the stage for the chapters that follow, which discuss the creation of maps and their application to crime analysis in more detail.

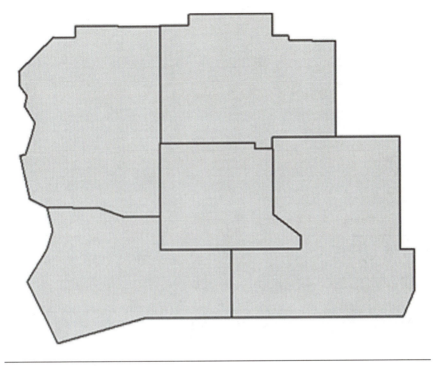

Figure 4.3   Polygon Feature Example

Figure 4.4   Image Feature Example

SOURCE: Photo courtesy of the Chula Vista (California) Police Department.

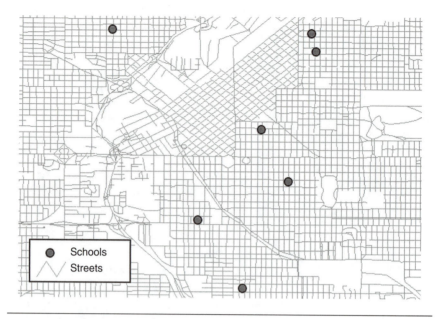

Figure 4.5   Single-Symbol Mapping Example

Single-Symbol Mapping

In **single-symbol maps**, individual, uniform symbols represent features such as the locations of stores, roads, or states. Figure 4.5 is an example of a single-symbol map showing school locations and streets.[1] An important thing to keep in mind about single-symbol maps is that a GIS places all points on such a map that share the same address directly on top of one another, making it impossible for the map to show how many points there really are. For example, in the map shown in Figure 4.5, if a middle school and elementary school share the same address, the GIS will have placed two gray circles in the same spot, so there is no way someone looking at the map can see all the schools in the area. This drawback of single-symbol mapping is particularly relevant for the mapping of crime and other police data, because crime and other police-related incidents often occur repeatedly at particular locations. Because of this, crime analysts use single-symbol mapping primarily to display geographic information in which there is no overlap; they employ other types of maps to convey information about multiple incidents at particular locations.

In addition, single-symbol maps are not useful when analysts are dealing with large amounts of data. Imagine the map in Figure 4.5 with the locations of 100 schools marked. The points would overlap, and the map would be difficult to read. Thus analysts use single-symbol maps primarily when they are working with relatively small amounts of data that do not overlap. Police agencies also often use single-symbol maps to communicate the locations of crimes within patterns to police personnel. (For numerous examples of how single-symbol maps are used in tactical crime analysis, see Chapter 9.)

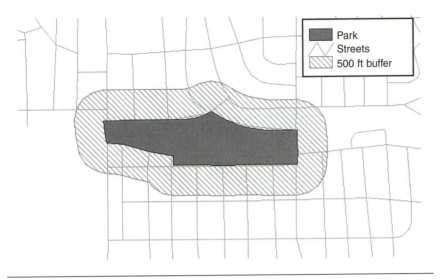

Figure 4.6   Buffer Map Example: One Buffer

Buffers

A **buffer** is a specified area around a feature on a map. Buffers can be set at small distances, such as 50 feet, or larger distances, such as 500 miles, depending on the purpose and scale of the map. Buffers help in crime analysis by illustrating the relative distances between features on a map. The example map in Figure 4.6 shows a park (polygon feature) with a 500-foot buffer, which could be used to show whether drug arrests were made within 500 feet of the park.

Buffers can also be used as polygons for data aggregation and comparison. Figure 4.7 shows two buffers (500 feet and 1000 feet) around nightclubs (point features), which analysts could use to compare incidents directly around the night-clubs to those farther out to see whether the activity has a spillover effect on surrounding neighborhoods.

Graduated Mapping

Crime analysts often use **graduated maps**—that is, maps in which different sizes or colors of features represent particular values of variables. Figures 4.8 and 4.9 are general examples of graduated size and graduated color maps, respectively (for discussion of specific techniques for creating these maps, see Chapter 12.)

In a graduated size map, the sizes of the symbols used for point and line features reflect their value. As noted above, single-symbol maps are not appropriate for displaying data about crimes that occur at the same locations repeatedly. Analysts use graduated size maps for this purpose, because these maps can account for multiple incidents at the same locations. However, like single-symbol maps, graduated size maps are subject to overlapping points if too many data are analyzed at once.

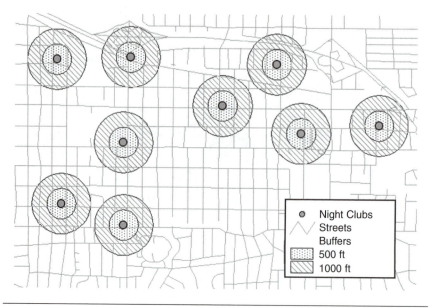

Figure 4.7　　Buffer Map Example: Two Buffers

Figure 4.8 is a map in which points are graduated by size according to the numbers of crimes at specific locations.

In a graduated color map, the colors of the symbols reflect their values; this kind of mapping can be used with points (in a single-symbol map only),[2] lines, and polygons. Figure 4.9 is a map that uses colors to show the total numbers of crimes in particular areas—the lighter shaded areas are those with fewer crimes, and the darker shaded areas are those with more crimes.

Chart Mapping

Chart mapping allows the crime analyst to display several values within a particular variable at the same time (e.g., variable = crime, values = robbery, assault, and rape). There are two types of chart mapping: pie and bar. In **pie chart mapping,** the relative percentages (represented by slices of a pie) of values within a variable are displayed. Figure 4.10 is an example of a pie chart map that depicts fights, drugs, weapons, and disorderly conduct incidents at nightclubs. The pies are placed at the locations of all the nightclubs in the area mapped, and the sizes of the pies are graduated to depict the total occupancy capacities of the nightclubs, which provides a relative comparison. Some of the nightclubs represented have had all four types of incidents, whereas others have had only two or three of the four, and the percentages (slices) are based only on the frequencies of the values included (not all types of incidents at all nightclubs).

In **bar chart mapping,** the relative frequencies (represented by bars) of values within variables are displayed. In the example in Figure 4.11, bar charts are placed at the locations of the nightclubs in the area mapped. This figure depicts the same

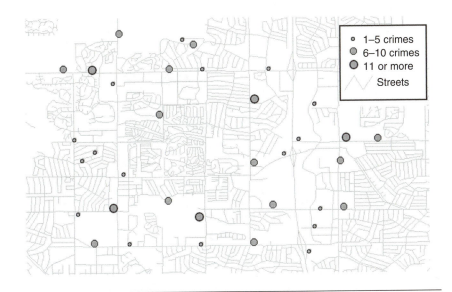

Figure 4.8   Graduated Size Map Example

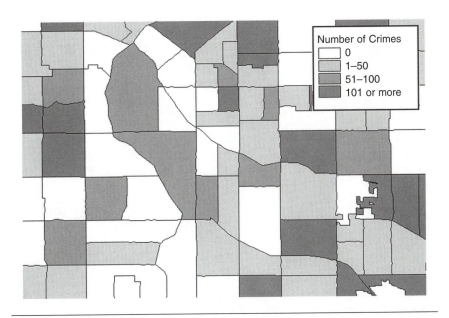

Figure 4.9   Graduated Color Map Example

data shown in Figure 4.10, but instead of percentages, the heights of the bars show the frequencies of incidents.

Density Mapping

In **density mapping**, analysts use point data to shade surfaces that are not limited to area boundaries (as is the case in graduated color mapping). In their most

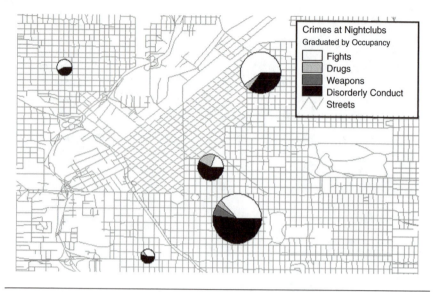

Figure 4.10   Pie Chart Map Example

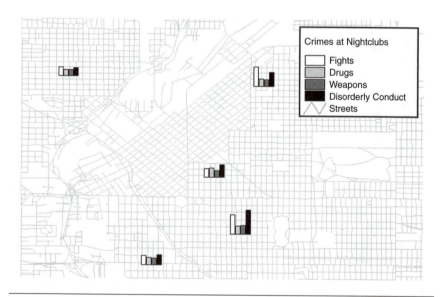

Figure 4.11   Bar Chart Map Example

basic form, density maps are shaded according to the concentration of incidents in particular areas. In the map shown in Figure 4.12, the darker colors represent areas in which the incidents are more concentrated, and the lighter colors represent those in which the incidents are less concentrated. Such maps are used to compare small variations in crime levels from one area to another rather than to compare levels of crime within fixed artificial geographic boundaries, as in area maps.(For more detailed explanation of density mapping, see Chapter 12.)

Figure 4.12   Density Map Example

Interactive Crime Mapping

Rather than a type of mapping, the term **interactive crime mapping** refers to simplified geographic information systems made available to novice users over the Internet. Many police departments have interactive Web sites where citizens and police officers can conduct basic crime mapping themselves. These applications typically are not flexible or sophisticated enough to be useful to crime analysts. To illustrate interactive crime mapping, Figures 4.13 and 4.14 depict selected screens found on the East Valley COMPASS (Community Mapping, Planning and Analysis for Safety Strategies) interactive Web site, which is hosted by the Redlands, California, Police Department (http://www.eastvalleycompass.org). Figure 4.13 shows the query screen of this site's mapping program, which allows the user to choose a particular type of data. In other queries, the user can request data for particular locations, areas of interest, or time frames. Figure 4.14 shows the single-symbol map resulting from a query, with its legend on the right-hand side and different types of functions (e.g., zoom, pan, identify) listed on the left. The user can manipulate the map with limited functions, query different data, and print maps and reports.

History of Crime Mapping

Even though crime mapping plays a significant role in crime analysis today, conducting spatial analysis and creating crime maps have only recently become common in policing and crime analysis, thanks to advancements in technology. Unlike crime analysis, the history of crime mapping begins not with the establishment of the first police force, but with researchers long before computers were invented.

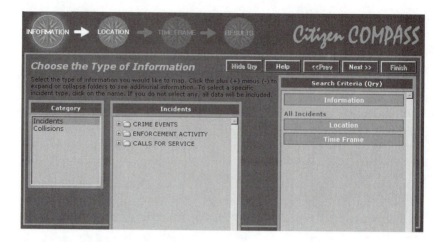

Figure 4.13   Interactive Map Example: Query Screen

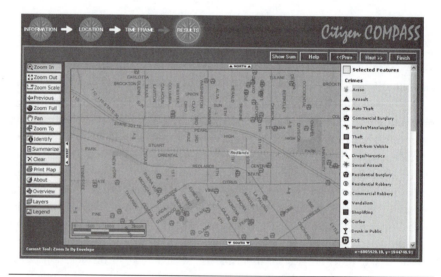

Figure 4.14   Interactive Map Example: Resulting Map

Beginnings of Crime Mapping

In the 1800s, European researchers who adhered to the school of thought known as the cartographic school of criminology examined the levels of crime within different areas (regions) and the relationship of these levels to sociological factors, such as socioeconomic status (Groff & La Vigne, 2002). For example, in 1829, Adriano Balbi, an ethnographer and geographer, and André-Michel Guerry, a lawyer, created the first maps of crime using criminal statistics for the years 1825 to 1827 and demographic data from the census. They examined crimes against property, crimes against persons, and levels of education in France and found that areas with high levels of crimes against property had a low incidence of crimes against people and that higher numbers of educated people lived in areas with more property crime (Weisburd & McEwen, 1997). Also during this period, the Belgian astronomer and statistician Quételet used maps to examine correlations between crime and transportation routes, education levels, and ethnic and cultural variations (Weisburd & McEwen, 1997).

United States: 1900–1970

In the United States, the use of crime mapping began a little later than it did in Europe. Because the United States was a relatively new country in the 1800s, reliable maps were not readily available and census data were not regularly collected, as they were in France and England at that time. The first substantive spatial analysis of crime in the United States was conducted in the 1920s and 1930s by urban sociologists in Chicago. Their crime research and related crime maps linked crime and delinquency to factors such as social disorganization and poverty. In fact, these scholars' spatial analysis of juvenile delinquency and social conditions in Chicago is considered to be one of the foremost examples of crime mapping in the first half of the 20th century (Groff & La Vigne, 2002).

Crime mapping was a theoretical component in the development of the concentric zone model, which contends that in an urban setting different types of zones (areas with different purposes) form around a central business district and that some of these zones are more prone to crime and disorder than are others. Researchers who analyzed the locations and distribution of gangs in Chicago based on the concentric zone concept found that gangs were concentrated in parts of the city where social control was weak and social disorganization was high (Weisburd & McEwen, 1997). Most of the early crime mapping conducted in both Europe and the United States examined aggregate levels of crime by area. However, evidence exists of a map that was created by hand in 1929 by Chicago school researchers in which the home addresses of more than 9,000 delinquents were clustered in particular areas of Chicago (Weisburd & McEwen, 1997).

Through the 1950s, 1960s, and 1970s, sociologists and others who were interested in crime and its causes continued to examine the sociological factors associated with crime. The explanations and geographic methods of analysis used remained fairly uncomplicated during this period, possibly owing to the researchers' focus on sociological factors and the lack of adequate technology (Groff & La Vigne, 2002). In the late 1960s, scholars began conducting spatial analysis of crime with the help of large computer systems and unsophisticated visualization methods (Weisburd & McEwen, 1997).

1970 to Present

From the late 1960s through the early 1980s, a group of researchers in England, Canada, and the United States shifted their focus of the study of crime away from what traditional criminology examined—criminal offender—and toward the criminal event and its context, including the physical and social environments that create opportunities for crime (Brantingham & Brantingham, 1981; Clarke,

1980, 1983; Cornish & Clarke, 1986). This movement affected crime mapping, as researchers shifted from aggregate analysis of crime and social factors to the analysis of discrete criminal events and their locations (for a more detailed discussion of this theoretical approach, see Chapter 5). Consequently, researchers began to incorporate information about geography and environment into their study of crime problems and related issues, such as rape (LeBeau, 1987) and a host of other crimes (Harries, 1980) as well as distribution of police personnel (Rengert & Wasilchick, 1985).

In the early 1980s, client server technology made geographic information systems more available, and this enabled a number of police departments to experiment with crime mapping in their everyday work (Groff & La Vigne, 2002). A project funded by the National Institute of Justice partnered researchers and practitioners in five U.S. cities to use innovative analytic techniques in studying drug markets and tracking their movements over time (Groff & La Vigne, 2002):

- In New Jersey, Rutgers University and the Jersey City Police Department implemented an experimental design to test problem-oriented policing responses to reduce violent crime.
- In Connecticut, the city of Hartford joined with Abt Associates, a private consulting firm based in Boston, to promote crime mapping as a way of encouraging community involvement in addressing crime problems.
- In California, the San Diego Police Department and the Police Executive Research Forum mapped drug incidents and drug markets with police interventions in an experiment that evolved into a crime mapping system.
- In Pennsylvania, Carnegie Mellon University and the Pittsburgh Bureau of Police developed a system in which thematic maps were created to show changes in crime by area over time.
- In Missouri, the Kansas City Police Department partnered with the Crime Control Institute to develop an innovative narcotics enforcement strategy aimed at reducing the violence and disorder associated with retail drug sales in residential neighborhoods.

These projects led the way for crime mapping partnerships between practitioners and researchers and demonstrated how communities could use GIS tools as a central part of crime control initiatives. The program was focused primarily on the use of geographic police data, but the participants found that examining other geographically based data contributed to their ability to target problem-solving strategies, brought together key partners with different perspectives, and facilitated the assessment of their joint efforts (Taxman & McEwen, 1997).

In the early to mid-1990s, significant improvements in computer technology and police data systems made electronic crime mapping a much more practical tool for police and researchers. GIS software became available for desktop computers as these computers became capable of processing large amounts of data quickly. In addition, police data on crimes, arrests, accidents, and calls for service became available electronically through computer-aided dispatch systems as well as through electronic records management systems (for discussion of these innovations, see Chapter 7).

Geographic data such as street and census information became widely available in electronic format and were provided free or at minimal cost by a variety of government agencies and commercial organizations. All of these developments helped to advance the field of crime mapping beyond manual methods and the use of large, costly mainframe mapping systems.

In 1993, the Illinois Criminal Justice Information Authority and the Sociology Department of Loyola University of Chicago joined forces to present a computer crime mapping workshop in Chicago. In a publication resulting from the workshop titled *Crime Analysis Through Computer Mapping* (Block, Dabdoub, & Fregly, 1995), participants—many of whom are top researchers and analysts in the field today—described spatial analytic techniques and offered practical advice for both police professionals interested in implementing computer mapping in their agencies and students of spatial analysis. This workshop was one of the first efforts to bring practitioners and researchers together to discuss crime mapping.

During the mid-1990s, the federal government, in a movement spearheaded by Vice President Al Gore, provided increased support for crime mapping technology and methods. Police agencies received federal funding to obtain crime mapping technology, and several programs were developed specifically to assist police agencies with the implementation of crime mapping. The U.S. Department of Justice's Office of Community Oriented Policing Services (the COPS Office) allocated a significant amount of funding for crime mapping software and equipment through a program called MORE (Making Officer Redeployment Effective). The primary objective of this funding was to "expand the amount of time current law enforcement officers can spend on community policing by funding technology, equipment, and support staff" (Office of Community Oriented Policing Services, 2004). Table 4.1 displays the details of the MORE funding, including how much of the money was allocated directly to crime mapping technology and staff. As the table shows, in a period of only 7 years the COPS Office provided more than $53 million to police agencies specifically for crime mapping.

Since 1995, the COPS Making Officer Redeployment Effective (MORE) program has provided funds in excess of 1.3 billion dollars to law enforcement agencies for the purchase of time-saving technology and civilian personnel. The time savings produced by these grants has resulted in the redeployment of officers to the street in order to enhance their community policing efforts. Some of the funds provided by MORE grants have been used to purchase crime mapping and GIS hardware and software. The COPS Office recognizes the important role that crime mapping plays in the in-depth analysis of community problems. This increased analytic capability improves the capacity of law enforcement to work with the community to develop more effective solutions to crime and social disorder problems.

—*Dr. Matthew Scheider, social science analyst, COPS Office*
(personal communication, October 8, 2003)

Table 4.1   Federal Funding for Crime Mapping

Year of Grants	Total Number of Grants	Total Funding ($)	Number of Grants for Mapping	Funding for Mapping ($)
1995	912	130,323,886	9	5,840,333
1996	1,050	187,426,110	25	6,439,829
1998	1,457	383,258,265	44	37,890,292
2001	536	78,554,321	6	1,623,859
2002	294	61,442,799	6	1,296,527
Total	4,249	841,005,381	90	53,090,840

SOURCE: Matthew Scheider, social science analyst, Office of Community Oriented Policing Services (personal communication, October 6, 2003).

To accompany the MORE funding, the COPS Office, in partnership with the Police Foundation, created the Crime Mapping Laboratory in 1997 to assist the policing community in integrating crime analysis and crime mapping into community policing and problem solving. Over the years, the lab has provided a wide range of training opportunities and technical assistance to the policing community and has published numerous reports and resource documents (updated yearly) on topics related to crime analysis, mapping, and problem solving. Its most recognized product is the newsletter *Crime Mapping News* ("Police Foundation Crime Mapping Laboratory," 2003, p. 1)

The Crime Mapping Research Center, now called the Mapping and Analysis for Public Safety (MAPS) program, was formed within the Department of Justice's National Institute of Justice in 1997 with the goal "to promote research, evaluation, development, and dissemination of GIS technology for criminal justice research and practice." The program provides "many beneficial services such as grant funding, annual conferences, information on training centers, publications, research, and more" (Mapping and Analysis for Public Safety, 2004).

Since its creation, the MAPS program has held annual conferences at which practitioners and researchers come together to discuss research and spatial analytic techniques. The program has also conducted a national survey of crime mapping, funded fellowships, developed training curricula, and published books on crime mapping. With the program's help, the United States has seen interest in and development of crime mapping and crime analysis techniques increase significantly among police departments and researchers.

In 1998, the National Institute of Justice created the Crime Mapping and Analysis Program (CMAP), the mission of which is "to provide technical assistance and introductory and advanced training to local and state agencies in the areas of crime and intelligence analysis and geographic information systems (GIS). GIS includes crime mapping, global positioning systems, automatic vehicle locator systems, and the use of this technology for the electronic home monitoring of community corrections clientele" (Crime Mapping and Analysis Program, 2004). CMAP has provided training to a significant number of crime analysts and officers in the field. In 2001, CMAP held a symposium on crime mapping topics that resulted in a publication titled *Advanced Crime Mapping Topics* (Bair, Boba, Fritz, Helms, & Hick, 2002), a collaborative document written by the attendees that includes articles on the role of crime mapping in crime series or investigative analysis, in operations research or resource allocation studies, in problem solving or applied research, and in discrete site analysis.

Another relatively recent influence on the use of crime mapping in policing is Compstat, a data- and mapping-driven police management strategy created by the New York City Police Department and adopted by other police agencies across the United States. A core component of Compstat is police officials' use of crime mapping software and analysis in weekly meetings to understand local patterns of crime and disorder incidents. Crime mapping is such an integral part of the Compstat program that during the 2001 television season, CBS's *The District,* a show based on New York's Compstat experience, highlighted crime mapping in every episode (Theodore, 2001).

To date, no historical study has been conducted on the adoption of crime mapping by police agencies, but David Weisburd, a distinguished professor in the field of crime and place, recently examined the rate of adoption of crime mapping in the 1990s through a number of surveys and a pilot study of his own and found that "crime mapping has become widely diffused among police agencies, that the diffusion process began in the late 1980s–early 1990s and gained momentum in the mid 1990s, and that the adoption of crime mapping appears to follow the standards curve of diffusion of innovation" (Weisburd & Lum, 2001, p. 7).

Current State of Crime Mapping

In 1997, the MAPS program conducted a nationwide survey to gauge the use of GIS technology for crime mapping throughout the police community. The researchers found that 13% of the 2,004 police departments responding to the survey reported using computerized crime mapping. It is interesting to note that 36% of larger departments (those with more than 100 officers) reported using computerized crime mapping, whereas only 3% of smaller departments (those with fewer than 100 officers) did so; this variation in the adoption of GIS technology by agency size is an important finding.

The MAPS survey also revealed that departments that were using crime mapping also geocoded data, mapped calls for service as well as various types of crime data, and primarily created single-symbol or graduated size and color maps. Most of the responding departments that were conducting crime mapping reported using visual analysis to identify hot spots and clusters of activity, and about one-fourth used statistical methods to do so. In addition, a majority of these departments reported maintaining several years of data for mapping purposes, which suggests that they may also conduct long-term (strategic) crime analysis (Mamalian & La Vigne, 1999).

The survey also showed that police departments were using mapping to visualize crime incident locations for officers and investigators, to make resource allocation (staffing) decisions, to evaluate interventions, to inform citizens about crime in their neighborhoods, and to identify repeat calls for service and crime locations. Factors that appeared to inhibit departments' implementation of crime mapping included limited financial resources, limited time, and lack of training (Mamalian & La Vigne, 1999).

No national studies of crime mapping have been conducted in recent years, but it seems safe to assume that the rate of adoption of crime mapping has slowed significantly in the United States for two major reasons. First, many, if not most, police agencies with more than 100 officers already have crime mapping technology in place, either for analysts or for officers. Smaller departments that do not yet have the technology may never adopt it, for financial and personnel (availability and training) reasons. Second, the focus of federal funding for law enforcement has shifted to homeland security since the terrorist attacks on New York City and Washington, D.C., of September 11, 2001. Although mapping plays a significant role in helping law enforcement prepare for and respond to acts of terrorism, local police departments are only one partner in this process and are likely to focus their mapping efforts on operational needs rather than terrorism concerns.

Another interesting element in the development of crime mapping is that in the past decade both crime analysis and crime mapping have evolved, but they have done so along different paths. This is evidenced by the differences in their histories (i.e., academic vs. police beginnings) and by the fact that, of the two, crime mapping has received greater funding, inspired the establishment of more organizations, and been the subject of more publications.

Crime Mapping as a Career Track

Even though many crime analysts utilize crime mapping in their daily work, many police agencies have established specific positions that are filled by people who specialize in spatial analysis of crime. These individuals, who are often called GIS analysts, are considered to be different from crime analysts. Salaries for GIS analysts are typically higher than those for crime analysts because of the specialized technical skills required and because police agencies must compete for qualified analysts with private companies offering high salaries. Compared with crime analyst positions, significantly fewer GIS analyst positions are available, for a number of reasons: (a) Smaller departments that conduct crime analysis typically have only one crime analyst position, and that is not a specialist position; (b) many police officials do not feel that filling a position with a person who works only on spatial analysis of crime is warranted; and (c) the number of potential applicants for GIS analyst positions (i.e., individuals who have both geography and criminal justice backgrounds) is relatively small.

Individuals with expertise in spatial analysis of crime may also find careers in organizations other than police agencies. The position of geographic profiler is one example; this kind of analyst is an expert in predicting the probable locations of criminals' residences based on the locations associated with their crimes (Rossmo, 2000). This position, which requires a full year of training, exists primarily in federal agencies (e.g., the Bureau of Alcohol, Tobacco, and Firearms and the FBI) rather than local ones, because many geographic profiles are based on crime series that cross jurisdictions. Positions are also available in government and nonprofit agencies that seek to work with police agencies through research or technical assistance (e.g., MAPS, CMAP, the Police Foundation, Abt Associates, the Institute for Law and Justice, and the Urban Institute). Police officers are also now receiving training in mapping, so the position of trainer of GIS for policing is becoming more common. Finally, individuals with advanced skills in policing and computer programming can work for private software companies that develop mapping software for police departments and crime analysts.

For undergraduate college students who are preparing for careers in the spatial analysis of crime, classes in geographic information systems and criminal justice are appropriate. Currently, no U.S. university offers a graduate program specifically in crime mapping, but many universities offer GIS certificates for majors in criminology who want to hone their spatial analysis skills.

Summary Points

This chapter has provided an overview of geographic information systems and crime mapping, describing the geographic features used in mapping and the various types of mapping, the history and current state of crime mapping, and crime mapping as a careers. The following are the key points addressed in this chapter:

- A geographic information system is a set of computer-based tools that allows the user to modify, visualize, query, and analyze geographic and tabular data.
- Crime mapping is the process of using a geographic information system to conduct spatial analysis of crime problems and other police-related issues.
- The three main functions of crime mapping are (a) to facilitate visual and statistical analyses of the spatial nature of crime and other types of events, (b) to enable analysts to link unlike data sources together based on common geographic variables, and (c) to provide maps that help to communicate analysis results.
- A GIS uses four types of geographic features to approximate real-world elements: points, lines, polygons, and images.
- In single-symbol maps, individual uniform symbols represent features.
- Buffers are areas that represent specified proximate zones around features on a map.
- In graduated maps, the sizes or colors of features represent the values of the variables.

- Chart maps, which can use either pie or bar charts, allow the illustration of several values within a particular variable.
- In density maps, areas without boundaries are shaded according to the concentration of incidents within them.
- The term *interactive crime mapping* does not refer to a type of mapping; rather, it refers to simplified geographic information systems made available to novice users over the Internet.
- The beginnings of crime mapping are different from the beginnings of crime analysis in that crime mapping began through the work of researchers (vs. police) in the 1800s and the early 1900s.
- The first substantive spatial analysis of crime in the United States was conducted in the 1920s and 1930s by urban sociologists in Chicago. This research focused on linking crime and delinquency to factors such as social disorganization and poverty.
- In the 1970s and 1980s, improvements in technology and academic developments encouraged the use of crime mapping in police agencies. However, the use of crime mapping did not increase dramatically until the 1990s.
- Federal funding in the form of grants and the establishment of crime mapping centers, improvements in technology and data collection, and the implementation of Compstat in police agencies across the United States fueled the rapid adoption of crime mapping in the mid- to late 1990s.
- Currently, most large police agencies use some form of crime mapping for one or more of the following purposes: to provide officers and investigators with information on crime incident locations, to make resource allocation (staffing) decisions, to evaluate interventions, to inform citizens about crime in their neighborhoods, and to identify repeat calls for service and crime locations.
- Crime mapping positions in police departments are sometimes separate from crime analysis positions and in many cases have higher salaries because of the high level of training and expertise required. Crime mapping positions are much rarer than general crime analysis positions.

Exercises

Exercise 4.1

Using the Internet, a newspaper, a magazine, or your local police department as your source, obtain an example of a map that displays crime information. List the following information about the map:

- Type of map (e.g., single symbol, graduated by size)
- Geographic area represented in the map (e.g., city, state, neighborhood)
- Data on the map (e.g., crime, population, accidents)
- Time period of the data (i.e., list dates)
- Creator of the map (e.g., agency and individual, if shown)

Discuss the following about the map:

1. What seems to be the purpose of the map?

2. Does the map seem to serve its purpose?

3. Is the map informative and helpful?

4. Does the map make sense?

Exercise 4.2

To review the specific concepts associated with geographic information systems, go online and complete Lesson 1 of the "Free Module: Learning ArcGIS 8." (This module includes conceptual material as well as exercises; it is not necessary to load the software and do the exercises.) Follow these directions to complete the lesson:

- Go to http://campus.esri.com. If you are already a Virtual Campus member, sign in with your member log-in and password. If you are not a member, click "Join now" under "Member Sign-In" and complete the form to become a member.
- Click on "Free Training" on the left-hand side of the page.
- Go to the 13th course, called "Learning ArcGIS 8, Part I."
- Look for the "Free Module" in the upper right-hand corner and click on "Enroll Today."
- Click on "Basics of ArcGIS."
- Click on "Lesson 1: Introducing GIS."
- Go to the bottom of the screen and read the section headed "Before you start" before starting.
- Follow the rest of the directions to complete the course. (*Note:* For this exercise, do only Lesson 1.)

Notes

1. The maps presented in this chapter are not "final" maps—that is, they are not complete maps that would be suitable for distribution to particular audiences. Rather, these maps are intended only to illustrate particular types of maps or techniques.

2. Both graduated color and graduated size cannot be displayed using the same points on a map. For example, if two robberies occurred at one location, the point for that location would be larger in size than points where only single robberies occurred. One cannot then shade that point to show that two different types of weapons were used in the robberies (one a gun and the other a knife).

5

Theory and Crime Analysis

Until recently, the everyday practice of crime analysis has involved only limited use of criminological theory. Crime analysts have tended to spend substantial amounts of time obtaining and cleaning data, counting incidents, and finding short-term patterns and considerably less time using theory to guide analysis. As the discipline develops, however, it is becoming more common for analysts to apply certain relevant criminological theories in their work.

The primary objective of crime analysis is to assist the police in addressing everyday crime and disorder. Sociological and psychological theories that explain the root causes of criminal activity, pointing to factors such as social disorganization, personality disorders, and inadequate parenting, are not relevant for crime analysis because police have little influence over these root causes. Police agencies, and crime analysts in particular, must focus on how and why crimes are occurring in particular situations in order to seek solutions for those immediate problems.

Over the past 30 years, significant developments have taken place in scholars' efforts to define and make sense of crime events as they happen "on the street." This branch of criminological theory, which is called **environmental criminology**, entails important concepts that can guide crime analysis and crime prevention efforts as well as evaluation of those efforts. This chapter provides a concise introduction to this theoretical framework. Although throughout this chapter's discussion I refer primarily to crime, the concepts presented can also be applied to disorder and other types of activity that are concerns for crime analysts and the police.

Environmental Criminology

Environmental criminology is different from traditional criminological theories in that it does not attempt to explain root causes of crime and why people become criminals. Instead, it focuses on offenders' patterns of motivation, opportunities that exist for crime, levels of protection for victims within criminal events, and the environments in which criminal events occur (Brantingham & Brantingham, 1990). The goal of environmental criminology is not to explain why a specific offender commits a specific crime but to understand the various aspects of a criminal event in order to identify patterns of behavior and environmental factors that create opportunities for crime.

For example, Jane Doe's wallet was stolen from her purse while she was working out at the gym; it was taken from her purse, which was in her car in the gym's parking lot. Environmental criminology does not seek to explain why Jane's wallet was stolen that day as an isolated incident or to examine what factors in the offender's background (e.g., bad parenting, poor education) made him or her steal the wallet. Rather, it focuses on how leaving a wallet in a parked car creates an opportunity for crime (i.e., no wallet, no crime) and on how routine behaviors of groups of individuals (e.g., women's avoiding taking their purses with them into the gym while they work out) facilitate the crime. A crime analyst working from this theory would ask questions such as the following:

- Have there been similar crimes in the same parking lot?
- Is the problem a function of victim behavior? (If so, other gym parking lots may have the same problem.)
- Does the problem have to do with this specific lot? Is it close to a major freeway? Does it lack adequate lighting or security personnel?

The crime analyst would examine the data to answer these questions and subsequently recommend ways in which the environment and victim behavior could be altered to eliminate opportunities for this type of crime.

Before this discussion proceeds any farther, several important concepts within environmental criminology require explanation.

The Crime Triangle

The core of environmental criminological theory is the concept of the **crime triangle** (Clarke & Eck, 2003), which is illustrated in Figure 5.1. The gray shading in the triangle at the center of the figure represents the idea that a crime occurs only when an offender and a victim or target come together at a particular place (a target is an inanimate object, such as property, a vehicles, or a building). The outer triangle represents certain types of people who can provide control over the three elements of victim/target, place, and offender. According to this theory, it is the lack of control of these elements that produces opportunities for crime. *Guardians* are people who protect victims/targets, such as victims themselves, owners of property, neighbors, and security guards. *Managers* are people who are responsible for places, such as hotel or store clerks and apartment building managers. *Handlers* are people who know offenders and are in positions that allow them to monitor and/or control offenders' actions, such as parents and parole officers.

In other words, for a crime to occur there must be a person who is willing and motivated to commit a crime, a vulnerable victim/target, and a place lacking sufficient oversight/guardianship. Returning to the example of Jane Doe's stolen wallet: A person who needs money (motivated offender) is walking through a parking lot, sees a purse in an empty car (vulnerable target), looks around and finds that no one

Figure 5.1   The Crime Triangle

else is present (lack of guardianship), and decides to break into the car and steal the wallet from the purse. This example illustrates a central concept of environmental criminology: that opportunities for crime are highly specific. If the offender had walked through the parking lot while another gym patron was there, or if there had been only two cars in the parking lot, the offender might have decided not to take the wallet because it was too risky.

This theory has important implications for crime analysis, in that it suggests that analysts can use specific techniques to identify and understand patterns of events, and that understanding, in turn, can inform police efforts to address or prevent crime. For instance, analysis of thefts from autos by location and time of day may show that cars are being victimized in a certain area of a shopping mall parking lot in the evening hours. Further examination may reveal that the affected area of the lot is near a movie theater and that people often leave the merchandise they have just purchased at mall stores in their cars while they go to the movies. Measures designed to facilitate potential victims' protection of their property (i.e., increase guardianship) would help to reduce the opportunity for this crime.

The three related theories discussed below are useful for helping crime analysts understand and anticipate how offenders and victims behave, why people come together, and how opportunities for crime are created. They provide insights into patterns of behavior at the individual level (rational choice theory), the social interaction level (crime pattern theory), and the societal level (routine activities theory).

Rational Choice Theory

According to **rational choice theory**, offenders make choices about committing crimes based on anticipated opportunities and rewards. The theory suggests that, if given a chance, or the right "opportunity," any person will commit a crime (Felson & Clarke, 1998). The motivation that a drug abuser with no money has to commit a robbery might be obvious, but it is more difficult to understand why seemingly non-criminal people commit crimes in certain circumstances; rational choice theory explains their motivation. For example, a person who would normally not steal may decide to steal a TV from a store during a riot because (a) access to the TV is easy (someone else has already broken into the store), (b) the likelihood of being caught is low (because of the chaos created by the riot), (c) the person could use a new TV, and (d) "Why not? Everyone else is doing it." The feeling of anonymity often changes the rational choice of both ordinary citizens and criminals.

It is also important to note that rational choice theory suggests that individuals will decide *not* to commit crimes when the risks are too high or the rewards are not adequate—an idea that differs from traditional criminological theory, which implies that criminal behavior is inevitable. Thus understanding why individuals "choose" to commit crimes in particular circumstances can lead to crime prevention based on this information.

Rational choice theory is useful for crime analysis and policing because of the importance of determining why offenders choose to commit particular crimes systematically. If offenders choose to offend based on the perceived risks and anticipated rewards of their crimes, an understanding of offenders' perceptions of risks and rewards can help police agencies and communities to take measures that can change the opportunities for crime and thus deter offending. For instance, again using the gym parking lot example, analysis may show that the cars being targeted are in the back row of the parking lot, farthest away from the gym's front doors. The offenders seem to be choosing these cars because of the lack of guardianship in this area—that is, because of the relatively low risk of their being seen while committing the crimes. Based on this finding, police might advise the gym's owners to take measures such as increasing lighting or installing security video cameras in the area to increase potential offenders' perceived risk of being caught.

Crime Pattern Theory

Crime pattern theory addresses the nature of the immediate situations in which crimes occur. According to this theory, criminal events are most likely to occur in areas where the activity space of offenders overlaps with the activity space of potential victims/targets (Brantingham & Brantingham, 1990; Felson & Clarke, 1998). An individual's activity space is that area familiar to him or her through everyday activities, such as where he or she lives, works, commutes, and goes shopping. The activity space of a target is, simply stated, its location.

Figure 5.2 illustrates a simple example of how the activity space of an offender (work, recreation area, and entertainment area) intersects with the activity space of a victim (home, social club, and recreation area). Crime pattern theory asserts that a crime event involving this offender and this victim can occur only within or stem from the intersection of their activity spaces (recreation). This is a relatively simple example, given that individuals' actual activity spaces are vast. More broadly, crime

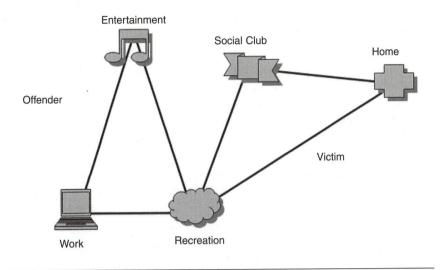

Figure 5.2   Offender and Victim Activity Space Example

pattern theory would suggest that a downtown area with retail stores, restaurants, and a movie theater would have a considerable amount of crime because many people frequent the area, including victims and potential offenders, and thus would be worthy of analysis. A crime analyst examining this area would break down the data into specifics about the various types of victims/targets and potential offenders who frequent the area to understand why they are there and how they come together. Such an area may have a major problem with thefts from vehicles and a problem with auto theft from parking lots because of the high volume of vehicle traffic as well as a problem with purse snatching because of the high numbers of victims on the street with cash. Crime pattern theory provides a structured way for crime analysis to view and investigate patterns of behavior.

Routine Activities Theory

Routine activities theory focuses on how opportunities for crime change based on changes in behavior on a societal level. For example, Cohen and Felson (1979) suggest that changes in Americans' routine activities were responsible for increases in crime rates in the United States from 1947 to 1974. They note that the number of Americans who routinely left their homes on a daily basis to go to workplaces increased significantly from 1947 to 1974. Thus guardianship over homes decreased, leaving opportunities for crimes such as residential burglary. In addition, with more people out in the working world, increasing the numbers of potential victims (individuals) and targets (cars), opportunities for crime such as robbery, rape, and vehicle crime also increased.

Looking again at the example of Jane Doe's stolen wallet, routine activities theory would argue that new opportunities for crime were created when working out at a gym became popular in Jane's community, and many gym patrons developed the habit of leaving their wallets and/or purses in their cars while they worked out. In recent years, the most significant example of a change in routine activity on a societal level is the increasing use of the Internet. The popularity of Internet usage has created opportunities for many new types of crimes as well as new ways of perpetrating age-old crimes; these include identity theft, dissemination of computer viruses, and the luring of children for sexual purposes.

It should be noted that routine activities theory also suggests that opportunities for crime can be decreased by changes in behavior, such as locking cars and increasing parental supervision of children.

Crime analysts working from the perspective of this theory ask questions about general patterns of behavior and the impacts of those patterns on crime opportunities. Local patterns of behavior, such as the prevalence of a particular type of drug in a community or the tendency of teenagers in an area to use drinking and driving as their primary form of entertainment on the weekends, are particularly important because crime analysis usually focuses on one city or a specific region.

Situational Crime Prevention

Situational crime prevention, a practice initiated in England in the 1980s, is based on the concepts of environmental criminology, which addresses why crime occurs in specific settings and seeks solutions that reflect the nature of those settings (Cornish & Clarke, 1986). Situational crime prevention consists of the specific actions that police take to address crime problems in local environments based on crime analysts' examination of those problems. In an article published in 1980, Clarke first presented a system for classifying the techniques that people and communities can use to reduce opportunities for crime that is based on the crime triangle and the theories discussed above. Cornish and Clarke (2003) recently updated this classification system.

Within the system, the first category of techniques is made up of those that prevent crime by increasing the offender's *perceived effort* to commit the crime. In simple terms, these techniques make it more difficult for the offender to commit the crime, thereby addressing the offender's motivation and anticipated rewards. Prevention techniques can be divided into five general types: target hardening (e.g., installing alarm systems, using steering-wheel locks), controlling access to facilities (e.g., reducing numbers of entrances/exits, installing gated barriers), screening exits (e.g., using electronic merchandise tags, requiring a ticket for exit), deflecting offenders (e.g., closing streets, implementing a police beat office), and controlling tools/weapons (e.g., restricting sales of spray paint to adults).

The second category consists of techniques that increase the offender's *perceived risk* in committing a crime. In other words, these techniques make the offender "think twice" because he or she perceives a possibility of getting caught. Prevention techniques can also be divided into five general types: extending guardianship (e.g., joining a neighborhood watch group, carrying a phone, not walking alone), assisting natural surveillance (e.g., improving street lighting, maintaining landscaping), reducing anonymity (e.g., requiring school uniforms, requiring taxi drivers to display identification), utilizing place managers (e.g., having two clerks on every shift at convenience stores), and using formal surveillance (e.g., installing video cameras and burglar alarms).

The third category in the classification system comprises those techniques that reduce the offender's *anticipated rewards* from committing the crime. In other words, these techniques reduce the value to the offender of the crime itself. These prevention techniques fall into the following five general areas: concealing targets (e.g., parking off the street, putting any valuables carried in a car in the trunk), removing targets (e.g., keeping a maximum of $50 in cash in a convenience store register), identifying property (e.g., licensing bicycles, etching a car's vehicle identification number on the car's parts), disrupting markets (e.g., monitoring pawn shops and street vendors for stolen merchandise), and denying benefits (e.g., installing removable faces on car stereos, attaching ink tags to clothing).

The fourth category in the system is made up of those techniques that reduce the offender's *provocation* for committing the crime. In other words, these techniques aim to change social and environmental conditions in ways that will diminish stress, conflict, and temptation to offend. These prevention techniques can be divided into five general types: reducing frustrations and stress (e.g., managing lines efficiently, providing comfortable seating and/or music or other entertainment for people waiting for service), avoiding disputes (e.g., reducing crowding in bars, establishing fixed cab fares), reducing emotional arousal (e.g., eliminating a bikini contest at a bar), neutralizing peer pressure (e.g., dispersing groups at schools, reassuring juveniles that "it's okay to say no"), and discouraging imitation (e.g., repairing vandalized property rapidly, censoring details of crimes in providing information to the media).

The final category of the classification system consists of techniques that address the offender's motivation by focusing on *removing excuses* for the crime. In other words, these techniques are intended to change social practices as a way of encouraging compliance with the law. These prevention techniques can also be divided into five types: setting rules (e.g., requiring written rental agreements, requiring registration for admittance to a hotel), posting instructions (e.g., installing signs specifying "No Parking" or "Private Property"), alerting conscience (e.g., installing a roadside speed display, posting signs that say, "Shoplifting is stealing"), assisting compliance (e.g., providing trash bins and containers for recyclables in public areas), and controlling drugs and alcohol (e.g., installing Breathalyzers in bars, refusing to serve alcohol to drunk individuals).

Situational crime prevention seeks to provide measures that are directly related to the immediate situations of criminal events, and just as the opportunities that facilitate crime may be unique, unique measures may be needed to prevent those opportunities. Even though crime analysts do not implement such crime prevention measures themselves, recommending them and evaluating their effectiveness once implemented can be an important part of crime analysis.

Repeat Victimization and the 80/20 Rule

Repeat victimization is the recurrence of crime in the same places and/or against the same people. A major finding of the research on repeat victimization is that people and places that have been victimized in the past have a higher likelihood of being victimized again than do people and places that have never been victimized (Farrell & Pease, 1993). This is an important theoretical consideration in crime analysis, not only because repeat victimization is common but also because it facilities the identification of patterns of opportunity. When the same group of people, location, or type of target is repeatedly victimized in different situations, the crime analyst has an opportunity to identify common characteristics among the crime events and understand why crime is occurring at a specific place or to a specific group. The phenomenon of repeat victimization also provides a focus for prevention, in that those who have been victimized in the past should be at the top of the list for the targeting of prevention measures.

Repeat victimization is broken down into the following four types, which provide for the identification of patterns of behavior as well as help to communicate the results of crime analysis in common terms:

1. **Hot dots** are people, individuals or groups of individuals, who are repeatedly victimized (Pease & Laycock, 1996). A hot dot could be one man whose car has been stolen four times or a group made up of older women whose purses have been stolen. The term *hot dot* is also used to refer to an offender who comes to the attention of the police repeatedly (Velasco & Boba, 2000).

2. **Hot products** are types of property that are repeatedly victimized, or, as Clarke (1999) puts it, "those consumer items that are most attractive to thieves" (p. 23). In order for an item to be a hot product, it must fit the following criteria: It must be "concealable, removable, available, valuable, enjoyable, and disposable" (p. 25). Examples include cell phones, laptop computers, and weapons.

3. **Hot spots** are specific locations or small areas that suffer large amounts of crime (Sherman, Gartin, & Buerger, 1989). Examples are particular shopping malls and particular neighborhoods.

4. **Hot targets** are types of places that are frequently victimized that are not necessarily in the same area (adapted from Velasco & Boba, 2000). Examples include beauty salons, convenience stores, day-care centers, bars, and fast-food restaurants. Repeated crimes occur in hot targets without involving the same victims or offenders (hot dots) or the same kinds of property (hot products). They are important to distinguish from other types of repeat victimization because similar places have similar opportunities for crime. For example, beauty salons, no matter whether upscale or downscale, typically are frequented mostly by women and keep large amounts of cash readily available.

An important concept that is related to repeat victimization is the so-called **80/20 rule.** In general, this concept comes from the observation that 80% of some kinds of outcomes are the result of only 20% of the related causes. This is true in many phenomena in nature; for example, a small proportion of the earthquakes that take place are responsible for a very large proportion of the world's earthquake-related damage. The same is true for many of the phenomena examined in crime analysis: A large proportion of offenders repeatedly target a small proportion of people and/or places, small numbers of locations account for large numbers of crime events, and a small proportion of offenders accounts for a large proportion of offenses (Clarke & Eck, 2003).

It should be noted that the numbers 80 and 20 are used here only to represent "large" and "small" amounts; the actual proportions change depending on the type of activity and the nature of the community in which it occurs. In relation to crime analysis, the 80/20 rule suggests that by focusing on the small proportion of areas, victims, and offenders where a large amount of activity is concentrated, police can get the most out of their crime prevention efforts (i.e., by addressing crimes at specific areas—say, 20% of the community—they can address 80% of the crime problem). (For discussion of the analytic techniques that crime analysts use to identify these relationships, see Chapter 11.)

Displacement and Diffusion of Benefits

In addition to using theory to understand opportunities for crime (environmental criminology) and to prevent crime (situational crime prevention), crime analysts use theory to understand why crime phenomena change. A crime phenomenon can change by being moved to another time and/or place or by taking on another form, which is called **displacement.** A problem can also change by being eliminated (partially or fully). In some circumstances, when one type of crime activity is eliminated, other types are affected as well (e.g., when prostitution is eliminated from an area, traffic problems and assaults on women also decrease in that area). This is called **diffusion of benefits.** Changes in crime phenomena are important to crime analysts because they can examine such changes on a regular basis (e.g., decreases in burglaries at medical offices) and use them in evaluating the outcomes of specific crime prevention programs (e.g., a program implementing restricted entry into an apartment community).

Displacement of Crime

Displacement occurs when crime or other types of activity shift to other forms, times, and locales instead of being eliminated. Crime analysts need to consider the following four types of displacement (Clarke & Eck, 2003):

1. **Spatial displacement** is the shifting of an activity from targets in one area to those in another area. For example, when police address prostitution in one area, the activity moves to another area of the city.

2. **Temporal displacement** is the shifting of an activity from one time to another. This can include changes in time of day, day of the week, and season of the year. For example, if police routinely patrol a particular area between 8:00 and 10:00 P.M., looking for gang members hanging out on the street, the

gang members may shift their behavior and hang out in the area either later or earlier in the day.

3. **Target displacement** is the shifting of the choice of one victim/target to a more vulnerable victim/target. That is, when one type of target is hardened, offenders focus on other types of targets. For instance, if the pay phones in a bus station are changed so that they take only credit cards and no coins, they become poor targets for offenders who want to obtain cash. Offenders in the bus station may shift from breaking into pay phones to breaking into coin-operated vending machines.

4. **Tactical displacement** is the shifting of tactics by offenders. This can happen when offenders find that their usual methods are no longer working or if they become more confident and reckless in committing crime. An offender might shift from conning his or her way into someone's home to steal valuables to breaking into the home, or an offender who has previously gone no further than exposing himself to women at a bus stop may shift to touching his victims.

In a comprehensive review of crime reduction studies, Hesseling (1994) found that not one study had reported complete displacement of any activity. Given the many forms that displacement can take, Hesseling explains, it is "empirically impossible to confirm the existence or magnitude of displacement" (p. 198). Yet some displacement of activity is possible, and crime analysts should examine the likelihood of displacement in specific cases. Crime analysis techniques can identify and describe any displacement of activity to help police agencies understand how crime activity changes and whether any changes seen are the results of crime prevention efforts.

Diffusion of Benefits

Research has shown that crime problems can be eliminated through the application of the principles of situational crime prevention, which aims to reduce/remove the opportunities for crime (Clarke, 1992). In addition, research indicates that when targeted problems are successfully eliminated, other problems are also often eliminated; as noted above, this is referred to as the diffusion of benefits (Clarke & Weisburd, 1994). For example, when police close down a hotel that has served as a hub for prostitution and drug dealing, other negative types of activity that have been taking place in the area of the hotel—such as robbery, theft, assaults, vandalism, and traffic concerns—decrease or even cease. Once opportunities to offend are removed by the closure of the hotel, offenders leave the vicinity; there are no longer any drug users robbing people nearby to get money to buy drugs at the hotel, any traffic problems caused by men driving past the hotel slowly as they seek prostitutes, and so on (Sampson, 2003).

Analysts can use crime mapping to determine whether crime or other activity has been spatially displaced and whether a diffusion of benefits has taken place as the result of a particular crime prevention effort or the change in opportunity for a crime. An analyst looking at the outcomes associated with the closure of the hotel in the example above can use buffers to identify areas 500 to 1,000 feet around the hotel to determine whether crime and disorder activity declined in surrounding areas.

Opportunity

Opportunity is the overarching theme of this chapter's discussion of how crime analysts understand and address patterns of crime events. To synthesize the concepts of environmental criminology, situational crime prevention, repeat victimization, the 80/20 rule, displacement, and diffusion of benefits, Felson and Clarke (1998), two of the original thinkers in this area, list the following 10 key points related to opportunity and crime:

1. Opportunities play a role in causing all crime.
2. Crime opportunities are highly specific.
3. Crime opportunities are concentrated in time and space.
4. Crime opportunities depend on everyday movements of activity.
5. One crime produces opportunities for another.
6. Some products offer more tempting crime opportunities.
7. Social and technological changes produce new crime opportunities.
8. Crime can be prevented by reducing opportunities.
9. Reducing opportunities does not usually displace crime.
10. Focused opportunity reduction can produce wider declines in crime. (pp. v–vi)

Summary Points

This chapter has provided an overview of the role of environmental criminological theory in guiding crime analysis. The following are the key points addressed in this chapter:

- Criminological theories that deal with immediate situational causes of crime are more relevant to crime analysis than theories that seek to explain the underlying sociological and psychological causes of crime or why people become criminals.
- Environmental criminology focuses on patterns of motivation for offenders, opportunities that exist for crime, and levels of protection of victims within the criminal event as well as the environment in which it occurs. The goal of environmental criminology is not to explain why a specific offender commits a specific crime but to understand the various aspects of a criminal event

in order to identify patterns of behavior and environmental factors that create opportunities for crime.

- The crime triangle illustrates the relationships among the elements that create crime opportunities: the offender's motivation, the vulnerability of the target/victim, the time and place of the crime event, and the lack of oversight/protection.
- Three theoretical perspectives help crime analysts understand and anticipate patterns of behavior that create opportunities for crime: rational choice theory (individual level), crime pattern theory (local level), and routine activities theory (societal level).
- Rational choice theory states that offenders make choices about committing crimes based on opportunities and anticipated rewards. It suggests that, if given a chance, or the right "opportunity," any person will commit a crime. It also suggests that a person will decide *not* to commit crimes when the risks are too high or the rewards are not adequate—an idea that differs from traditional criminological theory, which implies that criminal behavior is inevitable.
- Crime pattern theory helps to explain the nature of the immediate situation in which a crime occurs. According to this theory, criminal events are most likely to occur in areas where the activity spaces of offenders overlap with the activity spaces of potential victims/targets.
- Routine activities theory focuses on how opportunities for crime change based on changes in behavior on a societal level. Increasing use of the Internet is an example of a change in society that has created opportunities for crime.
- Situational crime prevention is a practice based on the components of the crime triangle. A classification system developed by Clarke specifies five types of crime prevention techniques—increasing the offender's perceived effort, increasing the offender's perceived risk, reducing the offender's anticipated rewards, reducing provocations for committing crime, and removing excuses for committing crime—each of which can be divided into five general kinds of techniques.
- Repeat victimization is the recurrence of crime in the same places and/or against the same people. A major finding from the research on repeat victimization is that people and places that have been victimized in the past have a higher likelihood of being victimized again than do people and places that have not been victimized.
- There are four types of repeat victimization: hot dots (people), hot spots (areas), hot products (property), and hot targets (types of places).
- An important concept related to repeat victimization is that of the 80/20 rule. This concept comes from the observation that 80% of some kinds of outcomes are the result of only 20% of the related causes. This suggests that by focusing their efforts on areas/people that are repeat victims or that account for a large amount of crime activity, police can maximize the impacts of a crime prevention strategy.
- Displacement occurs when crime or other types of activity shift to other forms, times, and locales instead of being eliminated. Crime analysis techniques can identify and describe any displacement of activity to help police agencies

understand how crime activity changes and whether any changes seen are the results of crime prevention efforts.

- Research has shown that crime problems can be eliminated through the application of the principles of situational crime prevention, which aims to reduce/remove the opportunities for crime. In addition, the successful elimination of targeted problems may also reduce other problems; this process is called the diffusion of benefits.

Exercises

Exercise 5.1

Think of a situation in which a crime has occurred in your own life or in the life of a family member, friend, or acquaintance. Answer the following questions in relation to that crime event:

- What was (or seemed to be) the offender's motivation to commit the crime?
- What was the nature of the place where the crime occurred?
- What was the nature of the target and/or behavior of the victim during the crime?
- How might the handlers, the guardians, and the managers have increased the opportunity for the crime to occur?
- How might the crime have been prevented? (Focus on the opportunities that enabled the crime to occur. For the offender, could anything have increased the perceived effort, increased the perceived risks, or reduced the anticipated rewards?)

Exercise 5.2

In order to understand your own daily movements (activity space) and the crime prevention measures you undertake without even thinking about them, create a "crime prevention activities log." For 7 days, record in this log *all* the activities/behaviors you engage in to prevent crime. The following is a suggested format for the log, with some examples:

Day	Time	Locatio	Behavior	Crime(s) Seeking to Prevent
Tuesday	7:00 P.M.	Mall parking lot	Locked car	Theft from vehicle Auto theft
Tuesday	10:00 P.M.	School parking lot	Walked with fellow student to parking lot	Rape Assault
Wednesday	10:00 A.M.	Home	Locked door	Burglary

PART II

Data and Technology

6

Crime Analysis Data

D ata collection and collation are significant components of the crime analysis process, and analysts spend a substantial amount of their time and energy on collecting and preparing data for crime analysis purposes. Police agencies use many different methods for collecting and managing their data, so analysts must deal with data that are in many different formats and of varying quality. This chapter provides a general overview of the most common data types as well as discussion of their use in crime analysis.

Key Terms

To ensure understanding of many of the basic concepts discussed throughout this and the following chapters, brief definitions of some key terms are in order.

Database

A **database** is a collection of data that have been organized for the purposes of retrieval, searching, and analysis through a computer. Databases can contain seemingly infinite numbers of records or cases. In crime analysis, a record or case would be a crime report, an accident report, or an arrest report. Within a database, the data are organized into a **matrix**, which is a table with individual cells organized in rows and columns. Each row contains all the information for one particular record (e.g., crime report) and each column contains information about one particular characteristic describing the data (e.g., date, time, location), as in Table 6.1. The columns are also called *variables* or *fields*. Most modern databases (e.g., Microsoft Access, SQL Server, Oracle) allow users to examine complex relationships among various tables through what are called *relational databases*.

Secondary Data

Secondary data are data that have been collected previously; such data are typically housed in electronic databases. The use of secondary data is common in crime

Table 6.1   Sample Data Table

Columns of fields or variables

Rows
of cases

Incident No.	Report Date	Crime Type	Address
2000013294	12/20/2000	Burglary	210 Anita Ct
2000141524	11/15/2000	Burglary	1350 Allesandro Rd
2000142509	11/23/2000	Criminal trespass	1065 W Colton Av
2000142640	11/18/2000	Burglary	1528 Calle Constancia
2000142676	11/18/2000	Burglary	953 Mendocino Wy
2000142878	11/27/2000	Criminal trespass	857 W Lugonia Av
2000143275	11/23/2000	Burglary	996 E Colton Av
2000143496	11/26/2000	Burglary	29 8th St
2000144169	11/26/2000	Burglary	32635 Greenspot Rd

analysis, because police agencies, city departments, and government entities routinely collect and store data that are relevant to the issues crime analysts examine. For example, police agencies collect crime reports, accident reports, and arrest reports, and city agencies collect data on street networks, keep business registries, compile information on usage of utilities, and collect tax and license data. The U.S. Bureau of the Census collects sociodemographic data, such as information about income, education, age, and race. Secondary data may be either qualitative (i.e., primarily narrative) or quantitative (i.e., numeric).

Primary Data

Because the secondary data that crime analysts use have been collected for purposes other than crime analysis, they are not always adequate to allow analysts to examine a topic fully. When that is the case, the crime analyst needs to collect **primary data**—that is, data collected specifically for the purposes of the analysis at hand. Analysts collect primary data through surveys, interviews, field research, and direct observation; such data may be coded and entered into a database or may be left in narrative form.

An example of the collection of primary data is the gathering of information about drug market areas. Typically, a crime analyst who needs such information cannot find it in any existing official database, and so needs to collect and organize the data him- or herself. The analyst might conduct interviews with detectives to locate drug market areas and then conduct field observation of the areas to collect data on characteristics, which he or she would then code into a database to be analyzed along with other data (e.g., drug arrests). Another example is a crime analyst's need to identify and document environmental characteristics of a particular type of location or neighborhood. In examining an ongoing problem of robberies at self-serve laundries, for instance, the analyst could record information about characteristics of the buildings and their surrounding areas, such as lighting, access control, and landscaping, and then examine these data to assist police in understanding why particular laundries experience robberies and others do not. For primary data to be both accurate and pertinent to the analysis, the crime analyst must invest explicit effort in collecting the data. (For further discussion of primary data, see Chapter 11.)

Geographic Data

Just as police agencies enter crime reports into computer systems, crime analysts enter data about the geographic features associated with crime and other activity into geographic information systems for analysis purposes. Chapter 4 introduced the four types of geographic data, or features, a GIS uses to represent objects or locations: point, line, polygon, and image features. The kinds of data associated with these features, also called *attributes,* are discussed below.

Point data. A point feature is a discrete location that is usually depicted by a symbol or label, as seen in Figure 6.1. Table 6.2 illustrates how a database would display the attribute data associated with each point. In this example, the points represent bus stops. The point circled on the map in Figure 6.1 corresponds with the first record (row) in the table. The variables in the database provide additional information about that location, such as the bus route number, address, bus number, and type of location of the bus stop.

Line data. A line feature is an element that can be represented by a line or set of lines. In Figure 6.2, the lines represent street segments. The circled line corresponds to the first record displayed in Table 6.3. Typically, each record in street data represents a street segment. The variables describe the attributes of that particular street segment and contain the addresses at the beginning and the end of the street segment. The variables "left from" and "left to" contain the addresses that start and end the range on one side of the street segment, and "right from" and "right to" contain the other side's range. The direction, street name, and type of street are also shown.

Polygon data. A polygon feature is a geographic area represented by a multisided figure with a closed set of lines. The polygons in Figure 6.3 show police districts. The circled district segment corresponds to the first record displayed in Table 6.4.

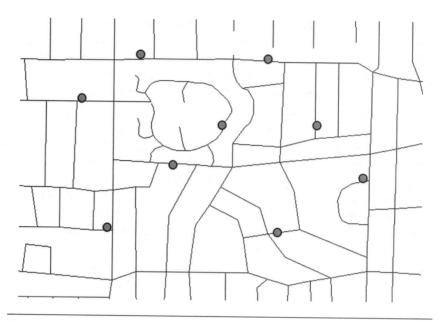

Figure 6.1   Point Feature Map

Table 6.2   Point Feature Attribute Data

Route No.	Address	Bus No.	Type of Location
0249	15 Exchange Pl	07302	Business
0249	169 York St	07302	Apartment
0249	111 1st St	07302	Business
0425	685 Grand St	07304	None
0425	344 Pacific Ave	07304	Business
0535	49 Fisk St	07305	None
0677	26 Journal Sq	07306	Apartment
0677	920 Bergen Ave	07306	Park
0677	438 Summit Ave	07306	Apartment
0677	921 Bergen Ave	07306	Park
1012	234 16th St	07310	Neighborhood

With the polygon feature, the unit of analysis is the area, so the lines (borders) of the polygon do not have attribute data—only the area itself does. In Table 6.4, the variable called "feature" describes the type of feature these data are, and "district" is the name/label for that polygon.

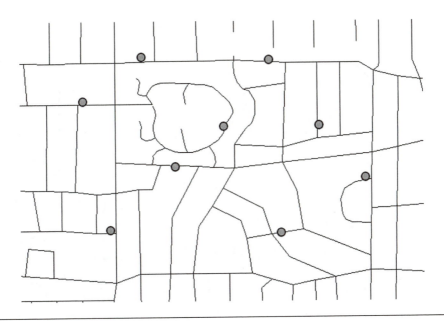

Figure 6.2   Line Feature Map

Table 6.3   Line Feature Attribute Data

Left From	Left to	Right From	Right to	Prefix	Street Name	Type
2201	2249	2200	2248	E	Columbia	Pl
2301	2399	2300	2398	E	Columbia	Pl
2101	2199	2100	2198	E	Columbia	Pl
2251	2271	2250	2270	E	Columbia	Pl
2273	2299	2272	2298	E	Columbia	Pl
2167	2231	2166	2208	E	Dartmouth	Cir
2101	2165	2100	2164	E	Dartmouth	Cir
2233	2299	2210	2299	E	Dartmouth	Cir
2999	2901	3030	2900	S	Fillmore	Way
3099	3001	3098	3032	S	Fillmore	Way
3099	2901	3124	2900	S	Milwaukee	Cir
2899	2701	2998	2700	S	Dallas	Way
2999	2901	3098	3000	S	Dallas	Way
2701	2899	2700	2898	E	Linvale	Pl
3081	3199	3074	3098	E	Yale	Way

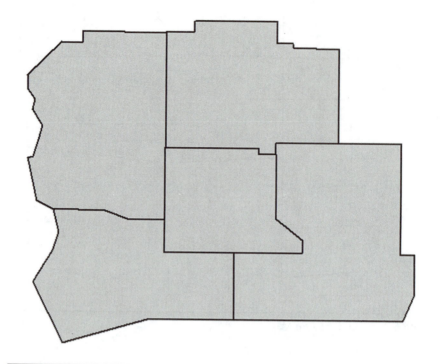

Figure 6.3   Polygon Feature Map

Table 6.4   Polygon Feature Attribute Data

Feature	District
Polygon	1
Polygon	2
Polygon	3
Polygon	4
Polygon	5

Image data. Even though an image feature has attribute data, those data are used only for the purpose of locating the feature within the GIS; such data are typically not used for analysis.

Tabular Data

Tabular data describe events that are not inherently geographic but that may contain geographic variables. Crime reports, accidents, and student information are examples of tabular data. The next section discusses the common types of both tabular and geographic secondary data used in crime analysis.

Databases Used in Crime Analysis

Databases are vital tools for conducting crime analysis and crime mapping because they allow analysts to use computers to analyze large numbers of observations efficiently. Crime analysts use many different tabular and geographic databases, but, for the sake of brevity, only the most commonly used types are detailed below.

Tabular Databases

Crime analysts most frequently use four types of secondary data: data on crime incidents, arrests, calls for service, and accidents (also called crashes).

Crime Incidents

The data about crime incidents used in crime analysis come from crime reports taken by police officers or other police personnel. Crime reports provide information for other databases that are linked to a **crime incidents database**, such as suspect, witness, victim, vehicle, and property databases. The crime incidents database contains information from each crime report concerning the nature of the crime, such as the type of crime and how, when, and where the crime occurred. The unit of analysis is the criminal incident; therefore, there is one record for each criminal incident. Crime incidents databases contain many variables; however, the following are the variables typically used in crime analysis:

- *Record number:* a unique number used to identify the crime and related information.
- *Date of report:* the date the crime was reported to the police. Crime statistics are tallied based on when crimes were reported rather than when they occurred.[1]
- *Type of crime* (state and federal): the type of crime the officer assigned to the event, as dictated by the laws of the state. Often, the corresponding federal code is also included.
- *Location of the crime:* the address where the crime occurred as well as the area, such as police district or beat and census tract. Some databases also include the type of location, such as vacant lot, single-family home, or commercial business.
- *Date and time of occurrence:* the date and time when the crime occurred. This can be different from the date of report and can also be a range of time if the exact time of the crime is not known (e.g., burglary, auto theft).
- *Method of the crime* (also called MO, or modus operandi): how the crime occurred, such as the point of entry, method of entry, weapon used, suspect's actions. Numerous variables are used to capture this information. (For further discussion of MO information, see Chapter 8.)

Table 6.5   Sample Crime Incidents Data Table

Incident No.	Report Date	Crime Type	Address	Beat	First Date	Last Date	Disposition
2000013294	12/20/2000	burglary	210 Anita Ct	11	12/11/2000	12/19/2000	Pending
2000141524	11/15/2000	burglary	1350 Allesandro Rd	24	11/15/2000	11/15/2000	Arrest
2000142509	11/23/2000	criminal trespass	1065 W Colton Av	12	11/20/2000	11/21/2000	Pending
2000142640	11/18/2000	burglary	1528 Calle Constancia	21	11/17/2000	11/18/2000	Pending
2000142676	11/18/2000	burglary	953 Mendocino Wy	16	11/17/2000	11/18/2000	Pending
2000142878	11/27/2000	criminal trespass	857 W Lugonia Av	13	11/23/2000	11/23/2000	Pending
2000143275	11/23/2000	burglary	996 E Colton Av	16	11/19/2000	11/23/2000	Arrest
2000143496	11/26/2000	burglary	29 8th St	19	11/15/2000	11/15/2000	Unfounded
2000144169	11/26/2000	burglary	32635 Greenspot Rd	11	11/23/2000	11/25/2000	Pending

- *Disposition:* the outcome of the incident (e.g., cleared by arrest, pending). A disposition is assigned when the initial report is written and is then updated if and when an investigation leads to arrest or another status.

Table 6.5 is an example of what a portion of a crime incidents database might look like, with each row representing a crime report and each column containing information about a particular characteristic, such as date, address, and disposition.

Arrests

When an arrest is made, an officer completes an arrest report that includes information specific to the arrest of that individual. These data are linked to the original crime report (if applicable). The unit of analysis is the arrest, so there is one record for every arrest. If one person is arrested multiple times, multiple arrest records are completed for that person. If three people are arrested for one crime, three arrest records are generated. Thus crime incidents databases and **arrests databases** do not have a one-to-one relationship. Crime analysts typically use the following variables found in arrest databases:

- *Arrest number:* a unique number used to identify the arrest.
- *Date and time of arrest:* the date and time of the arrest. This may be different from both the date of the report and the date and time of the crime occurrence.
- *Charge(s):* the specific crime(s) for which the arrestee is charged.
- *Location of arrest:* the address and area where the arrestee was at the time of the arrest. This may not match the location of the crime.
- *Location of residence:* the address of the residence of the arrestee.

Table 6.6   Sample Arrest Data Table

Arrest No.	Date	Hour	Charge	Address of Arrest	Fname	Lname	Race	Sex	DOB
20019615	7/20/2001	0235	14-269	West End Bv & W 1st St	John	Doe	B	M	02/11/62
20018395	12/11/2001	1400	14-269	W 1st St & N Sunset Dr	Robert	Smith	W	M	06/09/44
20015518	10/5/2001	2325	14-269	51 S Martin L King Jr Dr	Kevin	White	B	M	01/02/65 .
20012213	1/12/2001	2130	14-269	1500 E 1st St	Rodney	Jones	W	M	07/18/82
20016639	3/4/2001	0800	14-269.2	12 S University Dr	Karim	Williams	B	M	11/15/78

- *Physical description:* a description of the arrestee's physical characteristics, including height, weight, hair color, and eye color.
- *Date of birth:* the arrestee's date of birth. Note that date of birth, rather than age, is collected for identification purposes. Often, age is computed from this variable.

Table 6.6 is an example of what a portion of an arrest database might look like, with each row containing a record of one individual's arrest and the columns containing the characteristics of the arrest.

Calls for Service

Among the many activities carried out by police are responses to noncriminal activities, such as motor vehicle accidents, loud parties, and burglary alarm calls. Citizens call a police department's emergency number (i.e., 911) or a nonemergency number (e.g., 311) to request police services. Not all phone calls to the department warrant a police officer's response, and some citizens' calls are resolved in other ways. All citizen calls to which an officer does respond, whether the reason is criminal or noncriminal, are termed **calls for service**. More specifically, they are known as **citizen-generated calls for service**. Police classifications for such calls for service include, but are not limited to, the following:

- Robbery in progress
- Burglary in progress
- Burglary report
- Rape in progress
- Theft

- Homicide
- Shoplifting
- Family fight
- Assault
- Suspicious person
- Suspicious vehicle
- Loud noise
- Dog barking
- Accident
- Assist motorist
- 911 hang-up
- Burglary alarm
- Narcotics activity
- Check welfare
- Neighbor dispute
- Loud party
- Shots fired
- Criminal trespassing
- Speeding in neighborhood

Police officers also generate calls for service when they proactively identify activity in the field. An officer records a call for service by reporting it to the dispatcher. The police classifications for these types of calls, referred to as **officer-generated calls for service,** include those listed above as well as vehicle stops and subject stops.

Citizen-generated calls for service are more commonly used in crime analysis than officer-generated calls because citizen calls indicate the community's demand for police services. In addition, the volume of officer-generated calls for service is highly influenced by the volume of citizen-generated calls for service, because the number of citizen-generated calls influences the amount of time officers have to generate calls themselves. Therefore, crime analysts use officer-generated calls to examine officer activity and use citizen-generated calls to examine citizen demand for services and concerns about disorder.

The information on characteristics collected for a **calls-for-service database** results from a summary of the activity and communication of officers and dispatchers for individual calls. The call for service is the unit of analysis, and one record represents one call for service in the database. Both citizen- and officer-generated calls for service typically contain the following variables used in crime analysis:

- *Incident number:* a unique number assigned by the computer system and used to track the call for service. In many cases, this number is the same for all reports written as a result of a call for service, so a call for service and its resulting crime report can be linked together.
- *Date and time (received, dispatched, arrived, and cleared):* several time measurements collected for each call. These include when the call was received by the police call taker, when it was dispatched to an officer, when the first officer arrived at the scene, and when the call was closed or cleared. These variables

Table 6.7   Sample Calls-for-Service Data Table

Event_No	Date	Day	Call Type	Rec_ Time	Disp_ Time	Arv_ Time	Com_ Time	Priority	Location
00210621	7/4/1996	Mon	Robbery	0015	0016	0018	0129	1	16 Morton Pl
00203160	6/28/1996	Tue	Suspicious person	0015	0020	0025	0045	2	238 Carbon St
00239616	7/27/1996	Wed	Theft	0015	0030	0039	0052	3	253 Stegman St
00214600	7/7/1996	Thu	Domestic	0100	0101	0105	0312	1	48 Lienau Pl
00264094	8/16/1996	Fri	Robbery	0130	0132	0137	0345	1	560 Bramhall Ave
00249640	8/4/1996	Fri	Burglary report	0130	0139	0145	0201	3	608 Bramhall Ave
00231049	7/20/1996	Sat	Auto theft	0130	0142	0159	0235	3	68 MLK Dr

are used to compute other variables, such as response time (i.e., how much time elapses between a person's call to the police and an officer's arrival at the scene).

- *Type of call:* a number (e.g., 459 signifying burglary) or descriptive term (e.g., burglary alarm call) specifying the type of call.
- *Priority:* a number showing the call's level of importance. To manage the order in which officers respond to calls for service, police assign priorities to calls as they are received. A call's priority is correlated to its seriousness and is dictated by the individual agency's policies. Calls with an "emergency" priority are dispatched first.
- *Disposition:* description of the outcome of the call (e.g., "no action taken," "arrest," "crime report," "accident report," "unable to locate"). A call can have multiple dispositions.
- *Location of the call:* the address and area from which the call came. This is not necessarily the address of a particular incident; often the caller is unable to provide that information (e.g., loud noise coming from the next building).

Table 6.7 is an example of what a portion of a calls-for-service database looks like, with each row representing the summary information from one call for service and the columns containing characteristics of the call.

Accidents

Accidents, or crashes, are incidents in which vehicles collide with property or other vehicles. Accidents are a cause of concern in most communities, and responding to accidents accounts for a considerable amount of police officers' time, thus data on accidents are important in crime analysis. Typically, officers collect and report accident information in the manner dictated by the laws of their states. Each record in an **accident database** contains information about one accident, thus an

Table 6.8   Sample Accident Data Table

Report No.	Report Date	Acc_Date	Acc_Time	Location	Violation1
2003009877	1/5/2003	1/5/2003	0730	E Main Av & S Center St	Improper left turn
2003009882	1/12/2003	1/12/2003	0845	E Elliot Dr & S Apple St	Speed too fast for conditions
2003009878	1/7/2003	1/7/2003	1544	W Main Av & N Cherry Av	No signal
2003009883	1/15/2003	1/15/2003	0921	E Main Av & S Center St	Improper left turn
2003009879	1/28/2003	1/28/2003	1623	E Main Av & S Center St	Speed too fast for conditions

accident is the unit of analysis. Crime analysts typically use the following variables from accident databases:

- *Accident report number:* a unique number used to track the accident.
- *Date of report:* the date on which the accident was reported to the police.
- *Date and time of occurrence:* the date and time when the accident occurred.
- *Location of the accident:* the address at which the accident took place (in many cases an intersection). This information is often recoded into one variable from two others (street the accident "occurred on" and street the accident "occurred at").
- *Violations:* description of what traffic laws were violated, if any (e.g., "speed too fast for conditions," "improper left turn").

Table 6.8 is an example of what a portion of an accident database looks like, with the rows representing individual accidents and the columns containing their characteristics.

Other Databases

In addition to the types of databases discussed above, the following kinds are used less frequently in crime analysis:

- *Property database:* This database contains information about types of property that have been stolen, found, or used in the commission of crimes. The unit of analysis is the piece of property, thus multiple records for property can result from one criminal incident. This database is normally linked to the crime incidents database.
- *Vehicle database:* This database contains information about vehicles stolen, recovered, or used in the commission of crimes. The unit of analysis is the

vehicle, and each record includes information about the vehicle (vehicle identification number [VIN], make, model, color, and year) and the nature of the incident (date, time, location). This database is normally linked to the crime incidents database.

- *Persons database:* This database contains information about all individuals involved in criminal incidents, including witnesses, victims, investigative leads, suspects (some police agencies have suspect databases that are separate from their persons and arrest databases), and arrestees. In this database, the unit of analysis is the individual. Each record contains information about the individual (name, birth date, address, physical, description, aliases) and the nature of the contact (e.g., suspect, arrestee, witness, victim). This database is normally linked to the crime incidents database.
- *Field information database:* Many police agencies collect information from the field through "field interview cards" filled out by officers. This information is collected when an officer determines that a crime report is not necessary, but the agency would like to document the incident outside of the call-for-service record. (For further discussion of field information data, see Chapter 8.)
- *Traffic database:* In addition to accident data, police agencies collect data on traffic citations and vehicle stops. Particularly in the past few years, with the emergence of research on racial profiling, vehicle stop data have become a significant concern for crime analysis.

Geographic Databases

Crime analysts use many different types of geographic databases. Many of these are familiar to most people, because they represent elements of the real world and are used for purposes other than crime analysis. Among the types of geographic databases commonly used in crime analysis are those devoted to the following geographic features:

- *Point features*
    Police stations
    Schools
    Hospitals
    Businesses
    Retail stores/restaurants
    Offices
    Places of worship
    Government buildings
    Mass-transit stops/stations (e.g., bus stops, train stations)

- *Line features*
    Streets
    Highways
    Rivers
    Railroads
    Mass-transit routes (e.g., subways)

- *Polygon features*
  Parcels
  Buildings
  Census block groups and tracts
  Parking lots
  School campuses
  Airports
  City, county, and state boundaries
  Police areas (grid, beat, precinct, district)
  Drug markets
  Gang territories
  Areas targeted for special policing efforts

Geocoding

Before an analyst can use a geographic information system to analyze police tabular data along with geographic data, the tabular data must be geocoded. **Geocoding** is the process of linking an address (e.g., an incident address or the address of an offender's residence) with its map coordinates so that (a) the address can be displayed on a map and (b) the GIS can recognize that address in the future. Ordinarily in crime analysis, the address of a record (e.g., call for service, crime, arrest) is used along with street segment data in geocoding. Data can also be geocoded by other geographic variables, such as zip code, beat, or grid; however, geocoding by address is the focus of this discussion because that is the most common practice in crime analysis.

Geocoding is a five-step process in which the analyst prepares the geographic and tabular files, specifies the geocoding preferences, runs matches within the GIS, reviews the results, and respecifies parameters and begins the process again (Boba, 2001). Each of these steps is described briefly below.

Step 1: Preparing the geographic and tabular files. Data preparation plays a significant role in the crime analysis process, and geocoding is one reason this is so. Preparation of the tabular files typically occurs outside the GIS, because the data come from nongeographic sources (e.g., police records). The analyst's task in this step includes making sure the addresses within the tabular location variable are accurate and consistent. The most common problems affecting tabular data quality stem from data entry mistakes, including misspellings, incorrect abbreviations, inconsistent street types, and lack of compliance with city addressing conventions. For example, the address 136 East Main Street may be entered in many different ways, including the following:

- 136 E Main (missing information: St)
- 136 E Maine St (incorrect spelling)
- 136 E Mn St (inappropriate abbreviation)
- 136 E Main Av (incorrect suffix)

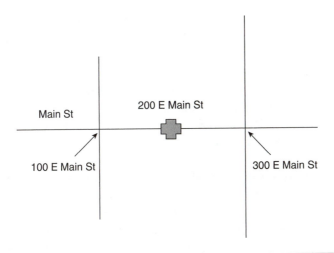

Figure 6.4   Geocoding: Street Segment Matching

- 136 East Main Rd (incorrect directional format and suffix)
- 136 E Main St (correct format)

To obtain accurate and complete geocoding results, the analyst must ensure that geographic data (e.g., street segment file) are up-to-date and accurate. This can be challenging in cities that are growing rapidly and undergoing changing street development.

Step 2: Specifying geocoding preferences. The analyst must determine and set the preferences for matching the reference data to the tabular data. Preferences include the spelling sensitivity of the matches (i.e., whether the tabular street names and geographic street names must be spelled exactly the same), address style (e.g., whether to match on address only or on address and zip code), and the acceptability of partial matches (i.e., whether to accept matches that are considered "close"). Geocoding produces a match score for each record that denotes how closely the address from the tabular file matches the street segments in the geographic file, with a score of 100 signifying a perfect match.

Step 3: Matching within the GIS. Once the preferences are set, the analyst's next step is simply pushing a button. GIS software packages use a fairly simple method to accomplish the placement of an address along a street segment. Each street segment contains a range of addresses, and the GIS places the point along the segment relative to its value within the range. For example, an address of "200 E Main St" would be placed halfway along a street segment that ranges from 100 to 300 East Main Street (see Figure 6.4).

Step 4: Reviewing results. After the geocoding process is complete, GIS software programs generate statistics showing the numbers and percentages of addresses that were matched successfully, addresses that were a partial match (i.e., with scores lower than 100), and addresses that were not geocoded at all. The ideal geocoding score is 100%, which means that *all* records from the tabular file were matched to the geographic file. Depending on the number of cases and the purpose of the analysis, a score of 95% may be acceptable, provided there is a legitimate reason perfection was not reached (e.g., cases that were not matched occurred outside the jurisdiction) and the missing cases will not compromise the analysis results. Whenever geocoding scores are lower than 100%, analysts should reexamine and correct the data and go through the geocoding process again.

Step 5: Respecifying parameters and geocoding again. Geocoding is a painstaking and often trying process, commonly requiring numerous adjustments and repetitions before a high enough score is achieved on a consistent basis. This is an important part of the crime analysis process (i.e., the data modification subcycle), because analysts may not be aware of data problems until they have undertaken geocoding.

Although geocoding in crime analysis most commonly places addresses by street segment, there is an accuracy issue with this method. The method uses a mathematical model to locate each address within an address range (e.g., "100 E Main St" is located halfway between 0 and 200 East Main Street), but in reality, addresses do not occur proportionally along street segments. Some addresses take up entire blocks, whereas others share space on a block, with one address behind another. Two methods of locating records on maps improve on geocoding to street segments:

- *Matching records to parcel data:* In this method, instead of street segment files with address ranges, parcel data are used to match an address to the center of the exact land parcel. This is particularly effective for single-family residences that have relatively small parcels and only one address or building per parcel. Figure 6.5 shows the address 200 East Main Street geocoded both to the street segment and to the parcel to illustrate the difference in the actual location on the map. However, this type of matching becomes problematic when large commercial parcels contain multiple addresses for multiple buildings, because the parcel data file contains only one address per parcel. In these cases, the addresses must be matched to the buildings. This is difficult because preparing the geographic files (i.e., addressing every building in a city) is time-consuming and expensive.
- *Matching records to latitude and longitude:* The most accurate and reliable way to locate records on a map is by using the exact latitude and longitude of the incident, as not all incidents happen at known addresses. To do this for crime and other police data, officers would have to carry global positioning system (GPS) devices to every scene to record the coordinates. Unfortunately, GPS technology is expensive, and in any case the GPS devices currently available are not always accurate.

Although these techniques are an improvement over geocoding to street segment, they are not used regularly in crime analysis because of the drawbacks noted.

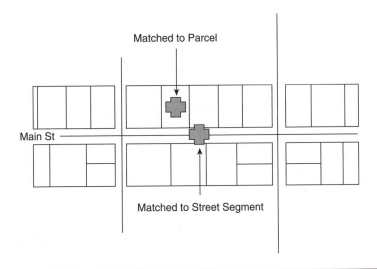

Figure 6.5   Geocoding: Parcel Matching

In time, as GPS technology improves in quality and becomes less expensive to use, crime analysis data will increasingly be located by latitude and longitude.

Data Considerations

The databases commonly used in crime analysis raise several important issues related to the inherent characteristics of the data used by all police agencies. These issues include (a) the fact that the data represent "reported" activity, (b) the distinction between local and federal data standards, (c) the appropriateness of the use of calls-for-service data to study crime problems, (d) the appropriateness of the use of arrest data to study crime problems and offenders, and (e) the integrity of the data. These issues are addressed in turn below.

"Reported" Activity

The databases examined in crime analysis represent activity "reported" or "known" to the police (e.g., crime incidents, arrests, accidents, calls for service) rather than all of the crime or other activity that actually occurs. Certain types of activity tend to be reported more consistently or come to the attention of the police more often than others. For example, incidents of rape, assault, and child abuse are vastly underreported; incidents of prostitution, drunken driving, and gambling are primarily discovered by the police rather than reported by victims; and incidents of auto theft and arson tend to be fairly accurately reported, given victims' need for documentation for insurance purposes. It is important that crime analysts be aware of the limitations of data on reported activity when they are analyzing and interpreting findings. For example, it is known that a very small proportion of the rapes that are committed are reported to police. Thus analysts should be aware that changes in rape statistics may not represent actual changes in the occurrence of rape; rather, they may simply come from changes in the level of reporting this crime. This issue is not limited to crime data; calls-for-service data, accident data, and other kinds of data also represent only activity that is known to the police and may not provide the entire picture concerning particular problems.

Local and Federal Crime Data Standards

Even though the crime analysis databases commonly used (e.g., crime reports, arrests, calls for service, and accidents) are similar across agencies, databases do vary by region, state, and even by police agency. Each agency has its own policies and procedures for recording activity, and this makes it difficult for crime analysts to compare statistics and combine databases. For this reason, the U.S. government developed a nationally based classification system, the Uniform Crime Report (UCR), in 1930 to keep consistent counts of crime across the United States. The UCR provides national standards for the uniform classification of crimes and arrests (for further details, visit the FBI's Web site at http://www.fbi.gov/ucr). UCR crime definitions are distinct and do not conform to federal or state laws.

As individual police agencies classify crimes based on the laws of their own jurisdictions, UCR reporting requires agencies to reclassify crimes according to UCR definitions and to provide only aggregate counts of (a) particular crimes (known as Part I crimes: homicide, rape, robbery, aggravated assault, burglary, larceny, motor vehicle theft, and arson) and (b) arrests for all crimes. In addition, UCR reporting requires the use of a hierarchical coding system (e.g., if one person is the victim of both rape and murder, only the murder is counted). Compliance with UCR reporting is voluntary, but most police agencies participate; currently more than 95% of the U.S. population is represented in UCR statistics. Police agencies report their counts monthly to state agencies, which report to the Federal Bureau of Investigation twice a year.

More recently, the federal government created the National Incident Based Reporting System (NIBRS) in an attempt to improve on the UCR. This system also requires the uniform classification of crime, without regard to local differences, but it tracks more crime types than the UCR does, and participating agencies submit individual records rather than aggregate counts to the FBI in electronic database form. Participation in the system is voluntary, and currently a minority of police agencies report NIBRS data, so the national crime statistics published yearly by the FBI are based on UCR figures.

UCR figures serve as the "official" crime statistics for local jurisdictions. However, because of differences among agencies in crime classifications and the UCR's use of hierarchical coding, figures from local crime and arrest data databases will *never* match the numbers reported to the FBI. It is imperative that crime analysts be aware of this fact, because they are often asked to explain differences between their crime analysis results and official figures.

Because different states' laws define crimes differently, the definitions provided here are from the FBI's Uniform Crime Report, the U.S. national crime reporting system. As the FBI (2003) states: "The Uniform Crime Reporting Program classifies offenses into two groups, Part I and Part II crimes. Each month, contributing agencies submit information on the number of Part I offenses (Crime Index) known to law enforcement; those offenses cleared by arrest or exceptional means; and the age, sex, and race of persons arrested. Contributors provide only arrest data for Part II offenses" (Appendix II). Part I offenses are defined as follows:

Criminal homicide—a.) Murder and nonnegligent manslaughter: the willful (nonnegligent) killing of one human being by another. Deaths caused by negligence, attempts to kill, assaults to kill, suicides, and accidental deaths are excluded. The Program classifies justifiable homicides separately and limits the definition to: (1) the killing of a felon by a law enforcement officer in the line of duty; or (2) the killing of a felon, during the commission of a felony, by a private citizen. b.) Manslaughter by negligence: the killing of another person through gross negligence. Traffic fatalities are excluded.

Forcible rape—The carnal knowledge of a female forcibly and against her will. Rapes by force and attempts or assaults to rape regardless of the age of the victim are included. Statutory offenses (no force used—victim under age of consent) are excluded.

Robbery—The taking or attempting to take anything of value from the care, custody, or control of a person or persons by force or threat of force or violence and/or by putting the victim in fear.

Aggravated assault—An unlawful attack by one person upon another for the purpose of inflicting severe or aggravated bodily injury. This type of assault usually is accompanied by the use of a weapon or by means likely to produce death or great bodily harm. Simple assaults are excluded.

Burglary (breaking or entering)—The unlawful entry of a structure to commit a felony or a theft. Attempted forcible entry is included.

Larceny-theft (except motor vehicle theft)—The unlawful taking, carrying, leading, or riding away of property from the possession or constructive possession of another. Examples are thefts of bicycles or automobile accessories, shoplifting, pocket-picking, or the stealing of any property or article which is not taken by force and violence or by fraud. Attempted larcenies are included. Embezzlement, confidence games, forgery, worthless checks, etc., are excluded.

Motor vehicle theft—The theft or attempted theft of a motor vehicle. A motor vehicle is self-propelled and runs on the surface and not on rails.

Motorboats, construction equipment, airplanes, and farming equipment are specifically excluded from this category.

Arson—Any willful or malicious burning or attempt to burn, with or without intent to defraud, a dwelling house, public building, motor vehicle or aircraft, personal property of another, etc.

Part II offenses, for which only arrest data are collected, are defined as follows:

Other assaults (simple)—Assaults and attempted assaults where no weapons are used and which do not result in serious or aggravated injury to the victim.

Forgery and counterfeiting—Making, altering, uttering, or possessing, with intent to defraud, anything false in the semblance of that which is true. Attempts are included.

Fraud—Fraudulent conversion and obtaining money or property by false pretenses. Confidence games and bad checks, except forgeries and counterfeiting, are included.

Embezzlement—Misappropriation or misapplication of money or property entrusted to one's care, custody, or control.

Stolen property; buying, receiving, possessing—Buying, receiving, and possessing stolen property, including attempts.

Vandalism—Willful or malicious destruction, injury, disfigurement, or defacement of any public or private property, real or personal, without consent of the owner or persons having custody or control. Attempts are included.

Weapons; carrying, possessing, etc.—All violations of regulations or statutes controlling the carrying, using, possessing, furnishing, and manufacturing of deadly weapons or silencers. Attempts are included.

Prostitution and commercialized vice—Sex offenses of a commercialized nature, such as prostitution, keeping a bawdy house, procuring, or transporting women for immoral purposes. Attempts are included.

Sex offenses (except forcible rape, prostitution, and commercialized vice)—Statutory rape and offenses against chastity, common decency, morals, and the like. Attempts are included.

Drug abuse violations—State and/or local offenses relating to the unlawful possession, sale, use, growing, and manufacturing of narcotic drugs. The following drug categories are specified: opium or cocaine and their derivatives (morphine, heroin, codeine); marijuana; synthetic narcotics—manufactured narcotics that can cause true addiction (Demerol, methadone); and dangerous nonnarcotic drugs (barbiturates, Benzedrine).

Gambling—Promoting, permitting, or engaging in illegal gambling.

Offenses against the family and children—Nonsupport, neglect, desertion, or abuse of family and children. Attempts are included.

Driving under the influence—Driving or operating any vehicle or common carrier while drunk or under the influence of liquor or narcotics.

Liquor laws—State and/or local liquor law violations except drunkenness and driving under the influence. Federal violations are excluded.

Drunkenness—Offenses relating to drunkenness or intoxication. Driving under the influence is excluded.

Disorderly conduct—Breach of the peace.

Vagrancy—Begging, loitering, etc. Includes prosecutions under the charge of suspicious person.

All other offenses—All violations of state and/or local laws except those listed above and traffic offenses.

Suspicion—No specific offense; suspect released without formal charges being placed.

Curfew and loitering laws (persons under age 18)—Offenses relating to violations of local curfew or loitering ordinances where such laws exist.

Runaways (persons under age 18)—Limited to juveniles taken into protective custody under provisions of local statutes.

Use of Calls-for-Service Data to Study Crime Problems

Occasionally, crime analysts use calls-for-service data rather than crime incidents data to study crime problems. In such cases, they use calls for service labeled as criminal activity that result in police reports to represent crime incidents. Analysis of crime based on calls for service can be misleading for several reasons, which also highlight the differences between these two data sources:

- *Crime type:* When a call comes in to a police department, the call taker assigns it a call type. In many cases, once on the scene an officer will discover that the incident is actually a different type. For example, a person calls the police department and says, "I've been robbed!" but the responding officer finds that in reality the person's house has been burgled. In many calls-for-service databases, the original call types noted are never updated, so these databases do not accurately represent the types of activities that actually occurred.

- *Date and time:* The date and time variables in calls-for-service databases reflect when each call was received, dispatched, and so on, not when each crime occurred, so such databases do not provide accurate information on when crimes occurred.
- *Location:* The location listed in a calls-for-service database may not be the location of the crime incident, but instead a nearby location or the location from which the call was made. The recording of apartment numbers in calls-for-service data is often haphazard and depends on the amount of information available (e.g., "a loud fight coming from the next building") and the diligence of the call taker (e.g., in determining the apartment number at which the incident is occurring, not where the call is originating).

Given these limitations, calls-for-service databases are more appropriately used in analyses of police officer activity (e.g., officer-generated traffic stops) and disorder activity (e.g., suspicious behavior, disorderly behavior, public drunkenness, noise complaints, and code violations) than in analyses of crime.

Use of Arrest Data to Study Crime Problems and Offenders

Arrests occur when sufficient evidence (probable cause) exists to indicate that persons have committed crimes, and crime analysts use arrest data to understand certain types of crimes as well as offenders. The use of arrest data in such analysis raises three main issues. The first is that arrests tend to reflect police activity. Certain types of crime are documented only through arrests (e.g., prostitution, gambling, driving under the influence of alcohol). Therefore, for example, if a police crackdown on prostitution occurs in February, analysis of arrests for prostitution will show a dramatic increase in February. This change, however, is the result of police action rather than an actual increase in prostitution activity. For this reason, crime analysts need to be aware of police practices that might influence arrests for certain types of crimes.

The second issue is that arrestees may not be representative of offenders, because offenders who are caught may be different (e.g., in intelligence and experience) from those who are not caught. The third issue is that arrest rates for certain crimes are extremely low, and analysts' use of a small number of offenders to understand the larger problem may be misleading. For example, an analysis of individuals arrested for auto theft may reveal that 60% of them are juveniles. Is there a juvenile auto theft problem? Before an analyst can draw any conclusion in this regard, he or she must know the overall arrest rate for auto theft. Property crimes typically have low arrest rates (16.5% for all property crime in 2002; FBI, 2003). Thus, if in the example the arrest rate is only 15%, juveniles were arrested in 9% of the auto thefts (60% of 15% is 9%). More generally, in this instance we are looking at only 15% of the cases—in 85% we have no information about who is committing auto thefts. Thus the answer to the question is that we do not know whether a majority of the thefts are being conducted by juveniles, but we do know that "of the people who are arrested" for auto theft, a majority are juveniles. These are two very different findings.

Data Integrity

The integrity of tabular and geographic police data can be affected by several factors that may influence crime analysis results, including the following:

- *Data entry:* Crime analysis relies primarily on secondary data, and the individuals who enter data often have no understanding of the importance of those data to crime analysis. In police agencies, these individuals include police officers, call takers, dispatchers, and records clerks. Their lack of awareness regarding the need for data accuracy can lead to carelessness and result in unreliable data. Data entry can be improved with technology (e.g., providing variable values, address-cleaning software) and proper training that includes information on the uses and importance of the data.
- *Timeliness:* A primary concern in crime analysis is that the data obtained are current and available in a timely manner. Missing or old data can affect the quality of crime analysis. For example, it is difficult to analyze crime patterns using data that are 6 months to a year old.
- *Validity:* Valid data are data that accurately reflect the concepts they are intended to measure. Issues of validity include the facts that, as discussed above, crime data reflect only "reported" crime, that calls for service do not represent crime incidents, and that arrests are a better indicator of police activity than of crime.
- *Reliability:* Reliable data are data that are the same in repeated observations. Two reliability issues related to police data involve changes in policies or laws (e.g., mandatory arrest for domestic violence offenses) and the coding of similar activities in the same way.
- *Data transfer process:* In many cases, crime analysts download, clean, and manipulate data before conducting their analyses. This process can affect data quality and integrity in that data can be inadvertently or unavoidably lost or reformatted. An issue associated with the data transfer process is data compatibility. Police departments are notorious for having data in many different formats, and converting and combining these data is often time-consuming and frustrating.
- *Data confidentiality/privacy:* Crime analysts are managers of police data; therefore, they are responsible for protecting the information and individuals represented within the data. Normally, the data used and created in crime analysis adhere to a jurisdiction's policies on privacy and confidentiality. In recent years, new ways of gathering and disseminating information have surfaced that require additional and more detailed policies, such as the use of the Internet and the use of mapping. Thus police departments need to include specific crime analysis concerns in their data protection plans.
- *Data management:* The term *metadata* refers to information about data. Every police department has its own set of procedures outlining how crime analysis data are to be collected and manipulated. However, many details regarding these procedures exist only in the memories of individual analysts. In the metadata process, this information is written down to ensure consistency in data handling and cleaning procedures, to provide guidelines for sharing work with others and keeping track of products and files created, and to reduce duplication of effort.

Summary Points

This chapter has provided an overview of the common tabular and geographic data used in crime analysis as well as discussion of the issues associated with the use of these data. The following are the key points addressed in this chapter:

- A database is a collection of data that have been organized for the purposes of retrieval, searching, and analysis through a computer.
- Secondary data are data that have been collected for purposes other than crime analysis and are housed in databases.
- Primary data are data collected—through surveys, interviews, field research, and direct observation—specifically for use in a particular analysis.
- Geographic data are data used primarily in mapping; in many cases, these data do not make much sense outside of a GIS. Four types of geographic data are used to represent real-world objects and locations: point, line, polygon, and image. The data associated with these features are called attributes.
- Tabular data describe events that are not inherently geographic but that may contain geographic variables.
- Crime analysts most frequently use four types of secondary data: data on crime incidents, arrests, calls for service, and accidents.
- Data about crime incidents come from crime reports taken by police officers and describe the nature of reported crimes, such as the type of crime and how, when, and where the crime occurred.
- Data about arrests come from arrest reports completed by officers and include information specific to individual arrests.
- Calls-for-service data are recorded in the dispatch center of a police agency and may be generated by either citizens or officers. A call for service is defined when an officer is dispatched to an incident or discovers an incident him- or herself.
- Accident (or crash) data are typically recorded in standardized ways dictated by state laws. Accidents are incidents in which vehicles collide with property or other vehicles.
- Among the police tabular databases used in crime analysis are property, vehicle, persons, field information, and traffic databases.
- Many types of geographic databases are used in crime analysis. Many of these are familiar to most people, as they represent elements of the real world and are used for a variety of purposes.
- Geocoding is a five-step process that is used to bring tabular and geographic data together for mapping. The steps are as follows: (a) preparing the geographic and tabular files for geocoding, (b) specifying the geocoding preferences, (c) matching within the GIS, (d) reviewing results, and (e) respecifying parameters and geocoding again.
- Two other ways of locating tabular data on maps are matching records to parcel data and using latitude and longitude. These methods are both improvements over geocoding but are more difficult to conduct.

- Important issues related to crime analysts' use of police tabular databases include the following: (a) the fact that the data represent "reported" activity, (b) the distinction between local and federal data standards, (c) the appropriateness of the use of calls-for-service data to study crime problems, (d) the appropriateness of the use of arrest data to study crime problems and offenders, and (e) the integrity of the data.
- Data integrity is affected by the following factors: data entry, timeliness, validity, reliability, the data transfer process, data confidentiality/privacy, and data management.

Exercises

Exercise 6.1

Using the Internet, find and copy or download a small set of police department crime data. Applying concepts discussed in this chapter, determine the type of data, the variables included, and the quality of the data.

Exercise 6.2

Make a list of types of geographic and tabular data, other than those mentioned in this chapter, that might be useful for crime analysis. Provide an example of the potential use of each kind of data in your list.

Note

1. Crime statistics are not based on when crimes occur because crimes are reported hours, days, weeks, months, and even years after they occur. Using report date is a static, reliable way of counting crime, but it may not provide a completely accurate picture of when crime is occurring (e.g., a high number of burglaries may be reported in January because people who were on vacation in December did not report the crimes until January).

7

Crime Analysis Technology

As noted in previous chapters, crime analysis relies heavily on computer technology, and over the past 15 years significant improvements in computer hardware and software have led to tremendous development in this field. This chapter provides a brief overview of the types of technology currently being used in the various stages of the crime analysis process.[1]

Computer Hardware

The computer hardware used for crime analysis is similar to that used in other disciplines that rely on the help of computers. Crime analysts use desktop personal computers to complete most of their work and use laptop computers for fieldwork and presentations. In many cases, police departments' crime analysis units have their own servers to house tabular data, geographic data, and software applications that are shared by users. Other kinds of hardware used in crime analysis include color laser printers that can produce high-quality documents quickly, plotters (printers that produce poster-size color maps for display), scanners, and digital cameras (used to obtain pictures of people and locations as well as to capture documents that are not available in electronic form).

Data Collection and Storage

The tabular and geographic data (secondary data) used in crime analysis are commonly obtained from three main kinds of data collection and storage systems: computer-aided dispatch (CAD) systems, records management systems (RMSs), and geographic data systems. The first two of these are typically located within police departments, whereas geographic data systems are maintained by city, county, or state governments. Other systems also produce data used in crime analysis, such as national data systems, court systems, and parole and probation systems, but CAD systems, RMSs, and geographic data systems are the most common data sources.

Computer-Aided Dispatch System

A **computer-aided dispatch system** is a highly specialized system that uses tele-communications and geographic display to support police dispatch and response functions (as well as those of public safety agencies, such as fire and ambulance services). Police departments use CAD technology to dispatch officers, to keep track of officers' locations and activities, and to track officer-initiated activity (e.g., traffic stops). Most communication between police officers and dispatchers is recorded in a CAD system. However, a CAD system is not a 911 system, which receives and records actual phone calls from citizens about emergency activity. Typically, a police department transfers key pieces of information about citizen calls for service from the 911 system to the CAD system, which records all information pertaining to dispatched calls. These data are often called *unit history* because they track officer activity. Typically, one record represents each communication, resulting in multiple lines of data for each call for service.[2]

As noted in Chapter 6, crime analysts do not need all of the information recorded about calls for service to conduct their analyses. The unit of analysis for calls-for-service data is an individual call, not each communication (as in unit history). Hence, for crime analysis purposes, analysts download summary data about calls for service from the CAD system, where there is one record for each call that includes variables relevant for crime analysis, such as time of the call, type of call, time officers dispatched to the scene, and disposition of the call. CAD systems collect, store, and allow downloading of data, but typically they do not include crime analysis capabilities. Other technology is used to conduct crime analysis.

Records Management System

A **records management system** is a data entry and storage system designed especially for police records. Some police agencies enter information directly into the RMS, whereas others download information to the RMS from other software programs, such as CAD or crime report–writing software. Ideally, the RMS contains all relevant data within the police agency and can include separate databases such as crime reports, arrest reports, persons information, property and evidence information, vehicle information, accident reports, field information, calls for service (i.e., snapshot data), and investigations. The contents of RMSs vary, but their purpose, to store crime incidents data and link them with related data, is consistent across different software products and police departments.

In addition to collecting and storing information, an RMS is used to check the quality of data, retrieve incidents, and provide information. Police agency employees, typically called records clerks, check data entry and police reports to be sure the information is accurate and the reports are in compliance with the appropriate laws and departmental policies. Police agencies also use RMSs to search reports and to locate individual reports for court cases and insurance purposes (e.g., accident reports) as well as to obtain lists of cases and summaries (e.g., the Uniform Crime Report). Like CAD systems, most RMSs do not have crime analysis capabilities;

analysts download data from these systems into other software in order to conduct crime analysis.

Geographic Data System

A **geographic data system** creates, maintains, and stores geographic data. Typically, city or county agencies use geographic data systems to create and maintain data concerning parcels, buildings, streets, roads, and highways, and to store aerial photographs and other geographic information to be used by various departments and agencies (e.g., planning, utilities). In addition, such agencies often obtain tabular and geographic data from other sources—such as census information, demographic information, and typological information—and store them along with local geographic data. It is important to note that crime analysts do not collect or maintain the data housed in geographic data systems; rather, they only borrow and use these data in their analyses.

Data Collation and Analysis

CAD systems, RMSs, and geographic data systems all produce data that are used in crime analysis, but these are not analysis systems; as noted above, other software is used for crime analysis activities. Crime analysts use four basic types of general desktop software applications to organize data as well as to conduct analyses: spreadsheet software, database management software, statistical software, and geographic information system (GIS) software.

Spreadsheet Software

A **spreadsheet** displays information in rows and columns of cells. **Spreadsheet software** applications allow users to create and change spreadsheets easily. In spreadsheet software, each unique entry or value is contained in a cell, and the user defines the type of data contained in each cell (e.g., time or date format, numeric or string variable). In addition, cells are usually named by rows and columns (called labels), and the software uses formulas to create relationships between cells. Most spreadsheet applications are multidimensional; that is, they contain multiple individual spreadsheets that can be linked together by formulas. If a change is made to one cell of one spreadsheet, that change is reflected in all other spreadsheets linked to that cell. Some powerful spreadsheet applications support graphics features such as charts and graphs. Many different kinds of spreadsheet software are available; some of the most widely used are IBM's Lotus 1-2-3 and Microsoft's Excel.

Crime analysts use spreadsheet software for both data organization and analysis purposes. An analyst typically downloads data into a spreadsheet, links with other databases, and reworks the data (e.g., makes consistent changes to addresses and creates new variables). Crime analysts also use spreadsheet programs for statistical analysis, as they provide a wide range of basic statistical capabilities. More advanced uses of spreadsheets include the creation of miniature computer programs (called macros) that can automatically execute tasks, such as summarizing data and formatting reports. Because spreadsheet applications are not actual database applications, they can be somewhat limited in their capabilities (e.g., Excel allows only approximately 65,000 records in one spreadsheet).

Database Management Software

Database management software (DBMS) allows users to enter, store, and modify data in and extract data from a database. CAD systems and RMSs are large database management systems that police agencies use to obtain and store data for crime analysis. However, crime analysts also use smaller desktop applications (most commonly Microsoft Access) to organize and analyze data. These database programs facilitate data entry, recognize multiple relationships among records, provide exporting capabilities, create automated reports, and provide powerful query tools, all of which are important in crime analysis. Typically, the analyst downloads data from larger systems into smaller desktop software or, when the agency does not have a large enough system, enters data directly into the desktop software.

Statistical Software

Statistical software accesses data obtained from spreadsheets and DBMS and facilitates data entry. The core purposes of statistical software are statistical computation and data manipulation, and these applications are designed to handle large numbers of records (e.g., more than a million). In recent years, the presentation and table-making capabilities of these applications have been dramatically enhanced.

Some crime analysis units use statistical programs such as SPSS (Statistical Package for the Social Sciences), SAS, and StataQuest. However, the use of spreadsheet and DBMS applications is much more common, because advanced statistical functionality is not particularly relevant to everyday crime analysis. Nevertheless, statistical software is available for those analysts who need to conduct advanced data manipulation and analysis that other types of applications cannot handle.

Geographic Information System Software

As noted in Chapter 4, a GIS is a set of computer-based tools that allows a person to modify, visualize, query, and analyze geographic and tabular data. It is a powerful software tool that enables the user to view the data behind geographic features, combine various features, manipulate data and maps, and perform statistical functions. As examples throughout this book highlight, crime analysts use **GIS software** primarily to bring data together through geographic variables, to analyze spatial relationships, and to display data through maps. A GIS utilizes data from other sources and does not have a specific capability for entering data even though it may have limited data entry, manipulation, and statistical functions. The most common GIS software packages used in crime analysis today are produced by ESRI (Environmental Systems Research Institute) and MapInfo.

Dissemination

Crime analysts use six basic types of software applications, alone or in combination, to create reports, publications, and presentations: word processing software, spreadsheet software, graphics software, publication software, presentation software, and software related to use of the Internet and intranets.

Word Processing Software

Probably the most commonly used nonquantitative software is **word processing software**, which allows users to create, edit, and print documents (e.g., Microsoft Word and Corel WordPerfect). Word processing software primarily supports the creation and manipulation of text, but it can also enable users to incorporate tables, charts, and pictures in documents. Crime analysts use word processing software regularly to create memos, reports, and bulletins.

Spreadsheet Software

In addition to using spreadsheet software to enter, manipulate, and analyze data, as described above, crime analysts use such software to create tables and charts that can stand alone, be inserted into reports or presentations, or be posted on the Web. Crime analysts often use the automated functions of spreadsheet software to produce reports that are disseminated repeatedly.

Graphics Software

Graphics software enables users to create and manipulate pictures and other images. The graphics programs widely used in crime analysis include Corel Paint Shop Pro and Adobe Photoshop. A crime analyst might use this software for tasks such as adding labels to an aerial photograph for a report, cropping a picture of a suspect, or creating a logo for the department's crime analysis unit.

Publishing Software

Crime analysis units often produce flyers, brochures, newsletters, and/or electronic reports for the public. **Publishing software**, such as Microsoft Publisher and Adobe

Illustrator, allows users to create professional-looking products. Additionally, software is available, such as Adobe Acrobat, that allows users to create electronic versions of reports that cannot be modified by others.

Presentation Software

Presentation software, such as Microsoft PowerPoint, allows users to create visual aids that can enhance in-person presentations of information, such as the presentations crime analysts often give to police personnel, community members, and fellow analysts at conferences. The slides this software creates can include text, tables, charts, maps, and other images. The software also allows users to prepare notes and outlines for presenters and includes printing capabilities.

Internet/Intranet

The **Internet** is a global network that connects millions of computers. (The terms *Internet* and *World Wide Web* are generally used interchangeably, although technically not everything on the Internet is also on the Web.) Independent computers connect to the Internet through a wide range of software applications (e.g., Netscape, Explorer). In recent years, police departments have been using the Internet to disseminate information to their communities (and to others) about crime and police activities. Many police department Web sites post maps and/or allow users to access specialized mapping applications so that citizens can find out about crime in their area. (For further discussion of police agencies' use of the Internet, see Chapter 14.)

In recent years, many public and private organizations, including police departments, have established computer networks known as **intranets.** An intranet functions much like the Internet, but it connects only a limited number of users, usually people associated with a particular organization. It is accessible only to selected users (usually organization members, employees, or other associated individuals), who log on with user IDs and passwords, and has security features (typically called a firewall) designed to prevent unauthorized individuals from gaining access.

Police departments have begun to use intranet applications to disseminate crime analysis information to their personnel. In many cases, information is provided through a crime mapping application that allows officers to query recent crime incidents and other activity by location and time period. The software that police departments use for both Internet and intranet dissemination of information is typically managed by the departments or their cities but is often created by outside vendors.

Specialized Crime Analysis Software

The kinds of software discussed so far have all been adapted for use in crime analysis but were not created specifically for that purpose. In addition to these, a number of software applications have been created specifically for crime analysis. These include smaller applications for data entry and creating reports as well as more comprehensive programs that provide numerous capabilities needed for the crime analysis process. Most of the applications designed specifically for crime analysis have been created to perform functions that are not available in other existing software. For example, the ATAC (Automated Tactical Analysis of Crime) software that accompanies this book was created to provide users with techniques specific to tactical crime analysis because these functions were not available previously in one comprehensive program.

The following list of software programs designed for crime analysis, compiled by the Police Foundation (2003), is in no way intended to be comprehensive; it is offered simply to illustrate the range of programs currently available.

- *ATAC* (Bair Software, Inc.; http://www.bairsoftware.com): This tactical crime analysis software allows data entry, manipulation, and analysis. It also provides temporal analysis and a function that identifies potential crime patterns. (This software is included on the CD-ROM that accompanies this book.)
- *Crime Analysis Extension* (National Institute of Justice and ESRI, Inc.; http://www.ojp.usdoj.gov/nij/maps/software.html): This free mapping software was developed through a partnership between the U.S. government and a software vendor; it contains specific mapping functions used in crime analysis.
- *CrimeStat* (Ned Levine and Associates; http://www.icpsr.umich.edu/NACJD/crimestat.html): This spatial statistical software works with GIS software to allow users to conduct analyses with various techniques using incident locations.
- *CrimeView* (The Omega Group; http://www.theomegagroup.com): This software links directly to an agency's CAD system or RMS and provides specific crime mapping and analysis techniques.
- *GeoBalance* (Corona Solutions; http://www.coronasolutions.com): This redistricting software identifies the best possible arrangement of police areas (such as beats and districts) based on several statistics.
- *RCAGIS (Regional Crime Analysis Geographic Information System)* (U.S. Department of Justice; http://www.icpsr.umich.edu/NACJD/RCAGIS): This software is intended for use by numerous agencies in a region with the same data format (all the data are linked into the software automatically). It includes various crime analysis and crime mapping functions.
- *School COP (School Crime Operations Package)* (Abt Associates; http://www.schoolcopsoftware.com): This mapping software program is specifically designed to allow users to enter, analyze, and map incidents that occur in and around schools.
- *Staff Wizard* (Corona Solutions; http://www.coronasolutions.com): This software helps to optimize the placement of current staff (patrol deployment) as well as determine staffing needs.

In addition to these commercially produced programs, many police departments have created their own software to perform crime analysis. For example, one analyst created a data entry module and database in Microsoft Access because his department had not yet acquired a records management system; he simply had no other way of accessing electronic data for analysis. Another analyst with advanced computer programming skills created a program in Visual Basic to speed up the process of address cleaning (bringing the time needed down from 4 hours to 30 seconds).

In many cases, because crime analysis is a fairly young discipline and police data are unique by agency, analysts and agencies find that off-the-shelf software is not a good fit with their data, analysis, and presentation needs. As a result, they hire computer experts to customize existing software or create new software that provides the functionality they require.

Summary Points

This chapter has provided an overview of the hardware and software used in crime analysis. The following are the key points addressed in this chapter:

- Crime analysis is a discipline that relies heavily on computer technology, both hardware and a variety of software programs.
- The hardware used in crime analysis is similar to that used in other disciplines that rely on the help of computers; it includes desktop personal computers, laptop computers, servers, laser printers, plotters, scanners, and digital cameras.
- Crime analysts obtain secondary data from three main kinds of data collection and storage systems: computer-aided dispatch systems, records management systems, and geographic data systems.
- A CAD system is a highly specialized system that uses telecommunications and geographic display to support police dispatch and response functions (as well as those of public safety agencies, such as fire and ambulance services).
- An RMS is a specialized data entry and storage system that contains relevant data within the police agency.
- A geographic data system creates, maintains, and stores relevant geographic data. Such a system is usually maintained at the city or county level, and crime analysts "borrow" data from it.
- Crime analysts use four basic types of general desktop software applications to manipulate data and conduct analyses: spreadsheet software, database management software, statistical software, and geographic information system software.
- Crime analysts use six basic types of software applications to create reports, publications, and presentations to communicate their analysis findings: word processing software, spreadsheet software, graphics software, publication software, presentation software, and software related to use of the Internet and intranets.
- Among the software applications that have been created specifically for crime analysis are small applications for data entry and creating reports as well as more comprehensive programs that provide numerous capabilities needed for the crime analysis process.

- Many police agencies do not find off-the-shelf software to be a good fit with their data, analysis, and presentation needs, so they hire computer experts to customize existing software or create new software that provides the crime analysis functionality they require.

Exercises

Exercise 7.1

Many local and county police agencies allow citizens to observe the 911 call-taking process and/or the work that takes place at agency dispatch centers. It is very important for anyone using police data for analysis to understand how those data are collected. With permission from your instructor, request a "ride-along," not with an officer but with your local 911 and/or dispatch center. While you are there, think about the following issues:

- How are calls documented in the system?
- Do the call takers use mapping to identify addresses and/or locate officers?
- Do the call takers use numerical codes or literal descriptions (words) to label crime and other activity?
- How can the data collected by call takers be accessed at a later time?

Exercise 7.2

Go to three of the Web sites mentioned above in the list of available crime analysis specialty software, and review the purpose and nature of each of the three software programs. Why do you think these software programs were developed?

Notes

1. Specific information about the software provided with this book is contained on the accompanying CD-ROM.
2. Crime analysts use "unit history" for the specific purpose of assessing staffing needs and scheduling officers, because it provides information about officers' specific activities on individual calls.

PART III

Tactical Crime Analysis

The focus of this book now shifts from description of concepts and data to presentation of the methods and techniques used in crime analysis. Part III is the first of three sections devoted to individual types of crime analysis. To repeat the definition provided in Chapter 2, tactical crime analysis is the study of recent criminal incidents and potential criminal activity through the examination of characteristics such as how, when, and where the activity has occurred to assist in pattern development, investigative lead and suspect identification, and case clearance.

The following two chapters provide an introduction to the data, analysis techniques, and products of tactical crime analysis. Chapter 8 includes a discussion of tactical crime analysis data and methodologies for identifying patterns, investigating leads, and clearing cases. Chapter 9 covers specific techniques that analysts can use to understand known crime patterns and provides examples of tactical crime analysis products. Although these chapters are introductory, the concepts discussed and the exercises and examples of the uses of software provided constitute a solid basis for an understanding of tactical crime analysis.

8

Data Collection and Pattern Identification

One of most important aspects of tactical crime analysis (TCA), and the first step in the crime analysis process, is the collection of the necessary data. This chapter describes the kinds of data used in tactical crime analysis and how crime analysts use these data to identify patterns, investigate leads, and clear cases.

Collection and Collation of Tactical Crime Analysis Data

The data used in TCA include information about how, when, and where crimes have occurred. TCA utilizes both quantitative and qualitative information from police reports. Quantitative data such as date, time, location, and type of crime typically come from specific variables that are collected in reports. Other quantitative variables are gleaned from the narratives of reports—that is, from qualitative information. Analysts create these variables by reviewing and categorizing information contained in reports, such as what the suspect said during the commission of the crime or unique property stolen. Analysts also examine additional qualitative information gathered from the field, such as from patrol briefings, ride-alongs, and discussions with officers and detectives.

Before the systematic use of computers in TCA, analysts recorded the data in paper matrices such as the one depicted in Figure 8.1. Analysts coded limited numbers of variables manually and examined them in order to determine patterns. The matrices used today look similar, as Figure 8.2 shows, but they are electronic, allowing analysts to include many more variables and to rearrange variables as needed for easier visualization. In addition, electronic matrices allow analysts to collect and review large numbers of cases quickly and easily—the only limitations lie in the creativity of the analyst.

Analysts can create such matrices in any number of programs, including Excel, Access, SPSS, Quatro Pro, and programs created specifically for tactical crime analysis. In this chapter, the examples presented come from the specialized program Automated Tactical Analysis of Crime (ATAC), which is included on the CD-ROM that accompanies this book.

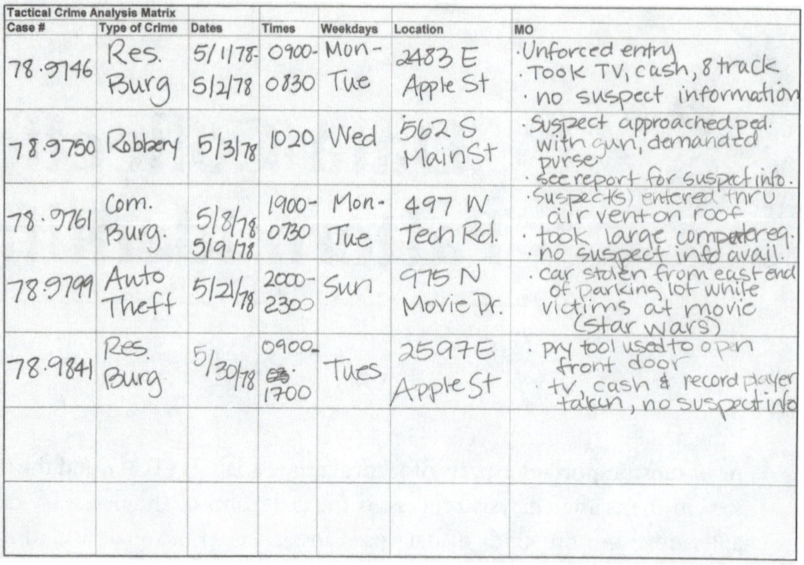

Tactical Crime Analysis Matrix						
Case #	Type of Crime	Dates	Times	Weekdays	Location	MO
78-9746	Res. Burg	5/1/78-5/2/78	0900-0830	Mon-Tue	2483 E Apple St	·Unforced entry ·Took TV, cash, 8 track ·no suspect information
78-9750	Robbery	5/3/78	1020	Wed	562 S Main St	·Suspect approached ped. with gun, demanded purse ·See report for suspect info.
78-9761	Com. Burg.	5/8/78 5/9/78	1900-0730	Mon-Tue	497 W Tech Rd.	·Suspect(s) entered thru air vent on roof ·took large computer eq. ·no suspect info avail.
78-9799	Auto Theft	5/21/78	2000-2300	Sun	975 N Movie Dr.	·car stolen from east end of parking lot while victims at movie (Star Wars)
78-9841	Res. Burg	5/30/78	0900-1700	Tues	2597 E Apple St	·Pry tool used to open front door ·tv, cash & record player taken, no suspect info

Figure 8.1 Paper Matrix Example

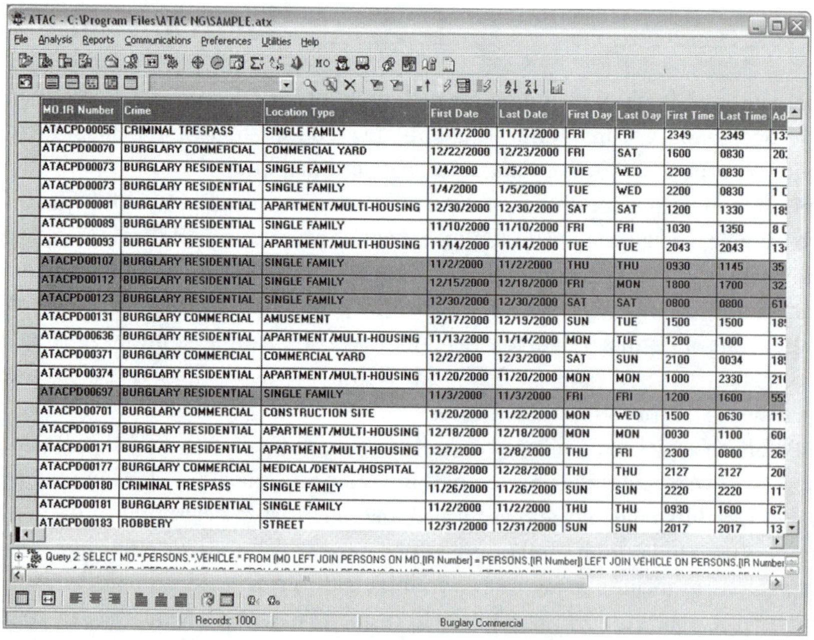

MO.IR Number	Crime	Location Type	First Date	Last Date	First Day	Last Day	First Time	Last Time	Ad
ATACPD00056	CRIMINAL TRESPASS	SINGLE FAMILY	11/17/2000	11/17/2000	FRI	FRI	2349	2349	13
ATACPD00070	BURGLARY COMMERCIAL	COMMERCIAL YARD	12/22/2000	12/23/2000	FRI	SAT	1600	0830	20
ATACPD00073	BURGLARY RESIDENTIAL	SINGLE FAMILY	1/4/2000	1/5/2000	TUE	WED	2200	0830	1
ATACPD00073	BURGLARY RESIDENTIAL	SINGLE FAMILY	1/4/2000	1/5/2000	TUE	WED	2200	0830	1
ATACPD00081	BURGLARY RESIDENTIAL	APARTMENT/MULTI-HOUSING	12/30/2000	12/30/2000	SAT	SAT	1200	1330	18
ATACPD00089	BURGLARY RESIDENTIAL	SINGLE FAMILY	11/10/2000	11/10/2000	FRI	FRI	1030	1350	8
ATACPD00093	BURGLARY RESIDENTIAL	APARTMENT/MULTI-HOUSING	11/14/2000	11/14/2000	TUE	TUE	2043	2043	13
ATACPD00107	BURGLARY RESIDENTIAL	SINGLE FAMILY	11/2/2000	11/2/2000	THU	THU	0930	1145	35
ATACPD00112	BURGLARY RESIDENTIAL	SINGLE FAMILY	12/15/2000	12/18/2000	FRI	MON	1800	1700	32
ATACPD00123	BURGLARY RESIDENTIAL	SINGLE FAMILY	12/30/2000	12/30/2000	SAT	SAT	0800	0800	61
ATACPD00131	BURGLARY COMMERCIAL	AMUSEMENT	12/17/2000	12/19/2000	SUN	TUE	1500	1500	18
ATACPD00636	BURGLARY RESIDENTIAL	APARTMENT/MULTI-HOUSING	11/13/2000	11/14/2000	MON	TUE	1200	1000	13
ATACPD00371	BURGLARY COMMERCIAL	COMMERCIAL YARD	12/2/2000	12/3/2000	SAT	SUN	2100	0034	18
ATACPD00374	BURGLARY RESIDENTIAL	APARTMENT/MULTI-HOUSING	11/20/2000	11/20/2000	MON	MON	1000	2330	21
ATACPD00697	BURGLARY RESIDENTIAL	SINGLE FAMILY	11/3/2000	11/3/2000	FRI	FRI	1200	1600	55
ATACPD00701	BURGLARY COMMERCIAL	CONSTRUCTION SITE	11/20/2000	11/22/2000	MON	WED	1500	0630	11
ATACPD00169	BURGLARY RESIDENTIAL	APARTMENT/MULTI-HOUSING	12/18/2000	12/18/2000	MON	MON	0030	1100	60
ATACPD00171	BURGLARY RESIDENTIAL	APARTMENT/MULTI-HOUSING	12/7/2000	12/8/2000	THU	FRI	2300	0800	26
ATACPD00177	BURGLARY COMMERCIAL	MEDICAL/DENTAL/HOSPITAL	12/28/2000	12/28/2000	THU	THU	2127	2127	20
ATACPD00180	CRIMINAL TRESPASS	SINGLE FAMILY	11/26/2000	11/26/2000	SUN	SUN	2220	2220	11
ATACPD00181	BURGLARY RESIDENTIAL	SINGLE FAMILY	11/2/2000	11/2/2000	THU	THU	0930	1600	67
ATACPD00183	ROBBERY	STREET	12/31/2000	12/31/2000	SUN	SUN	2017	2017	13

Figure 8.2 Electronic Matrix Example

Crime Report Data

TCA seeks to identify patterns of crimes that are not easily linked together. It focuses on crimes in which the offender and the victim do not know one another and on crimes that are predatory in nature. The types of crimes most often examined in TCA include the following (this list is adapted from Tempe Police Department, 2003):

- *Theft from vehicle*: the unlawful taking of property from inside or on a vehicle
- *Auto theft:* the taking of a motor vehicle
- *Vandalism:* the destruction or defacement of public or private property
- *Commercial burglary:* the unlawful entry or attempted forcible entry of a commercial structure to commit a felony or a theft
- *Residential burglary:* the unlawful entry or attempted forcible entry of a residential structure to commit a felony or a theft
- *Indecent exposure:* the exposure of a private part while another person is present, accompanied by recklessness about whether the other person, as a reasonable person, would be offended or alarmed by the act
- *Public sexual indecency:* the intentional or knowing engagement in sexual contact while another person is present, accompanied by recklessness about whether the other person, as a reasonable person, would be offended or alarmed by the act
- *Rape:* carnal knowledge of a person forcibly and against the person's will
- *Robbery:* the taking or attempting to take anything of value from the care, custody, or control of a person or persons by force or threat of force through violence and/or by putting the victim in fear

In some cases, the legal description of a crime is not as important as the type of behavior documented in the police report. Thus other types of crimes or police reports might also be examined in TCA if the activities they describe seem to be related to one of the crimes listed above, such as a kidnapping that might have been an unsuccessful rape or a criminal damage incident that seems more like an unsuccessful burglary.

Generally, TCA is not used to examine crimes in which the victim and offender know each other (e.g., burglary by an ex-roommate, date rape, or robbery of one drug dealer by another), crimes in which the acts are consensual (e.g., prostitution, drug dealing/buying, gambling), or crimes involving conflicts between acquaintances (e.g., assault and domestic violence).

Currently, no national standards dictate what characteristics (variables) police agencies should collect for TCA purposes. However, both standard practice in tactical crime analysis and the ATAC software organize the characteristics of a crime into three categories: modus operandi, persons involved in the crime, and vehicles involved in the crime. The number of characteristics known about the crime and the quality of that information vary by crime type, making some types of predatory crimes more difficult to link together than others. For example, robbery and rape incidents are rich with data because in each case a person (the victim) was present and is able to describe when, how, and by whom the crime was perpetrated. Conversely, auto theft incidents lack many characteristics because not only are there usually no witnesses to these crimes, but the targets themselves (the cars) are gone. TCA is still conducted on crimes with relatively few available characteristics, but the patterns are harder to specify and link to particular suspects. Described below are a wide range of characteristics that would be collected for incidents, depending on the information available.

Modus Operandi

Modus operandi (MO), a Latin term meaning literally "method of procedure," refers to the method of the crime—that is, the key elements of the crime incident itself:

- *What:* the type of crime (e.g., commercial burglary, residential burglary, rape).
- *How:* how the crime was carried out (varies by type of crime). Characteristics include but are not limited to the following:

    Point of entry: where the suspect(s) entered the property (e.g., front door, window, roof entry, unknown); especially important for property crimes

    Method of entry: how the suspect(s) entered the location (e.g., kick, pry tool, rock, drive in, unknown); especially important for property crimes

    Suspect's actions: what the suspect(s) did during the crime (e.g., beat the victim, tied the victim, acted compassionate toward the victim); especially important for persons crimes

    Action against property: what the suspect(s) did to the property (e.g., ransacked, set on fire)

    Object of attack: the type of person or property attacked (e.g., cash register, safe, clerk, pedestrian, car)

    Method of departure: how the suspect(s) left the scene (e.g., in car, on foot); especially important for persons crimes

    Weapon type: the type(s) of weapon(s) used in the commission of the crime (e.g., gun, pipe, simulated weapon)

    Property taken: the items stolen during the commission of the crime (e.g., jewelry, cash, TV)

- *Where:* where the crime was committed. Characteristics include but are not limited to the following:

    Address: the exact address where the crime occurred, including apartment, suite, or hotel room number if applicable

    Address name: the commercial name, if any, of where the crime occurred (e.g., ValueMart, Garden Apartments, Lucky's Convenience Store)

    Type of location: the category of location where the crime occurred (e.g., convenience store, apartment, storage shed, beauty salon)

    Area: area in which the crime occurred (e.g., reporting district, beat, grid, section)

- *When:* when the crime was committed. Characteristics include the following:

    Exact time and date of the crime: used when the exact time and date are known; typically for persons crimes

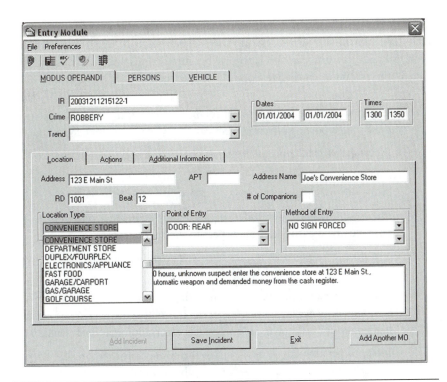

Figure 8.3   MO Data Collection Screen: ATAC

NOTE: This screen shot shows many MO characteristics captured and coded in a systematic way. The drop-down menu is available for all characteristics with arrows and provides a way for the user to code the information about the crime systematically. Notice also the area at the bottom where qualitative (narrative) information is kept.

First date and time: the first possible date and time the crime could have occurred (beginning of a time span); typically for property crimes that are not witnessed

Last date and time: the last possible date and time the crime could have occurred (end of a time span) (Note that the date of report is not included here because the purpose is not to count crimes but to examine when they occurred.)

Qualitative information about crime incidents may also be included in a TCA database. This would include information about incidents that does not fall within the characteristics listed above or that provides further explanation concerning MO (e.g., the suspect in a bank robbery sent all the women in the bank to the bathroom, or a rape suspect left a flower with each one of his victims). Figure 8.3 is an example of how MO data appear as collected in the ATAC program:

Persons

The data about a person involved in a crime typically include a description of the type of contact, the name/address of the person, a physical description of the person, and a description of the physical condition of the person at the time of the crime. The individual's actions during the crime are not included here; as noted above, these fall within the MO category, because actions are part of "how" the crime occurred and often change from incident to incident.

- *Type of contact*: the classification of the individual within the crime incident (made by the reporting officer in most cases). Categories include the following:

  Investigative lead: a person who is a potential suspect for a crime

  Known offender: a person who has been *convicted, not just arrested,* for any crime other than a sex offense

  Mention: a person mentioned in the report (entered if the person is a possible investigative lead or suspect in the crime)

  Sex offender: a person who has been *convicted, not just arrested,* for a sex offense

  Suspect: a person who was seen committing the crime or about whom there is enough evidence to "suspect" he or she committed the crime (The person's name may not be known; only a physical description may be available.)

  Victim: a person who is the victim of the crime (Information about property as victims—i.e., targets—is normally included in the MO category as type of location.)

- *Name/address/date of birth*: the name, address, and birth date of the individual, when these are known, as well as any aliases
- *Physical description*: a description of the person's static physical characteristics (i.e., characteristics that do not change from one day to the next) if they are known or as they are described by a witness or officer (if unknown). Characteristics include the following:

  Age: computed from the date of birth or a range for a suspect whose birthday is not known (e.g., suspect appeared to be between 25 and 35 years old)

  Sex (male or female): based on driver's license information of a known person or on a witness description

  Height: observed by an officer or a range based on a witness description (e.g., suspect appeared to be between 5 feet, 6 inches and 5 feet, 8 inches tall)

  Weight: observed by an officer or a range based on a witness description (e.g., suspect appeared to be between 210 and 230 pounds)

  Eye color: observed by an officer or based on a witness description

  Race/ethnicity: based on the person's self-classification on his or her driver's license or on a witness description (Note that these two classifications can be very different.)

  Build: the general body type of the individual (e.g., slight, medium, large, heavy, tall), based on an officer's observation or a witness description

Teeth condition: the nature of the individual's teeth (e.g., crooked, yellow, black, missing, gold), observed by an officer or based on a witness description

Hand use: whether the individual used one hand or another dominantly (e.g., held the gun in his right hand), based on a witness description

Scars, tattoos, marks, or other distinguishing characteristics: permanent unique visible characteristics (e.g., tattoos, scars, birthmarks, missing limbs), observed by an officer or based on a witness description

- *Physical condition:* a description of characteristics of the person that are not static (i.e., that can be different or changed on purpose from one day to the next or from one crime to the next). Characteristics include the following:

  Hair color: observed by an officer or based on a witness description

  Hair length: observed by an officer or based on a witness description

  Physical condition: the immediate physical condition of the person (e.g., intoxicated, belligerent, incoherent, nervous), observed by an officer or based on a witness description

  Facial hair: the type of facial hair (e.g., beard, mustache, goatee, clean shaven), observed by an officer or based on a witness description

  Appearance: the individual's general appearance (e.g., well-groomed, dirty, wearing a disguise, gang clothing), observed by an officer or based on a witness description

  Complexion: the texture and tone of an individual's skin (e.g., fair, tan, dark, pocked), observed by an officer or based on a witness description

  Speech: how the individual spoke during the crime (e.g., accent, slurred, quietly), based on a witness description

Not all of the characteristics mentioned above are collected for each crime incident, but this list provides a framework for collecting potentially important information about persons that can be used to link them to crimes and crimes to one another. In addition to this information on a suspect, a photograph of the person is attached to the information when available. Also, as in the case of MO data, an analyst can include qualitative information describing anything unique about the person that may not be covered by the previous characteristics or that provides further explanation (e.g., description of the exact clothing worn, including name-brand items). Figure 8.4 is an example of how persons data appear as collected in the ATAC program.

Vehicle

The third general category of information collected for TCA concerns vehicles. These data are important because vehicles often serve key roles in the commission of crimes. Offenders can use vehicles as transportation to and from the locations

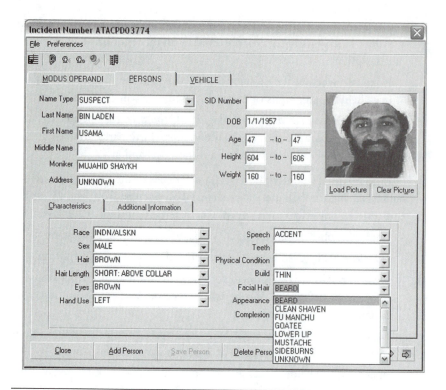

Figure 8.4   Persons Data Collection Screen: ATAC

NOTE: This screen shot shows many persons characteristics captured and coded in a systematic way. The drop-down menu is available for all characteristics with arrows and provides a way for the user to code the information about the crime systematically.

of their crimes, as weapons (e.g., running a person over), or as methods of entry (e.g., in a "smash and grab," the offender runs a vehicle through a storefront window and takes property inside). Stolen vehicles are often used in the commission of crimes.

Three types of information are collected about vehicles: official information, physical description, and the nature of the vehicle at the time of the incident. The official information on a vehicle consists of its vehicle identification number, or VIN, which is a unique identifier, and the license plate number and state of issue. In some cases, only a partial license number is available, but that information can still be useful, as computer search capabilities enable police agencies to examine motor vehicle databases for possible matches using various combinations of plate numbers and letters.

The physical description of a vehicle includes the make (e.g., Chevrolet, Ford, Honda), model (e.g., Corvette, Explorer, Accord), and style (e.g., four door, two door, hatchback, coupe, truck). Details such as the color, the model year, and the general type of vehicle (passenger, truck, SUV) are collected if a witness has seen the car, even if only briefly.

Information on the nature of the vehicle at the time of the incident includes its status (e.g., stolen, recovered, abandoned) and any other qualitative details available

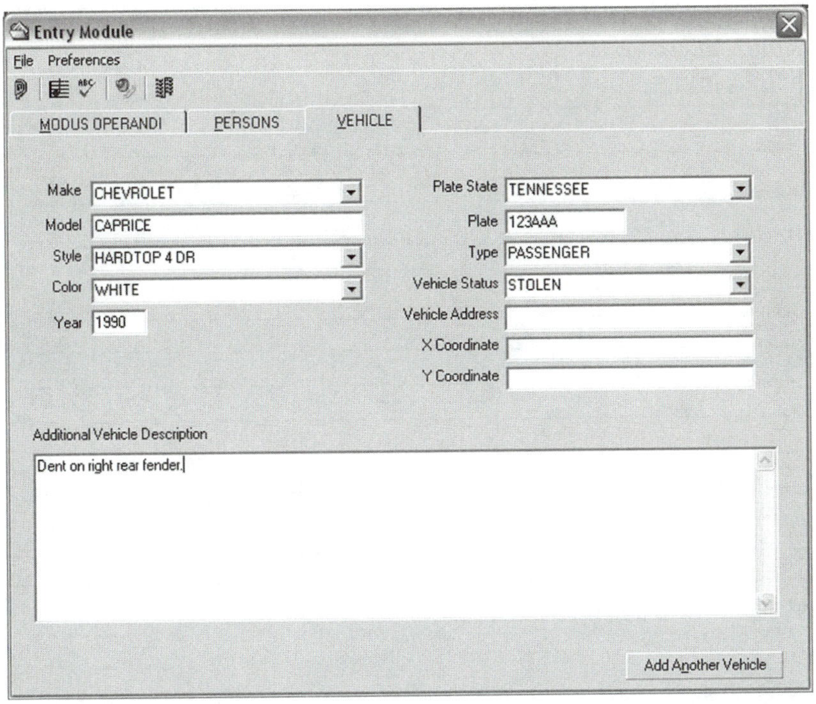

Figure 8.5   Vehicle Data Collection Screen: ATAC

about the vehicle (e.g., dent in the passenger door, front end has primer, vehicle found behind a convenience store). Figure 8.5 is an example of how characteristics about vehicles appear as collected in the ATAC program.

Field Information

Field information is another important type of data used in tactical crime analysis. In many police departments, patrol officers fill out **FI cards** (i.e., field information or field interview cards) when they respond to a call and find that there is not enough probable cause to take a police report, but additional information about the incident, the person, or a vehicle is worth collecting (e.g., a person acting suspicious in an area with an increased number of burglaries). FI cards are usually small (3 by 5 inches is typical) so that officers can easily keep them in their pockets and access them in the field. Figure 8.6 is an example of an FI card.

Not all types of incidents on which officers collect field information are useful in TCA, but analysts sometimes find that such information helps them to identify potential leads (e.g., when someone is stopped in a residential neighborhood for being suspicious during the time frame associated with a burglary pattern) or individuals who are continually being contacted by the police for suspicious behavior (e.g., individuals

```
┌──────────────────────────────────────────────────────────────────┐
│  ┌────────────────────────────────────────────┐                   │
│  │  Date/Time of Contact                        │                   │
│  │                                              │                   │
│  │                                              │                   │
│  └────────────────────────────────────────────┘                   │
│                                                                    │
│   Name  ─────────────────────────────   D.O.B. ─────────────────  │
│                                                                    │
│   Address ──────────────────────────    Apt.  ──────────────────  │
│                                                                    │
│   Height ──────── Weight ────────  Hair color ────── Eye color ─── │
│                                                                    │
│   Tattoos Marks Scars                                              │
│                                                                    │
│   Summarys  ─────────────────────────────────────────────────────│
│             ─────────────────────────────────────────────────────│
│             ─────────────────────────────────────────────────────│
│             ─────────────────────────────────────────────────────│
│             ─────────────────────────────────────────────────────│
│             ─────────────────────────────────────────────────────│
│                                                                    │
│   Reporting officer  ─────────────────────────────────────────────│
│                                                                    │
└──────────────────────────────────────────────────────────────────┘
```

Figure 8.6   Sample FI Card

sleeping behind commercial places and digging through garbage). The following four types of field information are most relevant in tactical crime analysis:

- *Suspicious person(s):* For example, officers may record information on person(s) contacted while loitering in a commercial area after business hours or person(s) driving or sitting in a vehicle under suspicious circumstances.
- *Suspicious vehicle(s):* For example, a resident may provide an officer with the license plate number and description of a vehicle that has driven through the neighborhood suspiciously on more than one occasion.
- *Person(s) warned for trespassing:* For example, officers may record information on such person(s) if they are engaged in disturbing or suspicious activity at specific locations.
- *Individuals with unique scars, marks, or tattoos:* Many police agencies compile databases on individuals with clearly identifiable, nonchanging characteristics such as visible scars, marks, or tattoos.

The field information used in TCA is not limited to these categories, however. Analysts may collect data on additional kinds of incidents, with the key question being, Could this person be linked to a crime that is being tracked in tactical crime analysis?

The data collected about an incident include general information about the characteristics of the incident, the person, and the vehicle involved. These variables are similar to those collected for crime incidents and allow analysts to examine field information and crime information together. Information about the incident includes the type of incident (e.g., suspicious person, trespass warning, suspicious vehicle); the date and time of the incident; the address of the incident, including apartment, suite, or hotel room number, if applicable; the address name and type of location; and summary information about the purpose and nature of the incident (e.g., individual warned for trespassing at ValueMart and left the premises).

In most cases, officers collect field information on known individuals, so information about many of the following characteristics of the person are available at the time of contact: name, aliases, date of birth, and home address; physical description (e.g., height, weight, race/ethnicity, sex); unique information (e.g., scars marks, tattoos); and physical condition at the time of the incident (e.g., appearance, hair color).

Finally, if a vehicle is involved, the information collected is the same as that collected in a crime incident (VIN, license plate information, make, model, style, color, and so on). Many police agencies also collect photos of individuals in the field (e.g., individuals with scars, marks, and tattoos) and link them to the field information.

Pattern Identification Methodology

Once tactical data have been collected, crime analysts use them to identify patterns, investigate leads, and clear cases. Pattern identification makes up most of the work in tactical crime analysis. This section describes the types of tactical crime analysis patterns, approaches to pattern identification, initial pattern identification, and pattern finalization.

Types of Patterns

The term *crime pattern* refers to a combination of attributes of particular crimes that distinguishes that collection of activity from other activity (Crime Mapping and Analysis Program, 2003). Tactical crime analysts categorize crime patterns into the following six main types, both to structure the identification of patterns and to provide a common language for communication about patterns within police departments and their communities; these types are not mutually exclusive (i.e., a pattern can be more than one type):

- *Series*: A crime **series** is a "run of similar crimes committed by the same individual(s) against one or various victims or targets" (Velasco & Boba, 2000, p. 2). For example, a Hispanic male suspect has robbed 10 separate people on the street by driving up behind a victim, jumping from his vehicle, and putting a gun to the back of the victim's head. The vehicle and suspect descriptions are similar in all 10 incidents. In most cases, unless the person is caught, there is no definite way to know whether particular crimes have been committed by the same person, but in TCA a pattern is called a series if it seems likely the crimes have been committed by the same person.
- *Spree*: A **spree** is a pattern characterized by a high frequency of criminal activity, to the extent that the activity appears almost continuous. Crimes in a spree involve the same offender(s) and usually occur over a short time span, with no "cooling off" period. This could be a few hours, a few days, or longer,

depending on the circumstances (Velasco & Boba, 2000). For example, the 1999 shootings at Columbine High School in Colorado would be classified as a spree, as would thefts from seven vehicles in a parking lot over a 2-hour period.

- *Hot spot*: A **tactical crime analysis hot spot** is "a specific location or small area where an unusual amount of criminal activity occurs that is committed by one or more offenders" (Velasco & Boba, 2000, p. 2). An example of a hot spot is an apartment community that normally has few crimes but has had a number of auto thefts, thefts from autos, and robberies during the past 2 months that may or may not have been committed by the same individual(s). Another example is an area with several parks in which there has been a noticeable increase in public sexual indecency and the suspect descriptions are different in many of the cases.

- *Hot dot*: Pease and Laycock (1996) coined this term to refer to "the victim who repeatedly suffers crime"; however, in TCA it refers more generally to "an individual associated with an unusual amount of criminal activity, either as an offender or a victim" (Velasco & Boba, 2000, p. 2). For example, a tactical crime analyst would categorize an individual who has been an offender, a victim, and a witness in five drive-by shootings as a hot dot. Another type of hot dot is a person who has been repeatedly contacted by the police for suspicious behavior and trespass warnings, but no criminal reports have been filed.

- *Hot product*: A hot product is a specific type of property that is the target in the same or different types of crime. Clarke (1999) coined this term, defining hot products as "those consumer items that are most attractive to thieves" (p. 23). In the context of TCA, a hot product is a type of property that has recently been targeted in crimes. For example, during a particularly cold December, the amount of firewood stolen from outside homes increased. Another example is a noticeable increase in the theft of car tire rims around a city.

- *Hot target*: A hot target is a type of place that is frequently victimized but is not necessarily in the same area as other targeted places of the same type (adapted from Velasco & Boba, 2000). For example, beauty salons would be categorized as a hot target if a higher-than-expected number of robberies have occurred at beauty salons around the city with different suspects. If a number of both burglaries and robberies have occurred at pizza restaurants, pizza restaurants would be considered a hot target.

Approaches to Pattern Identification

Two distinct approaches guide TCA efforts and are important starting points for pattern identification. In one of these approaches, analysts examine cases to identify patterns through deduction and induction; in the other, analysts identify patterns of persons and property crime by examining characteristics of the crimes and the persons involved.

Deduction and Induction

When a tactical crime analyst sets out to identify a pattern, one of two general circumstances exists: (a) The analyst has a large number of cases from which to determine a pattern, or (b) the analyst has one case to which others can be linked. In social science, these methods of inquiry are called **deduction** and **induction**, respectively.

A researcher using the deductive method starts with general ideas about the phenomenon of interest and moves to specific facts that support these general ideas. Thus in TCA, analysts using this method examine all cases together for commonalities that link individual crimes. Figure 8.7 illustrates how an analyst would deduce a pattern from a large number of incidents based on shared characteristics. The analyst in this case begins with all burglaries and then focuses in on commercial burglaries, then on those occurring in a certain area, then on those occurring in a certain type of location, and then on those occurring in that type of location on particular dates and at particular times. The decisions the analyst makes at each level are based on shared characteristics of the included incidents as well as critical thinking.

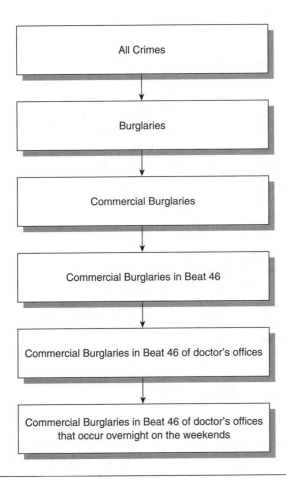

Figure 8.7   Pattern Identification: Deduction

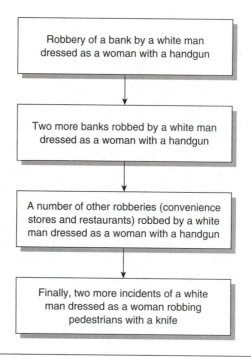

Figure 8.8   Pattern Identification: Induction

The inductive method, in contrast, involves taking individual facts or specific ideas and relating them back to general concepts. In TCA, an analyst using induction focuses first on one case/crime and then looks at many others for similarities. Figure 8.8 illustrates how an analyst would use the inductive method to find a robbery pattern. The first case is one in which a white man dressed as a woman robs a bank. Starting with this case, the analyst looks for cases with commonalities in the general population of robberies.

Tactical crime analysts find the cases with which they begin the inductive method of pattern identification in several different ways. One of these involves searching databases for anomalies (Crime Mapping and Analysis Program, 2003)—that is, identifying rare or distinctive characteristics that differentiate a particular crime from others (e.g., a robbery by a man dressed as a woman). Analysts also sometimes identify initial cases through exceptional incidents noted by police personnel, or cases may be brought to their attention by detectives who are interested in finding links to specific cases.

Persons Crime and Property Crime

Pattern identification in TCA is also guided by the distinction between persons crime and property crime patterns. That is, the characteristics that link persons crimes to one another are inherently different from those that link property crimes. **Persons crimes** are those crimes in which persons are the targets; they include robbery, sexual assault, indecent exposure, public sexual indecency, and kidnapping.

Because in persons crimes the victims are also witnesses (in most cases), such crimes provide analysts with abundant details about modus operandi, suspect characteristics, and the vehicles involved to use in pattern identification. In persons crimes, the types of patterns typically found are crime series or sprees; less commonly, analysts may identify patterns involving hot spots, hot dots, or hot targets. The following are examples of some specific patterns:

- *Indecent exposure series:* A suspect on a mountain bike approaches female pedestrians and exposes himself. Four incidents have occurred over a 1-month period, and the suspect's description, bicycle description, and actions are very similar in all four incidents.
- *Carjacking spree:* Three carjackings have occurred within the city in a period of 3 hours. Two suspects use a car to cut the victim off in traffic and force him or her to stop, then one suspect approaches the victim's car and orders the victim out of the car at gunpoint. That suspect drives away in the victim's car, and the other drives away in the suspect car.
- *Mall parking lot hot spot:* Several incidents of robbery of pedestrians and indecent exposure have occurred in a mall parking lot over a 1-month period. The crimes appear to have been committed by different people based on various suspect descriptions by witnesses.
- *Hot target, convenience store:* Several incidents of strong-arm robbery have occurred in the past week at a particular chain of convenience stores throughout the city, yet different MOs and suspect descriptions indicate that multiple suspects are responsible for the crimes.
- *Hot dot, pedestrians:* Several types of vehicles have been observed driving through a residential area during evening hours. On several occasions, the drivers of the vehicles have exposed themselves to pedestrians. Because the incidents have all occurred at night, officers have not been able to obtain detailed suspect and vehicle descriptions, but the targeted victims have consistently been people walking on the street.

Property crimes are those crimes in which property is the target; these include theft from vehicle, auto theft, residential and commercial burglary, criminal trespass, and criminal damage. Because witnesses are typically not present during the commission of such crimes, tactical crime analysts usually have little or no suspect information available to use in identifying patterns of property crime. Typically, analysts link such crimes together by examining information on types of crimes (e.g., residential versus commercial burglary), types of targets (e.g., office buildings, apartments, single-family homes), and locations (areas). The patterns most often identified in the analysis of property crimes are hot spots, hot targets, and hot products. For example:

- *Residential burglary hot spot:* Several residential burglaries have occurred in a specific neighborhood that has only one point of entry/exit. In all of the burglaries, suspects gained entry to the homes by breaking or prying open a rear window. Suspect information is not available, as there have been no witnesses to any of the incidents.

- *Apartment community hot spot:* Several incidents of residential burglary, criminal trespass, theft from vehicle, and criminal damage have occurred at the same apartment community. The number of incidents is much higher than usual, the incidents have occurred at various times of day during a 2-week period, and no suspect information is available.
- *Hot target, new home construction sites:* Numerous burglaries have occurred in the past 6 months at new home construction sites all over the city. Suspects break into or enter unlocked houses under construction and steal appliances or construction equipment. The incidents have all taken place at night, and no suspect information has been obtained, but different tire marks have been found at the scenes, indicating that several different types of vehicles have been used.
- *Hot product, pool equipment:* Several burglaries of residential backyards have occurred over a 2-month period; pool equipment is the only property that has been taken in the incidents.

Even though persons crime and property crime warrant examination of different characteristics, tactical crime analysts sometimes examine the two kinds of crimes together. For example:

- *Burglary and robbery series:* Four burglaries and two robberies have occurred in the same neighborhood. Suspect information is available for all of these incidents and is similar.
- *Burglary and carjacking spree:* A young man burglarizes a business suite late at night and leaves the scene by carjacking a vehicle. The man then crashes the vehicle into a retail store's front window, enters the store, and steals additional property. All of these incidents take place within a 1-hour period.
- *Water park hot spot:* Over the past 2 weeks, a water park has had an increased number of thefts from vehicles and auto thefts in its parking lot as well as an increase in public sexual indecency incidents inside the park.
- *Hot dot, Sam Spade:* The police have contacted Sam Spade several times for trespass warnings and suspicious behavior in the downtown area. Most recently, Sam has been a victim of a robbery.
- *Hot product, video games:* Over the past 2 months, several houses have been burglarized and video games have been the only property taken. In addition, several robberies have occurred in which video games have been taken from students walking home from school.
- *Hot target, beauty salons:* Several incidents of strong-arm robbery and commercial burglary have occurred at beauty salons throughout the city. In each incident, a large amount of cash was stolen from the cash register.

Initial Pattern Identification

To identify crime patterns, analysts must be skilled in critical thinking and be able to recognize commonalities among characteristics of crime incidents. Identifying a

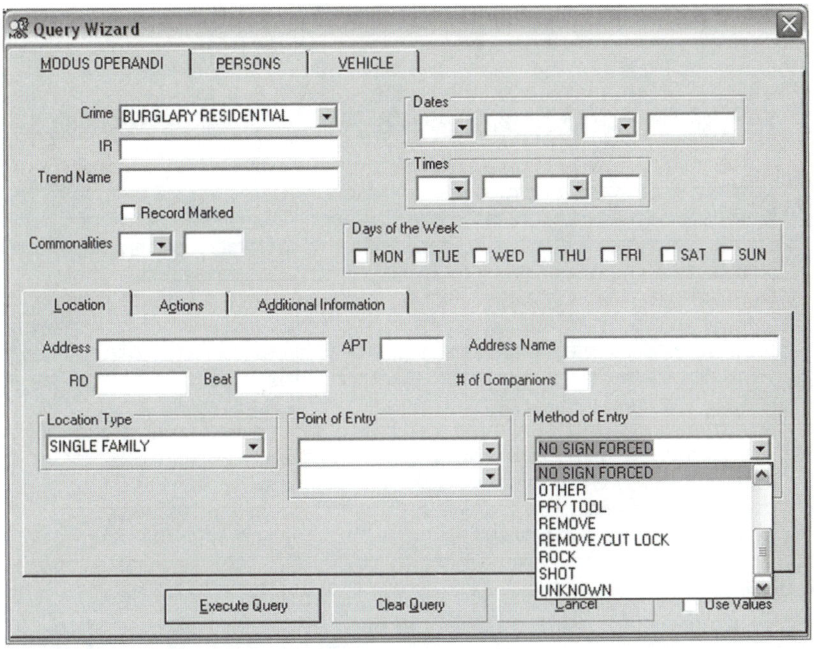

Figure 8.9   Query Screen: ATAC

pattern is a two-step process: The analyst must link together all of the cases that might make up a pattern (initial pattern identification) and then look closely at those cases to ensure that the pattern detected is sound (pattern finalization).

Tactical crime analysts use three general methods to arrive at the initial identification of a pattern. (Note that in any of these methods, analysts can examine cases inductively or deductively for persons or property crimes.) The most informal **pattern identification** method, referred to as **ad hoc linking**, consists of a person's linking cases by memory in the course of his or her everyday work. Even though this method is not systematic, analysts have identified many patterns this way. Most often, analysts follow up on ad hoc linking by applying one of the other two methods of pattern identification, which are more formal: the query method and the Trend Hunter method. The **query method** involves the use of critical thinking and the application of deductive/inductive methods as the analyst searches a database and links cases that have similar characteristics. The **Trend Hunter method** uses weights and thresholds within a computer system to identify patterns (Bair Software, 2004).

Query Method

In TCA, querying is an iterative process in which the analyst manipulates, searches, and sorts the characteristics of crimes in a database matrix to link crimes with similar characteristics. The analyst first uses induction or deduction to look for patterns of either persons or property crime. Figure 8.9 displays the initial query (selection) of an analyst using the deductive method to examine residential burglaries in which

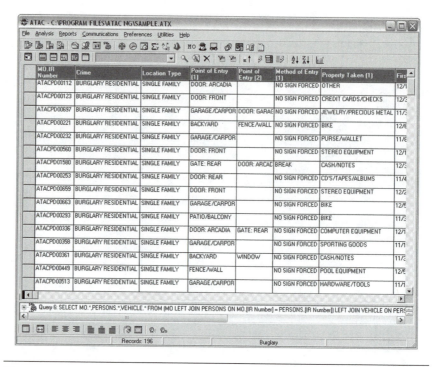

Figure 8.10   Query Results: ATAC

there was no sign of forced entry. In response to the query, the software selects only cases that meet all of the parameters set by the analyst. Figure 8.10 shows the list resulting from the query; note that it includes only residential burglaries for which the method of entry appears as "no sign forced."

To view the results more easily and to inspect them visually for patterns, the analyst might sort the cases. Figure 8.11 shows the cases sorted by the first point of entry, a second variable for point of entry, and then the method of entry. When the results are displayed in a matrix format, as in Figure 8.12, the analyst can see that there are a number of cases in which entry was made through the side gate and then the doggy door. These cases might be the beginnings of an initial pattern. The analyst might examine the similarities among cases further by using spatial analysis (crime mapping) and temporal analysis. (For explanation of these methods, see Chapter 9.)

The use of electronic data matrices is imperative in TCA, because analysts must be able to compare multiple cases and columns rapidly as well as scan fields quickly for pertinent information. For instance, to identify a robbery series, an analyst might organize the matrix so that those variables most salient to robberies—such as location type, weapon, suspect's actions against the victim, and suspect description—are contiguous, and thus easily examined together. To identify a residential burglary pattern, an analyst might organize the matrix so that the information on point of entry, method of entry, property taken, and location is close together. If the variables in a matrix are in fixed positions (e.g., as they were originally stored in the database or as they are in a paper matrix), the analyst is likely to find it difficult to see the

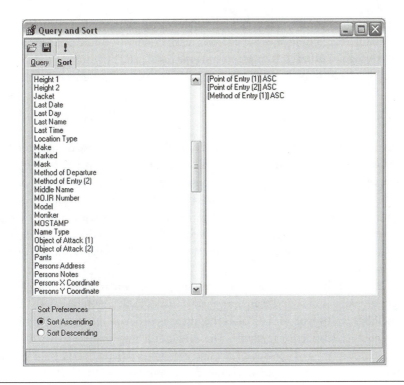

Figure 8.11   Sort Screen: ATAC

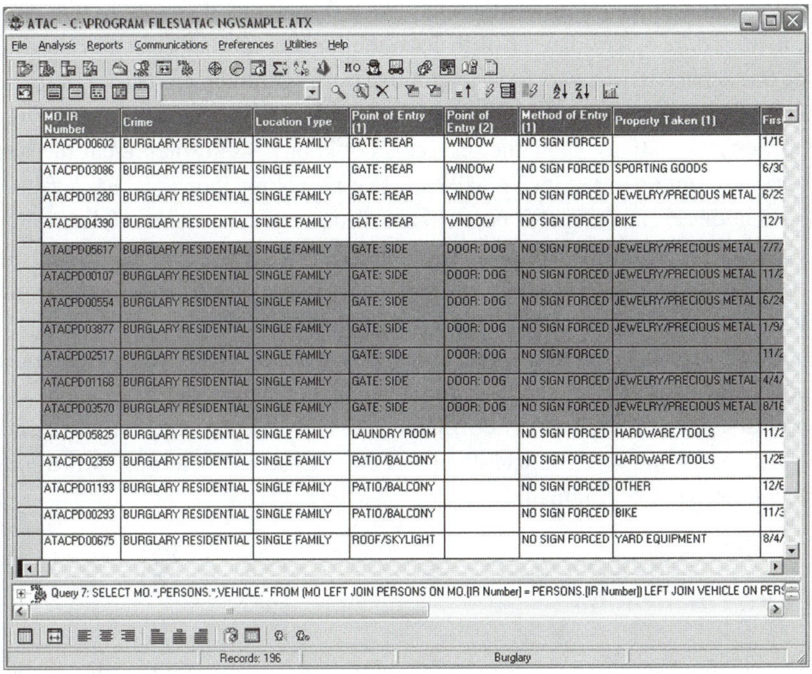

Figure 8.12   Resulting Query Sorted: ATAC

relevant variables by different crime types. The query method of analysis is simple yet powerful. It accommodates the analyst's need to examine information visually in order to recognize patterns. By manipulating the matrix and by grouping, sorting, and refining the results through data queries, the analyst can "see" patterns in the data.

Trend Hunter Method

Another way to identify initial patterns is through the mathematical method offered by the ATAC program's Trend Hunter feature. The analyst assigns weights to various characteristics of crimes and then uses Trend Hunter to sum up the weights for each case. The program highlights those cases that meet a particular threshold, indicating they have similar characteristics. This method may seem more scientific than the query method, but its results still rely on the analyst's critical thinking skills and experience, given that the analyst must determine the weights and the appropriate thresholds.

Once the weights are set, the analyst can instruct the program to do one of two things: (a) take one case and match its characteristics to the entire database (inductive method) or (b) look for any cases that meet a particular threshold of similarity to one another (deductive method). The program allows analysts to set different weights for property and persons crimes and even to set different weights for specific types of crimes (e.g., residential vs. commercial burglary).

Figure 8.13 shows the list of persons characteristics and the weights that an analyst might set for those characteristics in order to find a pattern in persons crimes such as robbery or sexual assault. The higher the number (or the greater the weight), the more important a characteristic is to linking these types of crimes. In this example, name, address, and date of birth have the highest values, because crimes that share these characteristics would be committed by the same person. The variables age, height, and weight also have the highest values because these characteristics are most important in situations where the suspect is not known, as they represent the static physical description of the individual. Note that race of the individual has a value of only 25 in this example. That is because, as noted previously, witnesses' descriptions of suspects' race/ethnicity are not always reliable (e.g., a very tan Caucasian man could be mistaken for Hispanic). The cases can also be linked by MO and vehicle characteristics, alone or together with the individual's characteristics.

Both the Trend Hunter and query methods produce lists of cases that appear related based on their having several characteristics in common. However, not all of these cases make up a sound pattern. Thus in the second step of pattern identification the analyst must examine all the cases more closely to determine which ones have the strongest commonalities.

Pattern Finalization

Pattern finalization is the process of refining a list of cases that are thought to be related by determining which cases on the list have key characteristics in common. For example, initial identification of a commercial burglary pattern might

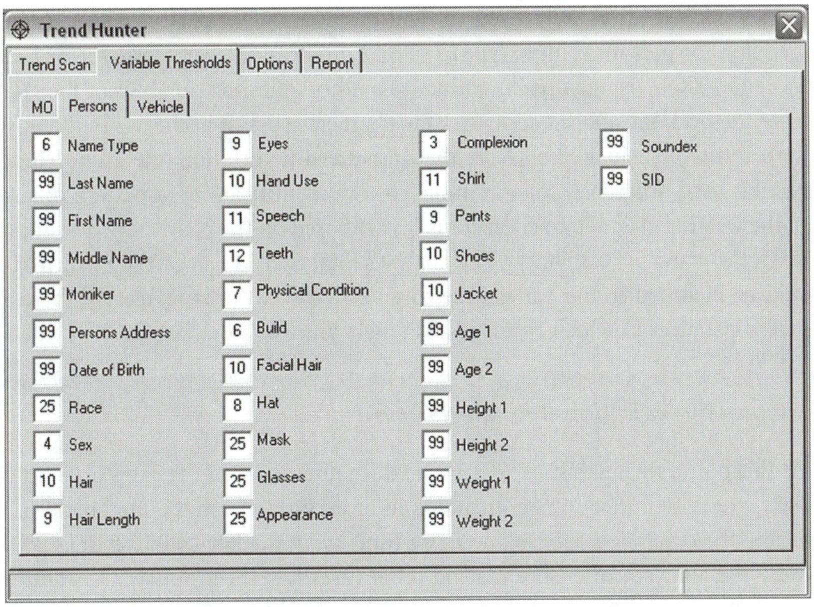

Figure 8.13 Trend Hunter Screen: ATAC

include all incidents in the preceding 2 months that occurred at businesses in a particular area. In the process of finalizing this pattern, the analyst might eliminate several cases that occurred on weekday afternoons because the rest occurred at night or on weekends. The methodology for finalizing a pattern is inductive and involves three steps: identifying the principal case, identifying other key cases in the pattern, and identifying any additional related cases (see Bair Software, 1999).

Identifying the Principal Case

The analyst's first step is to select one case from the initial list of cases that best represents the pattern. The analyst then uses this **principal case** to determine the other key cases in the pattern. The method that the analyst uses in determining the principal case is based on the key characteristics of that particular crime type (e.g., suspect description and MO for persons crime, address and type of location for property crime). Sometimes an analyst will identify two principal cases when two cases on the initial list share nearly all of the key characteristics. The following steps can be conducted for either one or two principal cases. If the analyst used the inductive method in the initial pattern identification, the case that began that identification would be the principal case.

Identifying Other Key Cases in the Pattern

To identify the cases that are strongly related to the principal case, the analyst must identify the characteristics most indicative of the pattern; these are usually the characteristics that were used to determine the principal case (e.g., suspect description for persons crimes; type of crime and location characteristics for property crime). Then, using either an inductive method of critical analysis or the Trend Hunter method, the analyst compares the characteristics of each case in the initial pattern to the principal case. (Note that in pattern finalization, the Trend Hunter method is used differently than in initial pattern identification; in pattern finalization, the weights assigned to characteristics are based on the characteristics' importance in the principal case only.) The analyst's final decisions regarding which cases should be included in the pattern are based on critical thinking; clearly, there are very few instances in which cases are absolutely known to be related.

Identifying Additional Related Cases

At this point, the analyst has determined whether most of the cases listed in the initial pattern identification are included in or excluded from the final pattern. By querying the original database one more time using the key characteristics of the pattern, the analyst can ensure that no other cases have been missed. In addition, the analyst needs to examine other databases that could contain cases related to the pattern, progressing from databases of current cases (e.g., those in the four most recent months) to older, or archived, databases. Here again, the analyst uses the key characteristics of the principal case to query the archived data.

Thoroughness is the key to the successful identification of patterns. Many police agencies maintain individual databases that may not be linked to the tactical data, and analysts should query these also for potential links to current patterns. In addition, analysts should solicit the help of neighboring agencies in identifying patterns, because criminals do not stay within police jurisdiction boundaries. In sum, before finalizing and distributing information about a pattern, an analyst needs to check all internal and external sources that might provide relevant data.

Even though the process of identifying patterns is systematic and involves specific techniques and methods, each pattern identification process is uniquely shaped by the analyst's critical thinking, which is driven by the analyst's experience and the crime pattern at hand. The pattern identification process is more intellectual than technical.

Identifying Investigative Leads

The second goal of TCA is to identify investigative leads for both individual cases and patterns. Many crimes do not have identified suspects (e.g., names and addresses of the individuals responsible for the crimes), so tactical crime analysts work to assist the investigative process by identifying potential suspects. Just as in identifying the principal case, the analyst's first step in identifying an investigative lead for a pattern is to find the most relevant and reliable suspect description or other information to which a person can be linked (e.g., date, time, and location of a burglary can be linked to the date, time, and location of field information of a suspicious person).

Thoroughness and critical thinking are as important in suspect identification as they are in pattern identification; analysts must take care to consider all potential suspects. For example, if witnesses have described a suspect as a pale black man or a dark white man, with an unidentifiable accent, it would derail the analysis to exclude either blacks or whites from a list of potential leads. In fact, given this rough description, the analyst would be wise to include Hispanics and Native Americans as well, given that both of these groups also include members who could fit the witnesses' description. In some instances, analysts can infer information about a suspect from the data available, such as strength (e.g., a door broken down during the crime), use of tools (e.g., evidence that a pry tool was used), and access to a location (e.g., the time span of the crime).

Once a key suspect description is identified, the analyst examines the characteristics of that description against various databases of offenders and suspect information (e.g., tattoo, height), such as the following:

- *Known offender database:* This database contains information on individuals arrested and convicted in a particular jurisdiction. A search of an offender database by location, type of crime, MO, and/or suspect description can produce the names of potential suspects for a particular crime. For example, such a search may turn up the name of a recently released offender whose description and MO (robbing banks containing a particular type of safe) match the key suspect description.
- *Registered sex offender database:* This database contains information on individuals who have been convicted of sex crimes. It is different from the known offender database in that it includes all sex offenders living in the jurisdiction no matter where they committed their crimes (i.e., sex offenders are required to register with the local police agencies in their residence cities). As with known offenders, analysts can search the sex offender database by description and type of crimes committed to identify potential suspects for related sex crimes (e.g., sex offenders convicted for abusing children living in the area of a current pattern of child abduction).
- *Field information database:* This database contains information about individuals who have exhibited suspicious behavior and the unique features of individuals. Analysts may identify potential leads by searching this database for information that matches a current pattern by time of day and day of week (e.g., suspicious vehicle in an area), unique features (e.g., a person with particular scars, marks, tattoos), or other unique information (e.g., a person found behind a commercial place with a hammer.
- *Vehicle database:* This is either a departmental database or a database maintained by the state's motor vehicle division that allows a search by various characteristics (e.g., VIN, plate number, make/model) of vehicles. Analysts search this database to identify the owners of vehicle used in the commission of crimes and thus identify potential suspects. Officers and citizens are more likely to identify vehicles than people, and vehicle ownership can be easily determined with tag information. As with a person, general information

about a vehicle is useful (dark blue, late 80s, 4-door sedan), but the more unique the feature, the more useful it is to match with a pattern or incident (e.g., license plate number or a unique bumper sticker combined with a damaged right front fender) (Bair Software, 1999).

In addition to these databases, analysts examine information provided by other sources, including individuals contacted by neighboring county sheriff offices, state troopers, private security companies, federal agencies, and others that collect data on offenders. Analysts often share these data through formal meetings and networks as well as through more informal methods (e.g., quick e-mail messages).

Clearing Cases

The third goal of TCA is to assist police in **clearing cases.** This is the process of linking unsolved cases to a recently solved case in order to close them and to enhance the prosecution of an individual suspect. It is important to note that tactical crime analysts assist in this process, but it is up to detectives to make the legal determinations (with probable cause) regarding whether or not particular cases are related. For example, a detective arrests a suspect for committing two residential burglaries in a particular area. An analyst searches data for the past 6 months and finds that four additional burglaries were committed in that area. The detective could use this information to interrogate the suspect (e.g., "Did you commit these as well?"), or the suspect could be matched to the other cases by fingerprints or DNA evidence. If the investigation is successful, six burglaries are cleared by the one arrest instead of two burglaries, the police department closes four additional burglary cases, and the prosecutor is able to charge the individual with more offenses.

By nature, clearing cases is an inductive process. It follows the method of pattern finalization in that one case (the solved case) is identified and compared with others to determine whether meaningful relationships exist. Another aspect of clearing cases is the closing of entire patterns. In this process, analysts reexamine formerly published information on known patterns for links to newly committed crimes or to determine whether anyone was arrested for any of the crimes in the patterns. For instance, a crime pattern was published about a rash of robberies in which the suspect was armed with an AK-47. Four months later, after no additional robberies, police arrest a man for a traffic violation and discover an AK-47 in his car. A crime analyst could check this person's description against the suspect description in the robbery pattern. Or perhaps a year after publication of the robbery pattern similar incidents are reported, and it appears that the same person has begun to commit robberies again after a long break. An analyst could identify a new pattern that includes both the new and older incidents.

Summary Points

This chapter has described techniques for collecting the data used in tactical crime analysis as well as approaches to pattern identification and methods for identifying patterns, investigating leads, and clearing cases. The following are the key points addressed in this chapter:

- One of most important aspects of tactical crime analysis, and the first step in the crime analysis process, is obtaining the necessary data. The data used in TCA include information about how, when, and where crimes have occurred. TCA utilizes both quantitative and qualitative information from police reports.
- TCA data are typically stored, viewed, and manipulated in a matrix format.
- TCA seeks to identify patterns of crimes that are not easily linked together by focusing on crimes in which the offender and the victim do not know one another and on crimes that are predatory in nature.
- The types of crimes examined in TCA typically include theft from vehicle, auto theft, vandalism, commercial burglary, residential burglary, indecent exposure, public sexual indecency, robbery, and sexual assault.
- Tactical crime analysts examine information about the modus operandi (method of the crime), the persons involved in the crime, and vehicles involved in the crime.
- Field information is another important data source used in TCA. Typically, field information is collected on suspicious person(s), suspicious vehicle(s), person(s) warned for trespassing, and individuals with unique scars, marks, tattoos.
- The term *crime pattern* refers to a combination of attributes of particular crimes that distinguishes that collection of activity from other activity. To structure the identification of patterns and to provide a common language for communication about patterns within police departments and their communities, tactical crime analysts categorize crime patterns into six types: series, spree, hot spot, hot dot, hot product, and hot target.
- Tactical crime analysts take two distinct approaches that focus their analysis efforts and are an important part of pattern identification. The first concerns how the cases are examined to identify a pattern (e.g., deductive and inductive methods) and the second concerns the use of different characteristics to identify patterns of persons and property crime.
- To identify crime patterns, analysts must be skilled in critical thinking and be able to recognize commonalities among crime characteristics. Identifying a pattern is a two-step process: The analyst must link together all of the cases that may make up a pattern (initial pattern identification) and then look closely at the cases to determine whether they should be included in or excluded from a pattern (pattern finalization).
- The three general methods of initial pattern identification are the ad hoc, query, and Trend Hunter methods.
- Pattern finalization is the process of refining a pattern by including only strongly related cases. The methodology for finalizing a pattern is inductive and consists of three steps: identifying the principal case, identifying other key cases in the pattern, and identifying any additional related cases.
- Identifying investigative leads is an inductive process that begins with identification of the most relevant suspect description or MO characteristics to match offenders.

- Tactical crime analysts use several kinds of databases to provide police with investigative leads; these include a known offender database, a registered sex offender database, a field information database, and a vehicle database.
- Clearing cases is an inductive process in which an analyst links unsolved cases to a recently solved case in order to close them and to enhance the prosecution of an individual suspect.

Exercises

Exercise 8.1

Develop a tactical crime analysis matrix on paper or in electronic form (e.g., using a spreadsheet program) with data from the following cases:

Case number 20030562: Between 2000 on January 13, 2003, and 0500 on January 14, 2003, a trailer/mobile home is burglarized. Entry was through an unsecured window, and a stereo was taken.

Case number 20030798: On February 2, 2003, at 1424, a man walks into a Nations Bank, points a gun at the teller, and hands her a demand note for money. The suspect then flees the scene in a car.

Case number 20030912: Between 0800 and 1730 on March 19, 2003, a storage shed door is pried open in the backyard of a single-family home.

Case number 20031059: Between 2130 on March 31, 2003, and 0630 on April 1, 2003, a criminal damage report is taken at a single-family home when the resident discovers the bedroom window screen has been pried off. No entry was made into the residence.

Case number 20031164: Between 2315 on April 25, 2003, and 0845 on April 26, 2003, an Applebee's restaurant is broken into (the front door pried open) and the safe is taken.

Case number 20031399: On May 5, 2003, at 0132, a man forces his way into a woman's camper and sexually assaults her at gunpoint. The suspect forces the woman to perform oral sex and then flees the scene on foot.

Case number 20031854: Between 0130 and 0545 on June 19, 2003, a Taco Bell is broken into (the front window broken with a rock). Cash from the safe and food are taken.

Case number 20031988: On July 4, 2003, at 0245, a man is robbed at gunpoint in an alley and his wallet is taken.

Case number 20032130: Between 1900 on July 24, 2003, and 0500 on July 27, 2003, the lock on a trailer at a construction site is cut and the trailer is burglarized and ransacked.

Case number 20032512: On August 21, 2003, at 1750, a woman who is walking home is forced into a car at knifepoint and is then sexually assaulted. The suspect then flees the scene in his car.

Your matrix will contain 10 records (rows) and the following 16 variables (columns):

- Case number
- Crime type
- First possible date
- Last possible date
- First possible time
- Last possible time
- Location type
- Location name
- Point of entry
- Method of entry
- Property taken
- Action against property
- Object of attack
- Suspect's actions
- Weapon type
- Method of departure

Exercise 8.2

Using the list of cases from the Excel file "Exercise 8.2_Pattern Identification" on the CD-ROM accompanying this book, identify a crime pattern according to the methods described in this chapter. Answer the following questions:

1. What type of pattern is it (e.g., series, spree, hot spot)? What information led you to this conclusion?

2. Which case is the principal case?

3. What are the three key characteristics you should use to match the principal case to other cases?

4. What are the remaining cases in the pattern? Why do you think these should be included? Justify your inclusion of each case.

9

Describing, Analyzing, and Disseminating Known Patterns

Given that the purpose of crime analysis is to assist police, once an analyst has finalized a pattern, an investigative lead, or other information, he or she must disseminate that information to personnel who can utilize it. This chapter focuses on the techniques that crime analysts use in describing, analyzing, and disseminating known patterns. Analysts can also use many of these techniques to understand commonalities of characteristics among crimes and to identify patterns, such as by mapping burglaries according to the times of day and days of the week on which they occurred. The chapter ends with descriptions of the products of tactical crime analysis and their uses.

Describing and Analyzing Known Patterns

The most basic techniques used in TCA focus on describing and analyzing how (e.g., crime type and MO analysis), when (i.e., time series analysis), and where (i.e., spatial analysis) patterns occur.

Crime Type and Modus Operandi Analysis

In most cases, tactical crime patterns are made up of multiple events of one type of crime. However, there are instances, as discussed earlier, in which different types of crimes make up a single pattern. For example, unsuccessful burglaries can be classified as criminal damage and examined along with successful burglaries. Also, public sexual indecency, indecent exposure, and rape can make up a pattern if an offender is escalating in violence or performs different behaviors depending on the circumstances. An important point is that police officers classify similar crimes differently based on specific legal criteria; however, the crime acts themselves may be similar in nature and can make up a crime pattern. A crime analyst needs to take both the classification and the nature of the activity into account in order to understand and describe the pattern.

Because MO characteristics can be very specific (e.g., a robber who forces the victim to strip), they can provide obvious links among cases that are months or even years apart. However, there is no way to establish a pattern definitely by MO alone (i.e., unless the offender is arrested and confesses, there is no way to be sure that a particular offender has committed all crimes with the same MO characteristics), so in most cases patterns are linked in other ways as well (e.g., suspect description, type of location). It is unlikely that an offender would deliberately or coincidentally copy another offender's vehicle or physical description, but it is easy to copy general MO characteristics; for example, suspect enters bank and demands money from a clerk using a gun and a note (Bair Software, 1999).

Another factor that can confuse the description and analysis of MO characteristics is that situational circumstances may result in an offender's altering his or her MO. For example, depending on how a victim reacts, an offender may use less or more violence within the same crime pattern. Also, characteristics that are based on witness descriptions are often problematic. Factors such as lighting, amount of time the victim and offender were together, and fear can influence the accuracy of information provided by witnesses. In addition, an offender may deviate from an established MO for some reason; for example, a burglar may not kick a door open (his usual MO) because a side window is open and it is much easier to enter that way. Crime analysts can use language such as, "The offender seems to be . . ." or, "It appears from the available information that . . ." to indicate the uncertainty of the MO characteristics within a pattern. The patterns that crime analysts identify represent their educated guesses about the relationships among incidents, so when communicating the findings, analysts should use language that reflects this.

Time Series Analysis

Among the most important characteristics of crime incidents, both for identifying patterns and for describing patterns, are the times of day, days of the week, and the order in which they occur. The method used to examine these characteristics is known as *time series analysis*. Tactical crime analysts focus on describing small numbers of cases, typically fewer than 25, so statistics of central tendency, such as mean and standard deviation, are not appropriate. Rather, counts and percentages are used to describe the temporal nature of patterns.

Exact Time

Exact time series analysis is the examination of incidents that have an exact time of occurrence, such as robbery and sexual assault. It is common practice in crime analysis to use military time and to round time variables to the nearest hour. Rounding makes the information slightly less accurate, but this is a necessary compromise to produce clear, understandable results. For example, the time of a crime that occurred at 9:35 A.M. would be rounded to "0900 to 0959," and the time of a crime that took place at 10:15 P.M. would be rounded to "2200 to 2259." Table 9.1

Table 9.1 List of Cases: Robbery Pattern

Case	Time of Occurrence	Rounded Time
1	8:56 P.M.	2000 to 2059
2	10:45 P.M.	2200 to 2259
3	4:33 P.M.	1600 to 1659
4	5:45 P.M.	1700 to 1759
5	12:02 P.M.	0000 to 0059
6	7:48 P.M.	1900 to 1959
7	9:55 P.M.	2100 to 2159
8	7:16 P.M.	1900 to 1959
9	10:30 P.M.	2200 to 2259
10	5:46 P.M.	1700 to 1759
11	10:22 P.M.	2200 to 2259
12	8:16 P.M.	2000 to 2059
13	9:25 P.M.	2100 to 2159
14	7:56 P.M.	1900 to 1959
15	9:12 P.M.	2100 to 2159

displays a list of cases in a robbery pattern, showing the exact times at which they occurred and their rounded times.

Even though it may be interesting to know the exact times of the crimes, the purpose of analysis is to organize the information so that a pattern can emerge. Table 9.2 shows the number of robberies by hour, which is a useful way of displaying information about the time events in a pattern. Although this information is an improvement over the list in Table 9.1, the results are even easier to understand when they are displayed in the form of a chart, as in Figure 9.1, which clearly shows that most of the robberies have occurred in the evening hours. This kind of format is useful for disseminating information about patterns to police.

Another way to display this pattern is to convert each robbery into a percentage of the total number of robberies. That is, the value of each hour is no longer 1; instead, it is a percentage of the total. In this example, because the total number of cases is 15, each case is worth 6.7% (i.e., 1/15). Table 9.3 shows the counts of robberies by hour converted to percentages. The resulting chart in Figure 9.2 illustrates the percentage values. Although the charts in Figures 9.1 and 9.2 look similar, they serve different purposes. Analysts can use charts that depict percentages to analyze unlike distributions (e.g., a pattern with 10 cases and another with 25 cases) in relation to one another.

Table 9.2   Number of Robberies by Hour

Hour of Day	Count
0000 to 0059	1
0100 to 0159	0
0200 to 0259	0
0300 to 0359	0
0400 to 0459	0
0500 to 0559	0
0600 to 0659	0
0700 to 0759	0
0800 to 0859	0
0900 to 0959	0
1000 to 1059	0
1100 to 1159	0
1200 to 1259	0
1300 to 1359	0
1400 to 1459	0
1500 to 1559	0
1600 to 1659	1
1700 to 1759	2
1800 to 1859	0
1900 to 1959	3
2000 to 2059	2
2100 to 2159	3
2200 to 2259	3
2300 to 2359	0

Exact Day of the Week

Using the same method for counting crimes by day of the week, Table 9.4 illustrates the frequency of crimes and the percentage of the total by day. Figure 9.3 depicts the count and Figure 9.4 the percentage of the total of crimes by day of the week. Crime analysts typically use bar charts to illustrate information about days of the week.

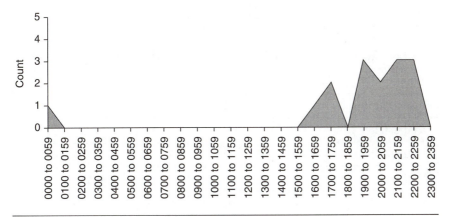

Figure 9.1   Chart: Number of Robberies by Hour

Exact Time of Day/Day of the Week

The two techniques described above illustrate information about time of day and day of the week separately. However, it is important for analysts to know what combination of day *and* time is most common among incidents in the pattern. Table 9.5 is the list of cases showing time of day and day of the week. Table 9.6 presents a **cross-tabulation** of these two variables, showing the count of crime by both time of day and day of the week.

Like the results in the examples above, these counts can be used to create a chart for visualization and dissemination of results, as in Figure 9.5. In this figure, the areas with the darker shading represent times and days when more crimes have occurred (note the legend); in this pattern, more robberies have occurred on Thursday, Friday, and Saturday evenings. It is important to keep in mind that such a chart is more useful if it displays more cases (e.g., note the numerous empty cells in Table 9.6) and is put to good use in strategic crime analysis, where larger numbers of cases are examined at once.

Exact Date: Intervals Between Events

Finally, an analyst may gain insight into the nature of a pattern by analyzing the number of days between crimes in the pattern. For example, a person committing robberies to support a drug habit may commit crimes closer together in time if his take in any given robbery is small. However, analysts must be careful not to assume too much about patterns or offenders when conducting this type of analysis, as many different factors can influence the time between incidents (e.g., weather, work, sickness, opportunity). Table 9.7 lists the dates of the crimes in the example pattern of robberies and the number of days between the events.

Figure 9.6 illustrates the information in Table 9.7 graphically, showing intervals that are proportional to the amounts of time between them. Analysts can also include information on intervals between events when mapping patterns, a technique discussed later in this chapter (in the section on spatial analysis). This type of analysis can

Table 9.3 Number and Percentage of Robberies by Hour

Hour of Day	Count	Percentage of Total
0000 to 0059	1	6.7
0100 to 0159	0	0.0
0200 to 0259	0	0.0
0300 to 0359	0	0.0
0400 to 0459	0	0.0
0500 to 0559	0	0.0
0600 to 0659	0	0.0
0700 to 0759	0	0.0
0800 to 0859	0	0.0
0900 to 0959	0	0.0
1000 to 1059	0	0.0
1100 to 1159	0	0.0
1200 to 1259	0	0.0
1300 to 1359	0	0.0
1400 to 1459	0	0.0
1500 to 1559	0	0.0
1600 to 1659	1	6.7
1700 to 1759	2	13.3
1800 to 1859	0	0.0
1900 to 1959	3	20.0
2000 to 2059	2	13.3
2100 to 2159	3	20.0
2200 to 2259	3	20.0
2300 to 2359	0	0.0

clarify whether there is a particular tempo to a pattern—that is, whether the pattern is accelerating, stable, or decelerating. In a pattern with an accelerating tempo, intervals between events decrease as the pattern progresses. In a pattern with a decelerating tempo, intervals between events increase as the pattern progresses. When the intervals between cases remain fairly consistent, the tempo is stable. By examining the intervals between cases in a pattern, a crime analyst can help to anticipate future incidents in the pattern.

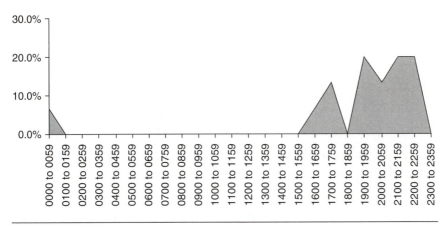

Figure 9.2   Chart: Percentage of Robberies by Hour

Table 9.4   Number and Percentage of Robberies by Day of the Week

Day	Count	Percentage of Total
Sunday	1	6.7
Monday	1	6.7
Tuesday	0	0.0
Wednesday	1	6.7
Thursday	3	20.0
Friday	4	26.7
Saturday	5	33.3

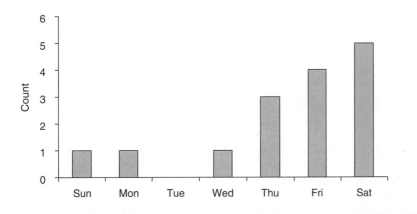

Figure 9.3   Chart: Number of Robberies by Day of the Week

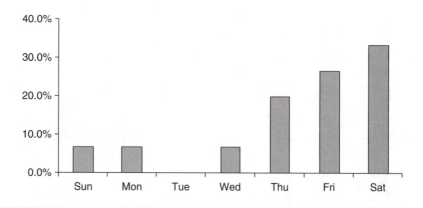

Figure 9.4   Chart: Percentage of Robberies by Day of the Week

Table 9.5   List of Cases: Time of Day and Day of the Week

Case	Time of Occurrence	Day of Occurrence
1	12:02 A.M.	Sunday
2	4:33 P.M.	Saturday
3	5:45 P.M.	Saturday
4	5:46 P.M.	Friday
5	7:16 P.M.	Saturday
6	7:48 P.M.	Thursday
7	7:56 P.M.	Thursday
8	8:16 P.M.	Friday
9	8:56 P.M.	Monday
10	9:12 P.M.	Saturday
11	9:25 P.M.	Saturday
12	9:55 P.M.	Friday
13	10:22 P.M.	Wednesday
14	10:30 P.M.	Thursday
15	10:45 P.M.	Friday

Weighted Time Span Analysis

Exact time of day and day of the week time series methods are not appropriate for types of crimes (typically property crimes) for which only time span information is available (i.e., the crime occurred between 7:00 A.M. and 5:00 P.M.). Although time

Table 9.6   Cross-Tabulation of Time of Day and Day of the Week

Hour of Day	Sunday	Monday	Tuesday	Wednesday	Thursday	Friday	Saturday
0000 to 0059	1						
0100 to 0159							
0200 to 0259							
0300 to 0359							
0400 to 0459							
0500 to 0559							
0600 to 0659							
0700 to 0759							
0800 to 0859							
0900 to 0959							
1000 to 1059							
1100 to 1159							
1200 to 1259							
1300 to 1359							
1400 to 1459							
1500 to 1559							
1600 to 1659							1
1700 to 1759						1	1
1800 to 1859							
1900 to 1959					2		1
2000 to 2059		1				1	
2100 to 2159						1	2
2200 to 2259				1	1	1	
2300 to 2359							

span information is not as accurate as exact time information, it can still help an analyst identify and understand a crime pattern. Two aspects of a crime-related time span are important: when the time span begins and ends, and the length of the time span. For example, a time span beginning at 4:00 P.M. and ending at 12:00 A.M. is very different from one beginning at 4:00 A.M. and ending at 12:00 P.M., even though both are 8 hours in length. Additionally, a time span of 1 hour is a much more accurate

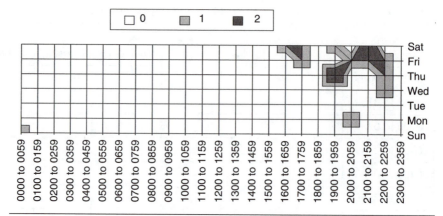

Figure 9.5   Chart: Time of Day and Day of Week

Table 9.7   Intervals Between Robbery Events

Case	Date of Occurrence	Days Between Events
1	12/7/2003	
2	12/13/2003	6
3	12/20/2003	7
4	12/26/2003	6
5	1/3/2004	8
6	1/8/2004	5
7	1/15/2004	7
8	1/16/2004	1
9	1/19/2004	3
10	1/24/2004	5
11	1/31/2004	7
12	2/6/2004	7
13	2/11/2004	5
14	2/12/2004	1
15	2/13/2004	1

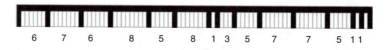

6   7   6   8   5   8   1   3   5   7   7   5   1   1

Figure 9.6   Graphic Depiction of Intervals Between Robbery Events

Table 9.8   List of Cases: Time Span Data

Case	First Possible Time	Rounded Time	Last Possible Time	Rounded Time	Length of Time Span	Weight of Each Hour
1	10:00 A.M.	1000 to 1059	3:15 P.M.	1500 to 1559	6	0.17
2	11:15 A.M.	1100 to 1159	2:30 P.M.	1400 to 1459	4	0.25
3	9:15 A.M.	0900 to 0959	7:15 P.M.	1900 to 1959	11	0.09
4	8:00 A.M.	0800 to 0859	5:00 P.M.	1700 to 1759	10	0.10
5	7:30 A.M.	0700 to 0759	5:30 P.M.	1700 to 1759	11	0.09
6	8:15 A.M.	0800 to 0859	4:30 P.M.	1600 to 1659	9	0.11
7	10:30 A.M.	1000 to 1059	1:30 P.M.	1300 to 1359	4	0.25
8	12:30 P.M.	1200 to 1259	6:30 P.M.	1800 to 1859	7	0.14
9	12:15 P.M.	1200 to 1259	4:30 P.M.	1600 to 1659	5	0.20
10	9:45 A.M.	0900 to 0959	6:15 P.M.	1800 to 1859	10	0.10
11	8:45 A.M.	0800 to 0859	5:15 P.M.	1700 to 1759	10	0.10
12	8:30 A.M.	0800 to 0859	4:30 P.M.	1600 to 1659	9	0.11

estimate of when a crime occurred than a time span of 5 hours. Thus it is important that analysts examine both aspects of time spans in time series analysis.[1]

In the **weighted time span analysis** method, each time span is assigned a value of 1, and each hour within the time span is a proportion of the time span.[2] For example, for a time span of 5 hours, each hour is one-fifth of the overall time span and is assigned a value of .20 (i.e., 1 hour is 20% of a 5-hour time span). Similarly, in a time span of 8 hours, each hour is one-eighth and thus is assigned a value of .125 (12.5%). Table 9.8 is a list of cases that shows, for each crime, the first possible time the crime occurred, that time rounded, the last possible time the crime occurred, that time rounded, the length of the time span, and the assigned value (weight) of 1 hour of the time span (e.g., in Case 1, with a time span of 6 hours, each hour in the time span is worth 1/6, or .17).

After assigning a value to an hour within the time span of each case, the analyst places these values in their appropriate hours of the day and examines these together. In Table 9.9, the rows represent the hours of the day and the columns are the values of the time spans for each crime in the pattern (e.g., in Case 1, hours 1000 to 1059 through 1500 to 1559 are weighted .17). The important columns are on the right: "Total" represents the sum of the values by hour of the day and "Percentage of Total" is "Total" for that hour of the day divided by the total of all the hours of the day (e.g., the "Total" for 1000 to 1059 is 1.12, which is 9.4% of 11.96, the total for all the hours of the day).

Table 9.9   Hour and Percentage Totals for Time Spans

Hour of Day	1	2	3	4	5	6	7	8	9	10	11	12	Total	Percentage of Total
0000 to 0059													0.00	0.0
0100 to 0159													0.00	0.0
0200 to 0259													0.00	0.0
0300 to 0359													0.00	0.0
0400 to 0459													0.00	0.0
0500 to 0559													0.00	0.0
0600 to 0659													0.00	0.0
0700 to 0759					0.09								0.09	0.8
0800 to 0859				0.10	0.09	0.11					0.10	0.11	0.51	4.3
0900 to 0959			0.09	0.10	0.09	0.11				0.10	0.10	0.11	0.70	5.9
1000 to 1059	0.17		0.09	0.10	0.09	0.11	0.25			0.10	0.10	0.11	1.12	9.4
1100 to 1159	0.17	0.25	0.09	0.10	0.09	0.11	0.25			0.10	0.10	0.11	1.37	11.5
1200 to 1259	0.17	0.25	0.09	0.10	0.09	0.11	0.25	0.14	0.20	0.10	0.10	0.11	1.71	14.3
1300 to 1359	0.17	0.25	0.09	0.10	0.09	0.11	0.25	0.14	0.20	0.10	0.10	0.11	1.71	14.3
1400 to 1459	0.17	0.25	0.09	0.10	0.09	0.11		0.14	0.20	0.10	0.10	0.11	1.46	12.2
1500 to 1559	0.17		0.09	0.10	0.09	0.11		0.14	0.20	0.10	0.10	0.11	1.21	10.1
1600 to 1659			0.09	0.10	0.09	0.11		0.14	0.20	0.10	0.10	0.11	1.04	8.7
1700 to 1759			0.09	0.10	0.09			0.14		0.10	0.10		0.62	5.2
1800 to 1859			0.09					0.14		0.10			0.33	2.8
1900 to 1959			0.09										0.09	0.8
2000 to 2059													0.00	0.0
2100 to 2159													0.00	0.0
2200 to 2259													0.00	0.0
2300 to 2359													0.00	0.0
Total													11.96	

As with the methods described above, a chart is useful for visualizing these results. Figure 9.7 illustrates the final column in Table 9.9, "Percentage of Total." The chart shows that the crimes in this pattern have time spans that generally cluster from 7:00 A.M. to 7:00 P.M., and that the time spans cluster between the hours of 11:00 A.M. and 2:59 P.M. (just over 52%, the exact number obtained from Table 9.9). Analysts can also use this method for weekday spans in which each day is weighted by the number of days in the time span (e.g., for a crime that spans over Monday,

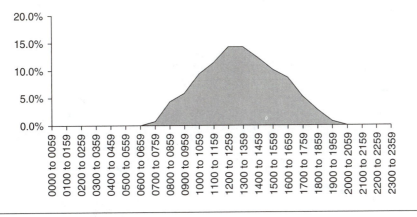

Figure 9.7   Chart: Weighted Time Spans

Tuesday, and Wednesday, each day would be weighted .33 and would be assigned to the appropriate weekday).

Spatial Analysis of Patterns

Another key characteristic of crime patterns is their geographic nature. Crime analysts use spatial analysis in several ways to identify and understand crime patterns. Scholars and practitioners are currently doing very advanced work in tactical spatial analysis, but the discussion below is confined to basic techniques.

Pattern Identification

The simplest, most straightforward way of using spatial analysis to identify and understand crime patterns is simply to map the incidents and look for clusters. The map in Figure 9.8 illustrates a complete list of crimes tracked in tactical crime analysis for a 4-month period. It is difficult to discern substantive patterns using such a map because it depicts all types of crimes combined. Taking a deductive approach, the analyst's first step is to query a particular type of crime or a shorter time period to focus the analysis. For example, the map in Figure 9.9 illustrates only commercial burglaries. Through this simple mapping of the incidents, particular clusters of activity become apparent. Figure 9.10 illustrates a closer examination of the circled area in Figure 9.9; this map reveals that there are several repeat locations and that many of the incidents have occurred on the same street.

As noted previously, in the analysis of property crimes, geographic proximity of incidents is a particularly important characteristic, and analysts often use mapping to identify property crime patterns. However, analysts need to consider more than just geographic locations of incidents when conducting pattern identification; to identify initial patterns, they must further examine characteristics such as MO, time, and day.

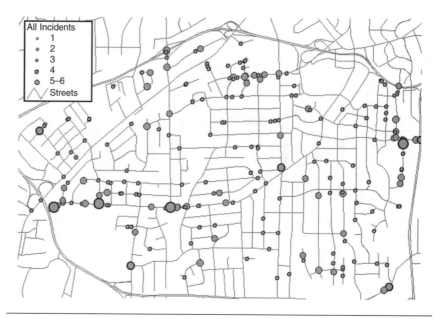

Figure 9.8   Graduated Point Map: All Incidents

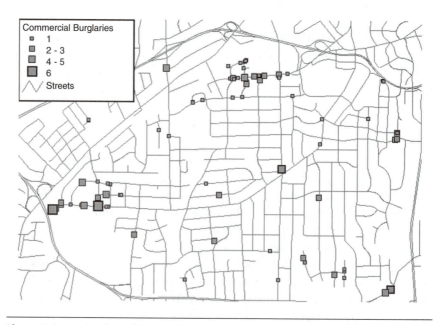

Figure 9.9   Graduated Point Map: Commercial Burglary Only

In contrast, persons crimes are initially identified through suspect and MO characteristics for series and sprees, but analysts may use mapping to identify hot spots and hot targets for these types of crimes. Figure 9.11 depicts robberies that have taken place in a particular area in which several locations have been robbed

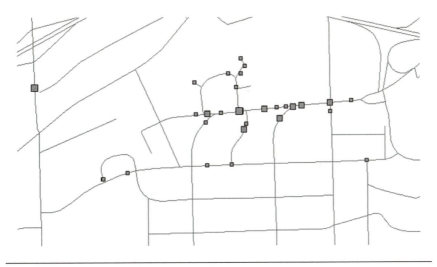

Figure 9.10   Graduated Point Map: Commercial Burglary Cluster

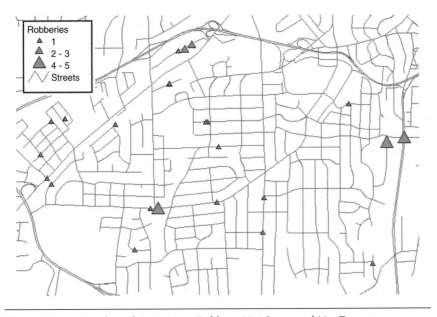

Figure 9.11   Graduated Point Map: Robbery Hot Spots and Hot Targets

repeatedly (note the locations with four to five robberies) in a relatively short period. The geographic nature of these crimes seems to warrant additional analysis for a hot spot or a hot target.

Describing and Understanding a Pattern

Once a pattern has been identified, the analyst can illustrate it spatially in several ways to describe and clarify the nature of the pattern. The first step is to create a

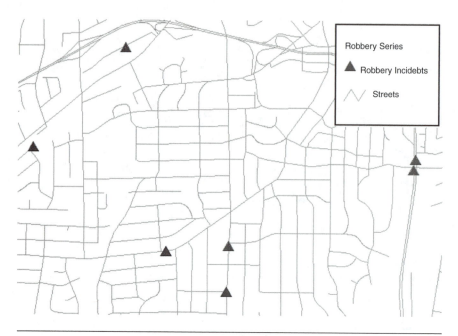

Robbery Series

▲ Robbery Incidebts

/\/ Streets

Figure 9.12   Single-Symbol Map: Robbery Pattern

single-symbol map of the crime pattern locations, making sure that each case is visible on the map (i.e., if there are two incidents at the same location, the symbols must be manually offset so that both are visible). Figure 9.12 is a single-symbol map of a robbery pattern (series).

The analyst can map the incidents with single symbols (instead of graduated symbols) and shading by unique value of variables (e.g., type of weapon used, method of entry, property taken, time of day) to begin to understand the spatial relationships among the crimes and their relationships to other key characteristics. Figure 9.13 illustrates the same pattern as in Figure 9.12, but with the points shaded by the type of weapon used in the crime. Although no clear pattern is discernible from this map, simultaneous examination of additional characteristics might yield interesting results (e.g., if the incidents in which a gun was used had two victims and the others only one).[3]

Figure 9.14 is another map with an example of unique shading that illustrates the order of occurrence of the incidents—that is, incidents are shaded by date. The older crimes are indicated by lighter shading, and more recent ones are indicated by darker shading. This map enables the analyst to examine the geographic and temporal progression of the pattern.

Another way of showing the spatial and temporal progression of a pattern is to connect the incidents with arrows that indicate the order of their occurrence, as in Figure 9.15. It is important to note that the straight lines in this map do not indicate the exact route the offender traveled, but only the order and general direction of the incidents. An analyst could also shade the symbols by another variable

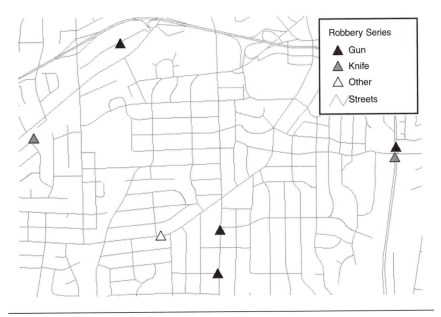

Figure 9.13   Single-Symbol Map Shaded by Weapon Type: Robbery Pattern

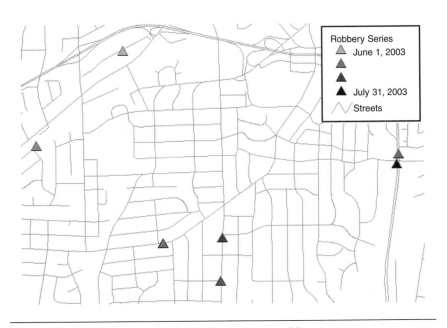

Figure 9.14   Single-Symbol Map Shaded by Date: Robbery Pattern

(such as property taken) and examine three characteristics at once on the map (e.g., geography, sequence, and property taken), or add other information for consideration, such as by labeling the sequence lines by number of days between events, as seen in Figure 9.16.

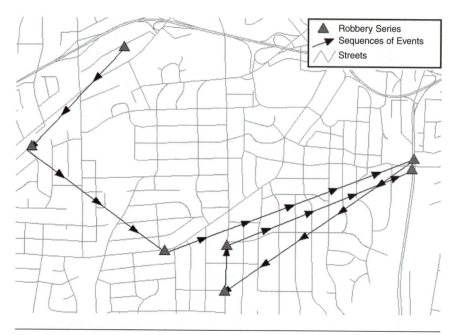

Figure 9.15   Single-Symbol Map With Arrows Showing Sequence of Events:
Robbery Pattern

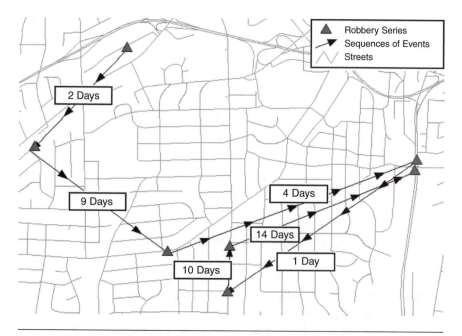

Figure 9.16   Single-Symbol Map With Arrows Showing Sequence of Events and
Labels Indicating Days Between Events: Robbery Pattern

Tactical Crime Analysis Products

To disseminate crime pattern and other tactical information to officers, detectives, and (in some cases) citizens, crime analysts often use a format known as a tactical crime analysis bulletin. Such a bulletin typically includes the following elements:

- *Summary:* a short, straightforward narrative of the incidents in the pattern
- *List of cases:* a list of the incidents highlighting key characteristics depending on the type of crime (e.g., MO information for persons crime; location type, point of entry, property taken for property crimes)
- *Suspect information:* the most reliable suspect description
- *Vehicle information:* the most reliable vehicle description
- *Investigative leads:* information on any suspects (e.g., suspicious persons or vehicles seen in the area at the time of the pattern, known offenders with a similar MO, sex offenders living in the area)
- *Time series chart*
- *Map of the incidents in the pattern*

Across the United States, such bulletins vary somewhat in format and content by police agency and often by analyst. Recently, the Police Foundation's Crime Mapping Laboratory developed templates for TCA bulletins based on an assessment of numerous bulletins from around the country (Velasco, Griffin, & Boba, 2001). Figure 9.17 depicts the template for a crime pattern bulletin containing all of the elements listed above.[4]

Police agencies also produce other types of bulletins, such as persons bulletins (i.e., summaries of crime activity attributed to one person) and property bulletins (i.e., summaries of crime activity concerning one type of property being targeted). Figure 9.18 shows a template developed by the Police Foundation for a persons bulletin (Velasco et al., 2001).

Crime analysts use TCA bulletins to inform police officers and detectives of ongoing crime patterns. When citizens are also provided with information about ongoing patterns, they receive "watered-down" versions of the bulletins created for police agencies; that is, bulletins intended for citizens exclude information that is not relevant to citizen safety, that might breach confidentiality, or that is likely to jeopardize an investigation. For example, if a burglary pattern contains privately owned locations (e.g., single-family residences), the bulletin for citizens would include only information about the MO, times, dates, and general locations; the specific addresses of the homes burglarized would not be provided. Exact address information would be provided for publicly frequented locations contained in the pattern; for example, if cars are repeatedly being burglarized in the parking lot of a particular nightclub, that location would be specified, because it would be important for citizens to have that information in order to protect their belongings.

Historically, tactical crime analysis bulletins have been distributed to police personnel on paper during briefings or in mailboxes. In recent years, however, many police agencies have begun to distribute bulletins through e-mail or by posting them on intranet sites. Police use the information that bulletins provide

[Agency Name]

Crime Analysis Unit – Crime Pattern Bulletin

Bulletin Number:
Date: May 20, 2005

[BULLETIN TITLE]

MO/Activity Summary:

*
*

Suspect Description(s):

*
*

Vehicle Description(s):

*
*

Day(s)/Time(s), (See [time of day and/or day of week] chart):

Area(s), (See map):

Please contact the Crime Analysis Unit at [telephone number or e-mail] if you have any questions or updates to the information contained in this report.

List of incidents:

Case No.	Date	Day	Time	Beat	Address	[Other]
1						
2						
3						
4						
5						
6						
7						
8						
9						
10						

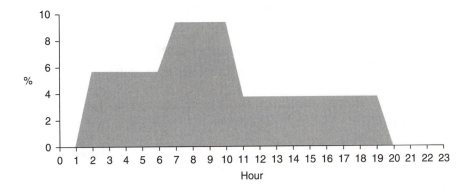

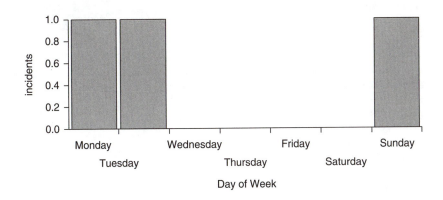

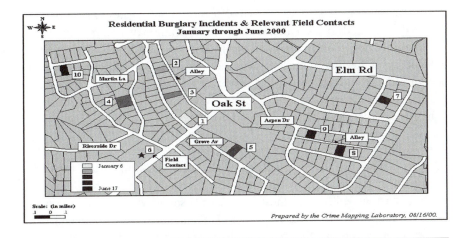

Figure 9.17   Template for a Crime Pattern Bulletin

[Agency Name]
Crime Analysis Unit – Persons Bulletin

Bulletin Number:
Date: May 20, 2005

[TITLE]

Name:

DOB:
Physical Description:
Markings:

Last Known Address:

Aliases:

Accomplices:

Please contact the Crime Analysis Unit at [telephone number or e-mail] if you have any questions or updates to the information contained in this report.

Summary of Subject's Activity:

-
-

Figure 9.18   Template for a Persons Bulletin

to raise citizen awareness, to try to catch offenders, to investigate crimes further, to clear old cases, and to prevent future crimes. A crime pattern can indicate the potential behavior of offenders, given the assumption that criminals are creatures of habit (i.e., if they find something that works, they tend to stick with it). A crime pattern can also indicate places and areas that are vulnerable to crime and that provide numerous opportunities for crime. The following are some examples of how police agencies make use of TCA information:

- In a convenience store robbery series, it is determined that two characteristics are common to all of the robberies: They occur late at night, and the victim is a female clerk working by herself. Two solutions are suggested: that police conduct surveillance of those convenience stores where female clerks are working alone late at night (apprehension) and that police recommend to the store managers that they have two clerks working late at night (prevention).
- A residential burglary pattern is occurring in an isolated suburban neighborhood. It is summer, and most of the burglars have entered through open

windows while the home owners have been away at work, but little more information is available about the offenders. Ten burglaries have occurred over the past 2 months. It is not realistic for police to conduct surveillance in the neighborhood 8 hours a day, 5 days a week, so officers attach a door hanger at each home in the area containing information on the general nature of the burglary pattern and offering suggestions for crime prevention.

- A sexual assault series is identified, and police release selected details about the assaults to the local newspaper (awareness and prevention). After the information is published, additional cases are reported that provide the police with further data on the suspect and the vehicle used in the crimes (apprehension).
- A commercial burglary pattern of 20 incidents at day-care centers is published in the police department. Two burglars are subsequently arrested for a burglary at a day-care center, and the detective uses the information provided in the bulletin to question the suspects, who then confess to 10 more crimes (clearing cases).
- A persons bulletin is published about a man who has been contacted by the police continually for disorderly behavior and has been warned for criminal trespass. The man is never arrested in this jurisdiction, but the bulletin provides his criminal history, which includes similar and more serious offenses. The next time the police contact the man, he is not just warned but arrested for this pattern of conduct (apprehension).

Summary Points

This chapter has described specific techniques that crime analysts use to identify and understand known crime patterns as well as the uses and formats of tactical crime analysis bulletins. The following are the key points addressed in this chapter:

- The techniques that crime analysts use to describe and understand crime patterns focus on how (e.g., crime type and MO analysis), when (i.e., time series analysis), and where (i.e., spatial analysis) patterns occur. Analysts also use many of the same techniques to understand the commonalities of characteristics and to identify patterns.
- Because MO characteristics can be very specific, they can provide obvious links among cases that are months or even years apart; however, there is no way to establish a pattern definitely by MO alone. Crime analysts can use language such as, "The offender seems to be . . ." or, "It appears from the available information that . . ." to indicate the uncertainty of the MO characteristics within a pattern.
- Among the most important characteristics of crime incidents, both for identifying patterns and for describing patterns, are the times of day and days of the week when they occur and the order in which they occur. These characteristics are examined in various types of time series analysis, including exact time analysis, weighted time span analysis, and analysis of days between hits.
- In spatial analysis, graduated symbol maps enable analysts to examine the geographic nature of crimes and identify initial patterns.

- In conducting spatial analysis of known patterns, analysts map individual incidents within patterns and shade the points by unique values of particular variables. Maps used in spatial analysis may also include lines to indicate sequences of events and labels to display patterns geographically.
- Crime analysts disseminate TCA information through bulletins that contain several standard elements: a summary of the pattern, a list of key characteristics, suspect information, vehicle information, investigative leads, time series charts, and a map.
- There are several types of TCA bulletins, including, but not limited to, pattern bulletins, persons bulletins, and property bulletins.
- Police use the information in tactical crime analysis bulletins to raise citizen awareness, to try to catch offenders, to investigate crimes further, to clear old cases, and to prevent future crimes.

Exercises

Exercise 9.1

Create a crime pattern bulletin for a pattern you have identified in a previous exercise. Use the following files on the CD-ROM that accompanies this book to guide the development of your bulletin:

- Exercise 9.1_ReadMe
- Exercise 9.1_Tactical Bulletin Template
- Exercise 9.1_Tactical Bulletin Template Instructions

Exercise 9.2

Conduct a search of the Internet for tactical crime analysis bulletins, and then examine their formats and the contact information they include. What changes do you think were made for distribution of these bulletins to the general public versus distribution to internal police personnel?

Notes

1. Some time series methods include examining "split time," or the middle of a time span, to determine when the pattern occurred. This method is not recommended, however, because it does not consider the beginning and end or the length of the time span, so the results provide the crime analyst with little relevant information.

2. Weighted time span analysis is also sometimes called aoristic analysis (see Ratcliffe, 2002). However, in crime analysis practice it is usually known simply as the weighted time span method.

3. In the spatial analysis process, numerous maps may be created but only a few may yield interesting results.

4. The actual template (formatted in Microsoft Word) used to create Figure 9.17 is included on the CD-ROM that accompanies this book. It is also available for download on the Police Foundation's Web site, at http://www.policefoundation.org.

PART IV

Strategic Crime Analysis

As discussed in Chapter 2, strategic crime analysis (SCA) is the study of crime and disorder problems and other police-related issues to determine long-term patterns of activity as well as to evaluate police responses and organizational procedures. The two primary purposes of strategic crime analysis are (a) to assist in the identification and in-depth examination of long-term problems and (b) to evaluate responses to problems as well as organizational procedures. The chapters in Part IV focus on the examination of problems; the evaluation of responses to problems and organizational procedures is a complex topic that is beyond the scope of this text.

In the context of crime analysis, a problem is defined as "a recurring set of related harmful events in a community that members of the public expect the police to address" (Clarke & Eck, 2003, Step 15). By examining crime rates, repeat victimization, hot spots, and the environment, crime analysts help to identify and create a picture of the underlying causes of problems such as street robbery, residential burglary, residential speeding, and false burglary alarms.

Part IV covers key areas of analysis for understanding problems and ends with a discussion of strategic crime analysis products. Chapter 10 defines problems in contrast to incidents and patterns and addresses the importance of both the context and the nature of a problem; Chapter 11 is devoted to discussion of temporal analysis, victimization, and the collection of primary data in SCA; Chapter 12 describes techniques for spatial analysis used in SCA; and Chapter 13 describes the products that come out of strategic crime analysis. Just as a carpenter uses a variety of tools for building different things, crime analysts apply different techniques in different situations. The chapters in Part IV present a toolbox full of different analysis techniques along with examples of situations in which they are especially useful.

10 Analyzing Problems

Definition, Context, and Nature of the Problem

The first tasks in analyzing a problem are to understand the environment in which the problem occurs and to describe the prevalence/magnitude of the problem. This chapter discusses various aspects of the context (environment) of a problem that crime analysts should consider and describes statistical techniques that analysts can use to describe the current nature of a problem. But first, it is important to be able to define a problem and develop hypotheses to direct the analysis process.

What Is a Problem?

In the context of crime analysis, a problem is defined generally as "a recurring set of related harmful events in a community that members of the public expect the police to address" (Clarke & Eck, 2003, Step 15). Although helpful, this definition is somewhat vague—it does not differentiate problems analyzed in strategic crime analysis (SCA) from patterns analyzed in tactical crime analysis. The following comparison of the concepts of an incident, a pattern, and a problem helps to clarify the meaning of the term *problem*. The most significant characteristic that varies among these three concepts is the temporal nature of the activity.

- *Incident:* An **incident** is one event that occurs over minutes, hours, or, in rare cases, days. One auto theft, one robbery, and one hostage situation (even if it lasts 2 days) are all examples of individual incidents. Analysis of incidents is conducted primarily by police officers and detectives while on the scene of those incidents or during follow-up investigation. Crime analysts assist with tactical analysis of incidents (e.g., by finding an investigative lead for a case through examination of a tactical crime analysis database or by locating a stolen piece of property in a database of pawn slips).
- *Pattern:* A **pattern** is a group of events, or multiple incidents, with similar characteristics that occur in a relatively short time span (over several days, weeks, or months). In rare cases, patterns can occur over years, but the events

in such patterns are typically characterized by having the same offender (e.g., serial rapist). Police agencies eliminate some patterns by arresting suspects or implementing crime prevention measures, whereas other patterns are parts of series of patterns that, over time, become problems.

- *Problem:* A **problem** is a set of related crime activities that occur over several months, seasons, or years. A problem may include multiple patterns (e.g., series, hot spots, hot targets). For example, 10 separate series of street robbery committed by different offenders may have been identified in an area over a 1-year period. Even though some of the offenders are caught, street robberies continue in this area. Thus it is something about the nature of street robbery and the opportunity for crime in this area that makes street robbery a persistent problem there, not individual offenders. Strategic crime analysis is warranted in this case, because strictly identifying patterns and apprehending individual offenders will not eliminate the problem.

Many of the techniques that crime analysts use to understand problems are applicable only for analyzing relatively large numbers of cases (e.g., 25 or more) over relatively long periods of time (e.g., at least a year). In addition, to understand a problem fully, analysts often need to invest substantial amounts of time and energy, thus problems must be significant enough to warrant the expenditure of such resources. Unfortunately, no hard-and-fast rule exists to help police agencies determine when a problem warrants strategic crime analysis.

In order to make sure that a problem is identified correctly and distinguished accurately from other problems, the crime analyst must classify two major characteristics of the problem: the environment in which it occurs and the type of behavior associated with it. Clarke and Eck (2003) have developed the following classifications for the environment and behavior of a problem:

Environments regulate the targets available, the activities people can engage in and who controls the location. Specifying an environment allows comparisons of environments with and without a problem. It also helps identify potential stakeholders and partners for addressing a problem. There are eleven distinct environments for most common police problems:

- Residential: Locations where people dwell. Houses, flats, and hotel rooms are examples. Though most are in fixed locations, a few are mobile, such as caravans.
- Recreational: Places where people go to have a good time. Pubs, nightclubs, restaurants, cinemas, playgrounds, and parks are examples.
- Offices: Locations of white-collar work where there is little face-to-face interaction between the workers and the general public. Government and business facilities are often of this type. Access to these locations is often restricted.
- Retail: Places for walk-in or drive-up customer traffic involving monetary transactions. Stores, branch banks, and post office branches are examples.
- Industrial: Locations for processing of goods. Cash transactions are not important activities in these environments and the public is

seldom invited. Factories, warehouses, package-sorting facilities are examples.

- Agricultural: Locations for growing crops and animals.
- Educational: Places of learning or study, including day care centres, schools, universities, libraries and churches.
- Human service: Places where people go when something is wrong. Courts, jails, prisons, police stations, hospitals and some drug treatment centres are examples.
- Public ways: Routes connecting all other environments. Roads and highways, footpaths and bike trails, and drives and parking facilities are examples.
- Transport: Locations for the mass movement of people. These include buses, bus stations and bus stops, airplanes and airports, trains and train stations, ferries and ferry terminals, and ocean liners and piers.
- Open/transitional: Areas without consistent or regular designated uses. These differ from parks in that they have not been designated for recreation, though people may use them for this. Transitional areas include abandoned properties and construction sites.

Behaviour is the second crucial dimension for classifying a problem. Specifying behaviours helps pinpoint important aspects of harm, intent, and offender-target relationships. There are six types of behaviour:

- Predatory: The offender is clearly distinct from the victim and the victim objects to the offender's actions. Most common crimes are of this type. Examples include robbery, child abuse, burglary, and theft.
- Consensual: The parties involved knowingly and willingly interact. This typically involves some form of transaction. Examples include drug sales, prostitution and stolen goods sales. Note, however, that assaults on prostitutes are predatory behaviours.
- Conflicts: Violent interactions involving roughly coequal people who have some pre-existing relationship. Domestic violence among adults usually involves this type of behaviour, though domestic violence against children and the elderly is classified as predatory because the parties involved are not roughly coequal.
- Incivilities: Offenders are distinguishable from victims, as in predatory events, but the victims are spread over a number of individuals and the harms are not serious. Many concerns that are annoying, unsightly, noisy or disturbing, but do not involve serious property damage or injury fall into this category. Some incivilities are troublesome regardless of the environment, while others are only troublesome in specific environments.
- Endangerment: The offender and the victim are the same person or the offender had no intent to harm the victim. Suicide attempts, drug overdoses, and motor vehicle accidents are examples.
- Misuse of police: A category reserved for unwarranted demands on the police service. False reporting of crimes and repeated calling about issues citizens can handle themselves are examples. This is a category of last resort—for use

Table 10.1   Problems, Environment, and Behavior

Problem	Environment	Behavior
Assaults in bars	Recreational	Conflict
Construction site burglaries of homes	Transitional	Predatory
Accidents at intersections	Public ways	Endangerment
Thefts from vehicles at a mall	Public ways	Predatory
False burglary alarms at factories	Industrial	Misuse of police
Street prostitution in a neighborhood	Public ways	Consensual
Intimate violence at work	Office	Conflict
Loud parties at an apartment complex	Residential	Incivilities
Robbery of bus drivers	Transport	Predatory

when the sole harm stemming from the behaviour is the expenditure of police resources and when none of the other types fit. (Step 16)

Table 10.1 displays a list of problems and their characteristics of environment and behavior to help illustrate these concepts.

Developing Hypotheses

Hypotheses are statements about a problem that can be true or false. They normally take the form of answers to questions posed about the problem that are based on theory and experience. Crime analysts typically have limited amounts of time to devote to particular analyses, and by developing hypotheses relevant to local problems, they can streamline their work and not waste time producing analysis results that are not relevant. The hypotheses developed for a problem suggest the types of data that need to be collected, direct the analysis of data, and help the analyst to interpret the results (Clarke & Eck, 2003).

Hypotheses are often developed after some initial analysis has been conducted; however, the majority of an analyst's time should be spent on testing specific hypotheses. For example, an initial analysis might show that a large number of auto thefts are occurring in a given jurisdiction compared with others nearby. A question arising from this finding might be: Why are cars being stolen in our jurisdiction? One hypothesis an analyst might develop in response is: The cars are being stolen so that they can be stripped and the parts sold. To test this hypothesis and gain some insight into the problem, the analyst might examine the data on the number of cars stolen in the jurisdiction that are later found (i.e., recovery rate). If this analysis shows that 85% of stolen cars are recovered in near-original condition, the hypothesis would be proven false; that is, the majority of stolen cars are not being stripped for parts.

In many cases, the questions that generate hypotheses begin with *Why*. For example: Why is more crime associated with this bar than with others in the area? Why are burglars taking plasma TVs? For any question, numerous hypotheses can be formulated, but theory and experience, as well as practicality (e.g., availability of data, whether the results might lead to an outcome the police could implement), dictate which hypotheses are tested in crime analysis. When developing hypotheses, analysts should tap into the expertise of others by reviewing studies that scholars have conducted on the problems they are examining and by soliciting the help of others in their agencies.

Context of a Problem

Once a problem has been identified, strategic crime analysis begins with an understanding of the context of the problem. An analyst investigates three general areas in order to understand the context of a problem. Depending on the problem, the analyst may already have some of the information needed as a result of his or her own experience but will likely have to seek out other information specifically. The first kind of information the analyst needs concerns the types and amount of data available for analysis; the analyst must have this information in order to plan the analysis process. The second kind of information needed concerns the nature of the police agency and the community it serves. Finally, the analyst needs to gather information from other police agencies and communities, national crime surveys, and the findings of academic research about the problem to determine the seriousness of the problem and gain insight into its nature and possible solutions.

Data

The data necessary for strategic crime analysis vary by type of problem (e.g., data on building permits in the case of construction site burglary, data on bank locations in the case of bank robbery). In the crime analysis process, the first step is obtaining the necessary data. In SCA, this entails determining the types, the accessibility, and the integrity of both available and potential data sources. Analysts identify internal data sources—such as databases on crime incidents, calls for service, arrests, traffic accidents, and citations—through agency personnel. They may also identify currently unavailable data sources that may become available in the future, such as sex offender registries and field information cards. It is also essential for analysts to obtain data from outside their police agencies. For example, police agencies typically do not create their own base maps; rather, they obtain such maps from other city or county departments, from sources on the Internet, and/or from commercial vendors.

By collecting information on the data that are available early in the analysis process, the analyst can decide quickly what analysis he or she can do immediately and what data have to be collected for additional analysis. Often, the information that analysts collect for one project are also used in subsequent analyses of other problems. Building a repository of both tabular and geographic data sources is an important part of being an effective strategic crime analyst. However, in most cases, in order to study particular problems in depth, analysts need to collect additional data directly. (For further discussion of primary data collection in SCA, see Chapter 11.)

Agency and Community

As environmental criminology stresses, patterns of opportunities that create crime and other problems are specific to time, space, and environmental circumstances. Thus, in order to analyze a problem, a crime analyst must understand the nature of the community in which the problem exists and the police agency that will address the problem. Some needed information is general and easy to obtain, such as population of the community served, the number of officers in the agency, and what types of agency (e.g., local police, sheriff, state police) and community (e.g., rural, urban, suburban, large/small) are involved. The analyst can use all of this information to make comparisons with other communities.

The other types of information that are necessary for problem analysis differ from problem to problem, and this information may not be as easily obtained. Generally, the analyst needs to understand the political nature of the problem in the community (e.g., racial tensions between groups), who the audience for the analysis results will be (e.g., chief of police, community groups, city council), whether any recent significant changes have taken place in the community (e.g., increase in immigration, significant population growth), and any unique characteristics the city may have (e.g., contains a nuclear power plant, has seasonal visitors).

Furthermore, to determine the scope and intensity of the analysis, it is important for the analyst to know why the particular problem is a concern and has been chosen for study. A police agency may select a problem for analysis because addressing the problem is a strategic goal of the agency or because the problem has been an issue for years in the community. If problem analysis is being conducted for these reasons, the analyst can expect to spend significant time and energy on the project. On the other hand, a problem may be chosen because an officer will be making a presentation on the problem at a community meeting, or the problem may be quite specific and short term. In such cases, the analyst can expect to spend relatively little time and energy on examining the problem.

Research

Crime analysts can also gather information about the contexts of particular problems from other practitioners who have dealt with similar problems and from researchers who have studied the causes of problems. Sometimes neighboring jurisdictions that share a community's problem provide data and analysis results to complement local analysis. Obtaining information about a problem from regional and national perspectives allows the analyst to make comparisons (e.g., national arrest rates for burglary are 15%, but local rates are only 3%). Finally, the findings of academic and practical research about problems provide analysts with insights into the causes of these problems, suggestions for data collection, descriptions of analytic techniques they can use to study problems, and information on the success or failure of attempts to solve the problems.[1]

Current Nature of a Problem

When first examining a problem, in addition to understanding the context, the analyst needs to get a sense of the nature of the problem. To do so, the analyst typically examines the relevant data that are immediately available within the police agency (e.g., crime reports, calls for service), using a variety of analytic techniques that describe the data. Depending on the problem selected and the purpose of the analysis, any number of techniques may be appropriate. For example, in examining a problem for the purpose of providing a report for a neighborhood meeting, the analyst might conduct only counts of different types of crimes over the past year and compare the counts with those of other jurisdictions or national levels. In contrast, a 5-year analysis of the problem of robbery as a strategic issue for an agency would include counts, examination of rates, averages by area, breakdowns by the type of robbery, and more. The basic descriptive statistics commonly used in strategic crime analysis are frequency or count, cross-tabulation, percentage, rate, mean, and standard deviation. These are discussed in turn below.

Frequency or Count

The **frequency** or count is the number of all categories of a variable. To compare the numbers of robberies that have taken place within police beats, a crime analyst would conduct a count of the variable "beat" in a data set of robberies, as in Table 10.2. The value with the highest frequency is known as the **mode**. In Table 10.2, Beat 4 represents the mode value of the variable beat. Another question that an analyst might answer by examining frequency is, How many bank robberies, street robberies, or other types of robberies were reported? Table 10.3 provides this information with a frequency of "type of robbery."

Crime analysts use frequency most often to gain an initial view of problems and to answer questions such as, How often are officers called to an address and for what types of problems? and How many rapes were reported last year? In variables that have numerous categories (e.g., addresses and types of calls for service), analysts sort the categories in descending frequency by highest count, because this makes them easier to examine. Tables 10.4 and 10.5 show the data from Tables 10.2 and 10.3, respectively, sorted in descending counts. This method is more efficient than looking down a long list to determine the most frequent category (e.g., a frequency of addresses); it provides immediate information about the category with the most cases.

Table 10.2   Number of Robberies by Beat

Beat	Number of Robberies
Beat 1	46
Beat 2	23
Beat 3	49
Beat 4	·84
Beat 5	12
Beat 6	19
Beat 7	38
Total	**271**

Table 10.3   Type of Robbery

Type of Robbery	Frequency
Bank	25
Street	50
Convenience store	75
Carjacking	12
Other	109
Total	**271**

Analysts also visualize frequency data by using bar or line charts, because this allows them to make relative comparisons easily. Figure 10.1 is a bar chart (also called a *histogram*) of the number of robberies per beat. Bar charts are typically used for categorical variables (e.g., beats and types of robberies), whereas line charts are used for ordinal variables (e.g., months).

Strategic crime analysts use frequency often, but they do not use this statistic alone to describe a problem, for the following reasons:

- Just because an address or area has the "most" incidents of a problem does not mean it is the "worst" area. Many times analysis is based on "reported" crimes and calls for service, so levels of reporting influence the statistics. Both "good" and "bad" neighborhoods can have low frequencies—the former because there is little or no activity to report, and the latter because few people report the activity that occurs.

Table 10.4   Number of Robberies by Beat Sorted in Descending Frequency

Beat	Number of Robberies
Beat 4	84
Beat 3	49
Beat 1	46
Beat 7	38
Beat 2	23
Beat 6	19
Beat 5	12
Total	**271**

Table 10.5   Type of Robbery Sorted in Descending Frequency

Type of Robbery	Frequency
Other	109
Convenience store	75
Street	50
Bank	25
Carjacking	12
Total	**271**

- In comparisons of units that are dissimilar, frequency may distort a problem (e.g., comparing an area of 200 square miles and a population of 300,000 to one of 20 square miles and a population of 10,000).
- Variables with large numbers of categories may be difficult to illustrate using simple frequency (e.g., frequency of addresses of all crimes, frequency of ages of suspects), and these long lists may be categorized into fewer, more general categories (e.g., addresses into areas, ages into categories).
- Frequency of a variable with small numbers can be meaningless. For example, frequency of homicide by year for a small community over 4 years may be 0, 1, 3, 0. Clearly, this does not tell us much about the homicide problem.

Thus analysts use frequency to formulate initial descriptions of problems but then employ other statistics to obtain more information about the current nature of those problems.

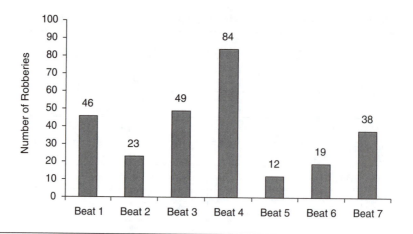

Figure 10.1   Bar Chart: Number of Robberies by Beat

Table 10.6   Cross-Tabulation of Type of Robbery by Beat

	Type of Robbery					
	Bank	Street	Convenience Store	Carjacking	Other	Total
Beat 1	5	7	11	2	21	46
Beat 2	1	4	8	0	10	23
Beat 3	6	10	15	4	14	49
Beat 4	10	15	19	2	38	84
Beat 5	0	4	2	0	6	12
Beat 6	1	6	6	0	6	19
Beat 7	2	4	14	4	14	38
Total	25	50	75	12	109	271

Cross-Tabulation

A cross-tabulation (also called a cross-tab) is a way to examine the frequency of cases within each category in more depth, using counts of two variables at once. The frequencies are computed for one variable separated into categories of the other, and vice versa. Using the data from the previous examples of robbery by beat and type of location, Table 10.6 shows the number of robberies within beats by type of robbery. The table indicates that most of the robberies (10) have occurred in Beat 4. Crime analysts use cross-tabs often to examine variables such as sex and race of

Table 10.7   Number and Percentage of Robbery by Type

Type of Robbery	Frequency	Percentage
Other	109	40.22
Convenience Store	75	27.68
Street	50	18.45
Bank	25	9.23
Carjacking	12	4.43
Total	**271**	**100.00**

arrestees, geographic area by crime type, and types of calls for service by address, time of day, and day of the week.

Percentage

A **percentage** is the proportion of the count of one category by the count of all categories of a variable multiplied by 100. For example, there were 46 robberies in Beat 1, which was 17% of the total, 271 (i.e., 46 divided by 271, and the result multiplied by 100). Table 10.7 shows the frequencies of robbery types along with the percentage of the total for each category.

Like frequencies, percentages can also be depicted in charts. The type of chart most commonly used for this purpose is a pie chart. When creating pie charts, crime analysts typically include no more than five to seven categories, so that the slices of the pie do not become too small to discern and label. Figure 10.2 illustrates the relative percentages of five types of robbery. Note that the figure caption includes information on the number of cases; this is important because it provides context for the percentages.

Cross-Tabulation Percentage

For every cross-tabulation table of frequencies, the corresponding percentages can also be computed; this allows the analyst to compare categories within the variables even if the frequencies of the categories are very different. Table 10.8 contains the first two rows of the cross-tab table from the previous example as well as the percentages. A comparison of Beat 1 and Beat 2 shows that even though Beat 1 has twice as many robberies as Beat 2, Beat 2 has *relatively* more street (17.4% vs. 15.2%) and convenience store robberies (34.8% vs. 23.9%).

The cross-tabulation percentages can also be computed by column. Table 10.9 contains the first two columns from the original cross-tab table with column

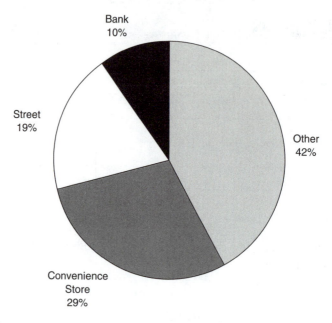

Percent of Robbery by Type (N=271)

Bank
10%

Street
19%

Other
42%

Convenience
Store
29%

Figure 10.2 Pie Chart: Percentage of Robbery by Type ($N = 271$)

Table 10.8 Cross-Tabulation of Number and Percentage of Type of Robbery by Beat: Row

	Bank	Street	Convenience Store	Carjacking	Other	Total
Beat 1	5	7	11	2	21	46
Percentage	10.9	15.2	23.9	4.3	45.7	100.0
Beat 2	1	4	8	0	10	23
Percentage	4.3	17.4	34.8	0.0	43.5	100.0

percentages that compare robbery types by beats. That is, Beat 4 accounts for 40% of all bank robberies and 30% of all street robberies (even though the actual number for bank robberies is lower).

Percentile

Percentages are also used to determine **percentile**, or a value above and below which certain percentages of cases lie. For example, when a student's score on a test

Table 10.9   Cross-Tabulation of Number and Percentage of Type of Robbery by
                   Beat: Column

	Bank	*Percentage*	*Street*	*Percentage*
Beat 1	5	*20*	7	*14*
Beat 2	1	*4*	4	*8*
Beat 3	6	*24*	10	*20*
Beat 4	10	*40*	15	*30*
Beat 5	0	*0*	4	*8*
Beat 6	1	*4*	6	*12*
Beat 7	2	*8*	4	*8*
Total	**25**	*100*	**50**	*100*

is in the 95th percentile, that means that the student has scored higher than 95%
and lower than 5% of other students taking that test. Percentile is computed from
the cumulative percentage of ordered data (e.g., test scores, months, age, income)
through addition of the percentages in the ordered sequence. Table 10.10 illustrates
the number of robberies per month (ordered values) as well as the percentage and
the cumulative percentage for each month. For example, the cumulative percentage
of April is 38.75%, which is the sum of January (11.44%), February (8.49%), March
(8.12%), and April (10.70%).

Percentiles are computed from cumulative percentages. For example, in Table
10.10, 57.20% of the cases are below June, which really means that 57.20% of the
robberies occurred before the end of June. This is interesting, given that one might
expect only half of the robberies to occur before the end of June, as that marks the
end of half of the year. Percentiles are often presented in terms of particular values
called *quartiles*—that is, the 25th, 50th, and 75th percentiles—or the 95th percentile,
as in the test score example above. In the example displayed in Table 10.10, the 95th
percentile occurs sometime in December, so this information is not useful. In crime
analysis, the exact cumulative percentage is most often used to indicate the percentile. For instance, using the example in Table 10.10, it is more realistic to say that
just over 90% of the robberies occurred before December 1 than it is to say that 95%
occurred "sometime in December."

The 50th percentile is also the **median**—that is, the value or potential value
(in that it does not necessarily occur in the distribution) above and below which
one half of all the values lie. In this example, the median month is June, because
50% comes between 47.60% and 57.20%. Again, in the case of crime analysis, where
the 50th percentile lies might not be as important in practice as knowing that more
robberies occurred in the first half of the year than in the second.

Table 10.10 Number, Percentage, and Cumulative Percentage of Robbery by Month

Month	Number of Robberies	Percentage	Cumulative Percentage
January	31	11.44	11.44
February	23	8.49	19.93
March	22	8.12	28.04
April	29	10.70	38.75
May	24	8.86	47.60
June	26	9.59	57.20
July	19	7.01	64.21
August	15	5.54	69.74
September	18	6.64	76.38
October	20	7.38	83.76
November	19	7.01	90.77
December	25	9.23	100.00
Total	**271**	**100.00**	

Rates

A **rate** is another statistic that is derived from frequency. In calculating rate, one variable (the denominator) is used to determine the relative difference between values of another variable (the numerator). In geographic information systems, this is often called *normalizing*. The rate used in crime analysis that is most recognizable to the layperson is crime rate, which is the number of crimes (numerator) in an area divided by the population (denominator) of that area.

Table 10.11 contains the frequency of robberies by beat and the rate per person (computed by dividing the number of robberies by the number of people). Notice that the number of robberies per person is a fraction and thus hard to understand (i.e., How can there be .011 robberies?). This is why crime rates are reported by 1,000s, 10,000s, or 100,000s (e.g., the number of robberies per 1,000 persons). To arrive at these rates, analysts multiply the rates of the crimes of interest by the chosen number of persons. In this table, notice that even though Beat 4 has the highest number of robberies (84), the robbery rate in Beat 4 (7.88) is not the highest because that area also has a large population. On the other hand, Beat 1 has significantly fewer robberies than Beat 4 (46), but its rate is much higher (11.47) because its population is lower.

When an analyst is examining a problem, using population to compute a rate may not always provide the most relevant information for comparison of levels of

Table 10.11   Number and Rate of Robberies per Population

Beat	Number of Robberies	Population	Robberies per Person	Robberies per 1,000 Persons
Beat 1	46	4,012	0.011466	11.47
Beat 2	23	8,752	0.002628	2.63
Beat 3	49	6,499	0.007540	7.54
Beat 4	84	10,659	0.007881	7.88
Beat 5	12	2,310	0.005195	5.19
Beat 6	19	2,564	0.007410	7.41
Beat 7	38	3,984	0.009538	9.54
Total	**271**	**38,780**	**0.006988**	**6.99**

the problem. For instance, it would not be appropriate to use population to compare commercial burglaries over several areas because people do not live at commercial businesses. A commercial burglary rate by population would show high rates in commercially zoned areas because the population counts would be low. In contrast, a rate of commercial burglaries by number of commercial businesses would show the relative number of burglaries in the areas according to the number of relevant targets, as seen in Table 10.12.

Analysts compute crime rates for other particular problems by using the appropriate variables for the comparisons they want to make. For example:

- Per dwelling or apartment unit (e.g., to compare the number of residential burglaries, because the target is the residential unit, not the number of people living in it)
- Per room (e.g., to compare hotels and motels of different sizes)
- Per building (e.g., to compare commercial districts by their relative size)
- Per square foot (e.g., to compare commercial areas in which buildings contain multiple floors of commercial space)
- Per capacity (e.g., to compare bars, nightclubs, or other service establishments, given that actual number of patrons is difficult to measure; note that occupancy rate and square foot are correlated and thus measure essentially the same thing)
- Per parking space (e.g., to compare parking lots, given that the number of spaces in a lot determines how many cars it can hold)
- Per acre (e.g., to compare parks or other land masses)
- Per building permit (e.g., to compare number of burglaries at construction sites by how many houses are under construction)

Table 10.12   Number and Rate of Burglaries per Target

Beat	Number of Burglaries	Number of Targets	Burglaries per 100 Targets
Beat 1	164	131	125.01
Beat 2	82	75	109.17
Beat 3	174	130	134.18
Beat 4	299	348	85.93
Beat 5	43	84	50.86
Beat 6	68	286	23.65
Beat 7	135	212	63.81
Total	965	1,266	76.21

Using such alternatives to determine rates does not always solve the comparison problem, however. For example, using parking spaces to determine relative size of a parking lot does not account for how much the parking lot is used. Other information, such as the length of time per day the parking lot is open and the amount of cars typically in the parking lot, would be more useful for comparison purposes. However, some kinds of information can be difficult to obtain and update regularly, so analysts may have to rely on the best type they can get; when they do so, they should use caution in communicating their results.

Crime analysts use three rates regularly to compare local crime problems with national crime problems as well as to describe particular general problems: crime rate, clearance rate, and recovery rate. A crime rate is typically the number of crimes in an area divided by the number of people living in the area. However, official crime rate figures are not that simple. The "crime rate" typically reported by police agencies and the FBI through the Uniform Crime Reports (UCR) program is called the **index crime rate. Index crimes** are *only* those crimes that the UCR tracks: homicide, rape, robbery, aggravated assault, burglary, larceny, motor vehicle theft, and arson. The index crime rate does not take into account any other types of crimes. Therefore, when analysts use UCR crime rates for comparison, they must be careful to compare only those index crime types.

The index crime rate is typically reported as the number of index crimes per 100,000 persons (number of index crimes divided by population, and the result multiplied by 100,000). At the local level, however, reporting crime rate by 100,000 persons may not be appropriate, especially in communities with populations smaller than 100,000 (i.e., reporting crime rate per 100,000 would give the impression that more crimes are occurring than actually are). If a town of 50,000 residents has 3,000 index crimes, this computes to an index crime rate of 6,000 crimes per 100,000 persons. Although it is important that analysts use "per 100,000" rates when comparing crime levels in their jurisdictions with national or state levels, those working in smaller jurisdictions can examine rates per 10,000 or 1,000 persons, depending on which is most relevant for comparing crime rates of smaller areas within a particular jurisdiction (e.g., census tracts, beats, precincts).

Another issue that crime analysts need to consider in using index crime rates at the local level is the distinction between property crime and persons crime. Most people think that violent crime is more common than property crime, even though the reverse is true. For example, in 2002, law enforcement agencies across the United States reported a total of 1,426,325 violent crimes to the FBI; in the same year, they reported 10,450,893 property crimes (FBI, 2003). Crime analysts need to be careful to separate the two types of crime into two different rates to avoid misinterpretation.

Another significant factor in the examination of a problem is the **clearance rate.** The Uniform Crime Report program acknowledges two ways in which crimes are cleared: (a) by arrest and (b) by exceptional means. A crime is cleared by arrest if at least one person is arrested for the crime, charged with the commission of the crime, and turned over to the court for prosecution. The UCR counts the number of crimes cleared, not the number of individuals arrested; the arrest of one individual may clear several crimes, and the arrest of many individuals may clear only one crime. A crime is cleared by exceptional means if circumstances beyond police control prevent the clearing of the crime by arrest. For the UCR program to count a crime as cleared by exceptional means, the police agency must have the following: knowledge of the offender's identity; enough evidence to support arresting, charging, and turning over the offender to the court for prosecution; and knowledge of the offender's exact location so that law enforcement can make an arrest (FBI, 2003). Examples of exceptional clearance include death of the offender, victim's refusal to prosecute, and denial of extradition.

Clearance rates are typically reported as percentages. For example, if 200 robberies were reported in the past year and 90 of them were cleared, the clearance rate would be 45 per 100 robberies, or 45%. Like national crime rates, national clearance rates are based on index crimes only. When analyzing problems, crime analysts use clearance rates to determine the numbers of cases for which arrests have been made and to compare local to national rates (e.g., to see if the local clearance rate of a crime is much lower than the national rate).

Finally, the **recovery rate** is the percentage of vehicles that have been stolen in a jurisdiction and subsequently recovered (i.e., found) anywhere. Analysts use this rate to help understand the nature of an auto theft problem. For instance, if the recovery rate in a city is 90% (i.e., 9 out of 10 stolen cars are later found), it is clear that the city's auto theft problem does not primarily involve offenders who dismantle cars for resale of parts.

Mean and Standard Deviation

The mean, also known as the average, is the sum of the values of a variable divided by the number of values. It is used with ratio or interval variables. It is important to compute the **standard deviation** along with the mean because it provides, in simple terms, a standardized, average variation of the values from the mean

---

Table 10.13   Cross-Tabulation of Robbery by Month and Year

Month	2001	2002	2003
January	12	13	19
February	16	11	23
March	6	5	15
April	3	8	19
May	7	6	18
June	14	5	26
July	4	16	31
August	12	46	22
September	12	51	24
October	11	45	20
November	9	10	29
December	13	4	25

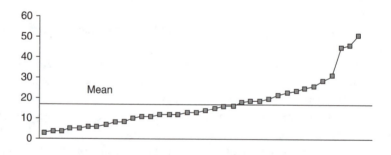

Figure 10.3   Robbery by Month (Lowest to Highest) and Mean Line

and helps indicate the shape of a data distribution. Table 10.13 is a cross-tabulation of robbery by month and year. The average number of robberies per month for the 3 years shown is 16.94, and there are some very large and small numbers in the distribution (e.g., 51 and 3). The standard deviation for these data is 11.89, indicating that the distribution is skewed (i.e., there are not equal numbers of values above and below the mean). Figure 10.3 is a depiction of the values in the distribution of months, sorted lowest (3) to highest (51), along with a line representing the mean value of all the months. By charting the actual values, we can see that most of them are below the mean and that 3 months are much higher than the others (on the right of the chart), distorting the mean.

If we were to remove those three unusually high values (called *outliers*), the mean for the distribution would change from 16.94 to 14.18 and the standard

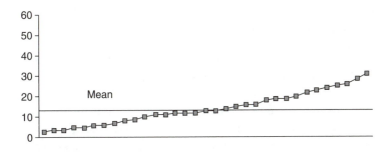

Figure 10.4   Robbery by Month (Lowest to Highest) and Mean Line: Outliers
Removed

deviation would change from 11.89 to 7.71, indicating that the values are more
closely clustered around the mean. The distribution would look like Figure 10.4.
However, an analyst cannot simply remove cases from a distribution; this example
is offered only to show how extreme numbers can affect the mean. As this illustrates, the mean may not be the most appropriate statistic to use to describe distributions that include extreme outliers.

Normally, numbers that are more than two standard deviations from the mean are
considered outliers. In crime analysis, outliers can indicate unusually high amounts
of activity that require further examination. In the first example, the mean plus
two standard deviations is 40.72 (16.94 + 11.89 + 11.89 = 40.72), which indicates that
any months with more than 41 robberies are outliers (e.g., August, September, and
October 2002) and may require further analysis.

The following are additional examples of ways in which an analyst can use mean
and standard deviation to understand the nature of a problem:

- The average number of incidents (e.g., different types of crimes and calls)
  per area
- The average number of incidents per month
- The average number of incidents per week
- The average age of victims
- The average age of offenders
- The average crime rate per area
- The average number of calls for service per apartment unit in the city

Crime analysts use mean and standard deviation primarily with data sets that
include more than 35 cases. These statistics are less reliable for describing data sets
with fewer than 35 cases, because 1 or 2 unusual cases can significantly influence the
final results. This is not a hard-and-fast rule, however, and analysts should closely
examine the results of the statistics in every database, especially smaller ones.

Summary Points

This chapter has provided a definition of the term *problem* in the context
of crime analysis and has discussed the techniques that crime analysts use to gain

understanding of the context and current nature of a problem. The following are the key points addressed in this chapter:

- A problem is a recurring set of related harmful events in a community that members of the public expect the police to address. A problem differs from an incident (one event that occurs over minutes, hours, or, in rare cases, days) and from a pattern (a group of events that are similar in nature that occur over several days, weeks, or months) in that the set of related activity that makes up a problem occurs over several months, seasons, or years and includes multiple incidents and patterns.
- In order to make sure that a problem is identified correctly and distinguished accurately from other problems, the crime analyst must classify two major characteristics of the problem: the environment in which it occurs and the type of behavior associated with it.
- Environments regulate the targets available, the activities in which people can engage, and who controls the location. The types of environments are as follows: residential, recreational, offices, retail, industrial, agricultural, educational, human service, public ways, transport, and open/transitional.
- By specifying the behaviors associated with a problem, the crime analyst can help to pinpoint important aspects of harm, intent, and offender-target relationships. The types of behavior are as follows: predatory, consensual, conflicts, incivilities, endangerment, and misuse of police.
- Once a problem has been identified, strategic crime analysis begins with an understanding of the context of a problem. An analyst investigates three general areas in order to understand the context of a problem: (a) information about the types and amount of data available for analysis, (b) information about the nature of the police agency and the community it serves, and (c) information about the problem from other police agencies and communities, national findings, and academic research for comparison.
- In addition to understanding the context, the crime analyst must get a sense of the nature of the problem. This begins with the application of a variety of statistical techniques to the study of available data; the statistics used include frequency or count, cross-tabulation, percentage, rate, and average.
- The frequency or count is the number of all categories of a variable. The value with the highest frequency within a variable is the mode. By displaying frequencies in descending order, an analyst can view counts easily as well as determine the mode.
- A cross-tabulation (or cross-tab) is a count of two variables at once.
- A percentage is the proportion of the count of one category by the count of all categories of a variable multiplied by 100.
- For every cross-tabulation table of frequencies, the corresponding percentages can also be computed; this enables analysts to compare variables with different values.
- A percentile is a value above and below which certain percentages of cases lie. The 50th percentile is also known as the median.
- A rate uses one variable (the denominator) to determine the relative difference between values of another variable (the numerator). In the most common

use of rates, population serves as the denominator. However, this is not always appropriate for studying problems, and other denominators are also used in crime analysis.

- Crime analysts use three rates regularly: index crime rate, clearance rate, and recovery rate.
- The mean is the sum of the values of a variable divided by the number of values. It is used with ratio or interval variables and should be reserved for use with data sets having relatively large numbers of cases because it is very sensitive to unusually large or small values.
- It is important to compute the standard deviation along with the mean because it provides, in simple terms, the average variation of the values from the mean and indicates the shape of a data distribution.

Exercises

Exercise 10.1

Using Clarke and Eck's (2003) classifications of the environments of problems and the behaviors involved in problems, develop a matrix and place the following problems in the appropriate categories (note that these categories are taken from the titles of POP Guides available from the Center for Problem-Oriented Policing at http://www.popcenter.org).

- Assaults in and around bars
- Acquaintance rape of college students
- Bullying in schools
- Loud car stereos
- Burglary of retail establishments
- Burglary of single-family houses
- Rave parties
- Robbery at automated teller machines
- Disorderly youth in public places
- Drug dealing in privately owned apartment complexes
- Speeding in residential areas
- Street prostitution
- Thefts of and from cars in parking facilities
- Disorder in budget motels
- Robbery of taxi drivers
- Student party disturbances on college campuses
- Bomb threats against schools
- Sexual activity in public places
- School break-ins
- Open-air drug dealing
- Bank robbery
- Street racing

Exercise 10.2

Fill in the numbers that should appear in the final column of this table:

Beat	Number of Robberies	Population	Robberies per Person	Robberies per 10,000 Persons
Beat 1	46	4,012	0.011466	
Beat 2	23	8,752	0.002628	
Beat 3	49	6,499	0.007540	
Beat 4	84	10,659	0.007881	
Beat 5	12	2,310	0.005195	
Beat 6	19	2,564	0.007410	
Beat 7	38	3,984	0.009538	
Total	**271**	**38,780**	**0.006988**	

Note

1. The best source of information about problems addressed in strategic crime analysis comes from a project funded by the Center for Problem-Oriented Policing in which prominent researchers in policing compile all the relevant research findings and practical information about individual problems and synthesize this material into relatively short, straightforward reports called POP Guides. For more information and access to the POP Guides, visit the POP Center's Web site at http://www.popcenter.org.

11

Analyzing Problems

*Temporal Analysis, Victimization,
and Primary Data Collection*

In addition to the context and general nature of problems, strategic crime analysis focuses on the temporal nature of problems, on victims and repeat victimization, and on the collection of data specific to particular problems. This chapter describes the techniques or tools that analysts use to study the temporal and victim-related aspects of problems and to collect primary data on problems.

Temporal Analysis

Temporal analysis is the analysis of data in relation to units of time. In general, tactical crime analysts examine small numbers of cases in relatively short time periods (using a method known as time series analysis), such as hours and days, whereas strategic crime analysts examine larger numbers of cases over short time periods (e.g., time of day/day of week) as well as over longer periods, such as weeks, months, seasons, and years. Temporal analysis is important for understanding problems because it establishes baselines of activity and can reveal new trends, such as increases and decreases in problem activity. The discussion of temporal analysis techniques in this chapter is introductory; the techniques presented are relevant for most crime analysis data, because the majority of such data have some type of temporal variable.

By Year

The largest time unit used in strategic crime analysis to describe a problem is a year. Most crime statistics collected on a national level and by local police agencies are tabulated by year, allowing analysts to make comparisons to previous years and across jurisdictions. Different types of statistics can be computed and displayed according to temporal variables (e.g., frequency of crime, crime rate, and average crime). In addition, temporal variables are normally displayed in line charts, because this is a

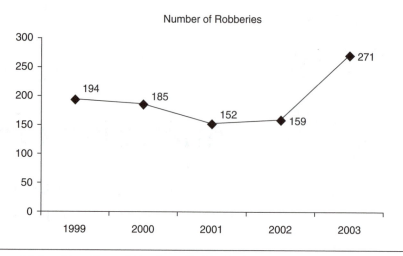

Figure 11.1 Line Chart of Number of Robberies by Year

clear way to show continuity and chronological order. Crime analysts typically do not use bar charts for this purpose, because such charts imply distinct categories within variables. Figure 11.1 is an illustration of a line chart showing the frequency of robbery for 5 years.

Another comparison by year might include robbery rates of cities of similar size and nature (e.g., rural vs. urban). Table 11.1 provides the information necessary to make a chart comparing the rate of robbery per 100,000 persons in a city to the national rate. The table shows that City Y began with a higher rate than the country in 1999 and 2000, but the rate has been lower in the most recent years. In the last year shown, there was a significant jump in both population and robberies; however, the population growth has not been as high as the increase in robberies, resulting in a relatively high rate (199.3). Unfortunately, national figures are not available as quickly as local figures, so it is not possible to tell whether the nation had the same increase in robbery in 2003. Although this table provides sufficient information about robbery rates, displaying the data in the form of a line graph, as in Figure 11.2, allows a viewer to understand the information at a glance.

By Month or Quarter

Crime analysts report statistics as well as study problems by month, as do most businesses and other organizations. A month is a small enough unit of time to allow the analysis of variation over a year, and at the same time it is large enough to produce a sufficient amount of data to examine. Crime analysts also study statistics by quarter (i.e., a period of 3 months) when the numbers by month are too small to analyze. Analysts use the techniques described here when examining data for both month and quarter.

Figure 11.3 illustrates the number of robberies by month for the past 3 years. Notice that this figure contains many more data points than Figure 11.1, resulting

Table 11.1   Number of Robberies, City Rate, and National Rate

Year	Number of Robberies	City Y Population	City Y Rate	National Rate
1999	194	120,000	161.7	150.1
2000	185	122,000	151.6	144.9
2001	152	125,000	121.6	148.5
2002	159	126,000	126.2	145.9
2003	271	136,000	199.3	Not available

SOURCE: U.S. robbery rates obtained through the FBI's Web site at http://www.fbi.gov.

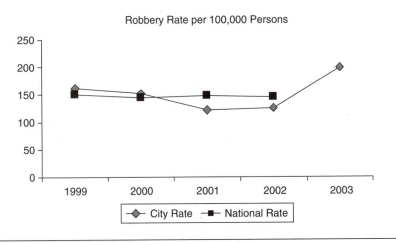

Figure 11.2   Chart Comparing City and National Robbery Rates

in peaks and valleys within the year. This type of chart allows the analyst to make month-to-month and seasonal comparisons (e.g., holiday season, summer). For example, from Figure 11.3, it appears that the number of robberies is relatively low in the period from March through May each year.

Another way of showing these data is to depict the totals for the same months alongside one another, so that monthly patterns are visible over many years, as in Figure 11.4. This figure indicates that each year robberies increase in June. Another common way of presenting data by month is to show only a single year by month for a particular crime, so that increases and decreases within that year are easily compared, as in Figure 11.5.

One problem with using months to identify variations in problem activity is that months are not equal units—they vary in length from 28 to 31 days. A 3-day period can make a big difference in monthly counts of crime and other activity. One way

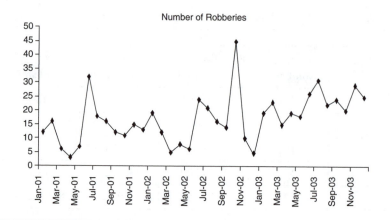

Figure 11.3   Number of Robberies by Month

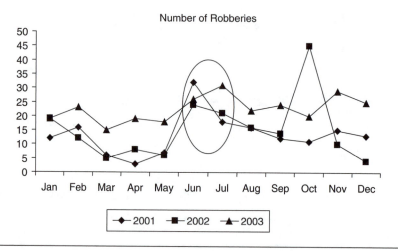

Figure 11.4   Number of Robberies: Comparison of Months for 3 Years

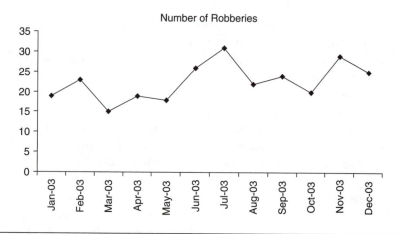

Figure 11.5   Number of Robberies by Month: 1 Year

Table 11.2   Average Number of Robberies per Day by Month

Month	Number of Robberies	Average Robberies per Day
January 2003	19	0.61
February 2003	23	0.82
March 2003	15	0.48
April 2003	19	0.63
May 2003	18	0.58
June 2003	26	0.87
July 2003	31	1.00
August 2003	22	0.71
September 2003	24	0.80
October 2003	20	0.65
November 2003	29	0.97
December 2003	25	0.81
Total	**271**	

in which crime analysts correct for this problem is by computing the mean number of occurrences of the activity of interest per day for each month. In this example, instead of January and February having robbery frequencies of 19 and 23, respectively, they have averages of .61 and .82 (i.e., 19 divided by 31 and 23 divided by 28) per day. Table 11.2 and Figure 11.6 illustrate the rate of robberies per day for each month.

By Week

Another problem with using month as the time unit for analysis is that months vary in the numbers of individual weekdays they contain; that is, one month may contain five Fridays and the next month may have only four. These variations can affect the counts of certain types of activity that are particularly heavy on weekends as opposed to weekdays, for example. Analysts address this problem by comparing time periods by intervals of set numbers of weeks (e.g., 4-week, 2-week, or 1-week intervals). Within such intervals, each unit of time has the same amount of days and the same types of days (e.g., four Fridays, four Saturdays). Figure 11.7 shows the same data as Figure 11.6, but displayed by 4-week periods instead of by months. Notice how the values within Figure 11.7 are smoother, with less extreme jumps from one time period to the next, because there are more data points and they are equal in length and in types of days. In conducting temporal analysis, crime analysts

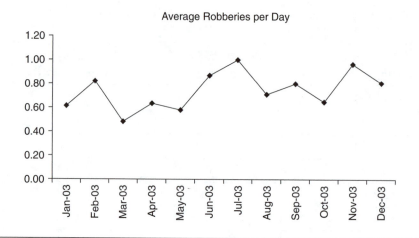

Figure 11.6   Chart: Average Number of Robberies per Day by Month

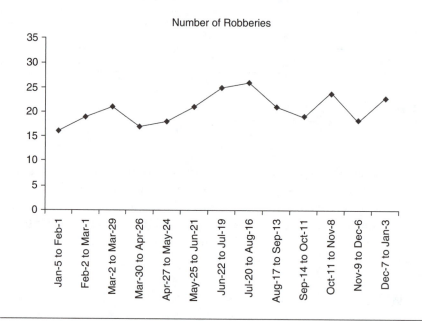

Figure 11.7   Number of Robberies per 4-Week Period

need to be careful to select appropriate time units—that is, units that will provide enough data in each unit to allow them to draw substantive conclusions.

By Time of Day/Day of Week

Both tactical crime analysts and strategic crime analysts examine data by time of day and day of the week. This technique is appropriate in tactical crime analysis in certain situations (as discussed in Chapter 9), but it is even more useful in strategic crime analysis because more cases are available. Table 11.3 contains data on the

Table 11.3   Cross-Tabulation of Robberies by Time of Day and Day of Week

	Sunday	Monday	Tuesday	Wednesday	Thursday	Friday	Saturday	Total
Midnight	8				3	1	10	22
1:00 A.M.	10	2	3	4	1	2	6	28
2:00 A.M.	2		1		1		4	8
3:00 A.M.								0
4:00 A.M.								0
5:00 A.M.		1			2			3
6:00 A.M.				1		1	1	3
7:00 A.M.	2						1	3
8:00 A.M.			3					3
9:00 A.M.		1		2		1		4
10:00 A.M.			1	3	1			5
11:00 A.M.			2		3		3	8
Noon		1						1
1:00 P.M.	5				3	4	3	15
2:00 P.M.	1		2			2		5
3:00 P.M.		4		2			1	7
4:00 P.M.	2				1			3
5:00 P.M.							2	2
6:00 P.M.						2		2
7:00 P.M.	2	3	5	1			2	13
8:00 P.M.	4		2	2		4	5	17
9:00 P.M.	1	5	2	3	5	11	15	42
10:00 P.M.	4	2	6	4	9	9	12	46
11:00 P.M.	3	4	2	1	7	8	6	31
Total	**44**	**23**	**29**	**23**	**36**	**45**	**71**	**271**

frequency of robberies over the past year by time of day and day of the week, and the chart in Figure 11.8 illustrates these data. Analysis of Figure 11.8 indicates that over the past year robberies have occurred throughout the week between 8:00 P.M. and 11:00 P.M. and have been more frequent on Fridays and Saturdays during those times.

Weighted Time Span Analysis

The weighted time span method, as described in Chapter 9, is also useful for determining temporal patterns of problems for which the exact times of occurrence

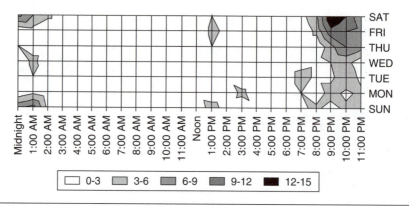

Figure 11.8   Chart: Robberies by Time of Day and Day of Week

are not known. This is frequently the case for property crimes such as burglary, auto theft, and vandalism, which are often not discovered until some time after the crimes have taken place. Figures 11.9 and 11.10 show the time spans for commercial and residential burglaries over a 1-year period, with 250 and 175 burglaries, respectively. It is easy to discern general patterns from these charts and to make comparisons between the two types of burglaries (e.g., commercial burglaries are occurring at night and residential burglaries are occurring primarily during the day).

Percentage Change

Percentage change is the amount of relative increase or decrease between two values over two time periods. That is, it expresses the amount of change as a proportion of the value at the first time period (Time 1), or the difference between a measurement at Time 1 and a measurement at Time 2, divided by the measurement at Time 1, and then multiplied by 100 (to arrive at a percentage). The formula for arriving at percentage change is as follows:

$$\frac{\text{Time 2} - \text{Time 1}}{\text{Time 1}} \times 100 = \% \text{ Change.}$$

For example, in 2002, 256 crimes were committed in Smalltown, and in 2003, 320 crimes were committed there. The percentage change of crime in Smalltown is computed as follows:

$$\frac{320\,(\text{Time 2}) - 256\,(\text{Time 1})}{256\,(\text{Time 1})} \times 100,$$

or

$$\frac{64}{256} \times 100 = 25\%.$$

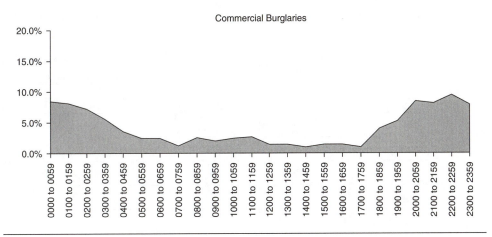

Figure 11.9   Weighted Time Span Chart: Commercial Burglaries

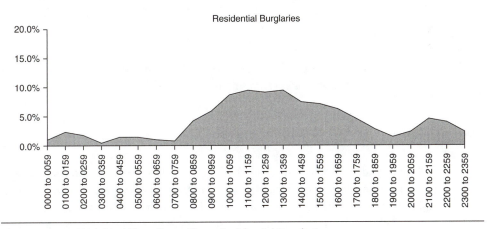

Figure 11.10   Weighted Time Span Chart: Residential Burglaries

Thus Smalltown experienced a 25% increase in crime from 2002 to 2003. Crime analysts examine percentage changes in overall numbers within cities or break down percentage change figures for subsections of cities to determine more specifically where increases and decreases in activity have taken place. Percentage changes can be used for yearly, quarterly, or monthly comparisons. Table 11.4 contains data on the change in frequency and the percentage change of robbery by beat for 2002 and 2003. It shows that even though the overall number of robberies has increased by 70%, the numbers within individual beats have fluctuated differently.

Note that Table 11.4 shows no robberies in Beat 5 in 2002 and "N/A" (for "not applicable") appears in the last column for that beat instead of a percentage change value. This is because one cannot divide a number by zero, thus it is not possible to compute any percentage change for Beat 5. In such a case, the crime analyst must revert to using the actual change in the number, reporting, for example, that "the number of robberies in Beat 5 increased by 12 from 0." Also, note that Beat 6 experienced a 533% increase in robberies, even though the actual increase (16 robberies) is not nearly as high as in some other beats (e.g., 26, 34, 28). The percentage change

Table 11.4   Actual and Percentage Change in Robbery by Beat From 2002 to 2003

Beat	2002	2003	Change	Percentage Change
Beat 1	20	46	26	130
Beat 2	36	23	−13	−36
Beat 3	15	49	34	227
Beat 4	56	84	28	50
Beat 5	0	12	12	N/A
Beat 6	3	19	16	533
Beat 7	29	38	9	31
Total	159	271	112	70

in Beat 6 is high because the value at Time 1 (3) is relatively low, and when numbers are low, even slight increases can result in large percentage change values.

Victims and Repeat Victimization

To understand the underlying causes of crime or disorder problems, analysts need to understand who and/or what the victims of those problems are. Research suggests that "lightning does strike twice"—that is, individuals and targets that are victimized once are likely to be victimized again (Groff & La Vigne, 2002). Thus an understanding of victimization can lead to the prediction and prevention of future victimization. The simplest way in which analysts examine the victimization patterns associated with particular problems is by conducting cross-tabulations of the data. For instance, Table 11.5 displays frequency data on the type of weapon by the type of target for robbery incidents. The table shows that most robberies occur on the street (27.68%) and are committed with a gun (53.14%). More specifically, more than half of the robberies that have occurred in retail stores have involved the use of knives (10 of 19 robberies), which is a different pattern than is found for the rest of the targets. Such a difference might indicate the need for further analysis.

The term *repeat victimization* refers to patterns of activity in which there is a "recurrence of crime in the same places and/or against the same people" (Pease, 1998, p. 1). As discussed in Chapter 5, repeat victimizations can be divided into four types: hot dots (i.e., people as repeat victims and offenders), hot products (i.e., products as victims), hot spots (i.e., areas with unusually high amounts of activity), and hot targets (i.e., types of places that are repeatedly victimized). Crime analysts use these categories to identify the types of repeat victimization that are occurring within particular problems. Researchers Farrell, Sousa, and Weisel (2002) recommend that

Table 11.5   Cross-Tabulation of Robberies by Type of Target and Type of Weapon

| Type of Target | Type of Weapon Used | | | | | |
	Gun	Knife	Hands	Other	Total	Percentage
Bank	15	3	5	2	25	9.23
Convenience store	29	11	7	3	50	18.45
Street	46	19	8	2	75	27.68
Carjacking	10	2	0	0	12	4.43
Fast-food restaurant	9	6	2	2	19	7.01
Liquor store	12	4	1	5	22	8.12
Retail store	3	10	5	1	19	7.01
Others	20	16	10	3	49	18.08
Total	**144**	**71**	**38**	**18**	**271**	**100.00**
Percentage	**53.14**	**26.20**	**14.02**	**6.64**	**100.00**	

analysts use at least 3 years of data in determining repeat victimization. That is, analysts should look for duplicate individuals or places in data sets covering 3 years. Ideally, those 3 years would be "rolling." For example, for a victimization occurring on December 15, 2001, the analyst would examine data from December 15, 2001, through December 15, 2004, for repeats, and for a victimization occurring on January 29, 2002, the analyst would look at data from January 29, 2002, through January 29, 2005. Thus the date of each victimization would dictate the data examined. However, when obtaining data for 3 years is not realistic, analysts studying repeat victimization should examine at least 1 year of data (i.e., counting repeat victimizations within a year from the first incident).

A concept closely related to that of repeat victimization is the "80/20 rule." As discussed in Chapter 5, this concept comes from the observation that 80% of some kinds of outcomes are the results of only 20% of the related causes. The numbers 80 and 20 in the name of this "rule" are meant only to represent "large" and "small" amounts; the actual proportions change depending on the type of activity and nature of the community in which it occurs. Clarke and Eck (2003) recommend that a crime analyst take the following steps to determine whether the 80/20 rule is operating in regard to a given problem:

- Identify the people or places the rule might apply to.
- Get a list of these people or places with a count of the number of events associated with each person or place.
- Rank order the people or places according to the number of events associated with each—most to least.

Table 11.6 80%/20% Calculation for Robberies by Address

1	2	3	4	5	6	7
Rank	Address	Number of Robberies	Percentage of Robberies	Cumulative Percentage of Robberies	Percentage of Addresses (N = 106)	Cumulative Percentage of Addresses
1	134 E Main St	25	9.23	9.23	0.94	0.94
2	254 S Clover Av	17	6.27	15.50	0.94	1.89
3	8012 N Grand Blvd	15	5.54	21.03	0.94	2.83
4	8210 N Grand Blvd	10	3.69	24.72	0.94	3.77
5	1430 E Main St	9	3.32	28.04	0.94	4.72
6	365 W Haverty Rd	9	3.32	31.37	0.94	5.66
7	3401 N Staple Dr	8	2.95	34.32	0.94	6.60
8	210 S Daisy Rd	7	2.58	36.90	0.94	7.55
9	4598 N Roan Rd	5	1.85	38.75	0.94	8.49
10	132 E Main St	5	1.85	40.59	0.94	9.43
	Addresses with 4 (N = 5)	20	7.38	47.97	4.72	14.15
	Addresses with 3 (N = 15)	45	16.61	64.58	14.15	28.30
	Addresses with 2 (N = 20)	40	14.76	79.34	18.87	47.17
	Addresses with 1 (N = 56)	56	20.66	100.00	52.83	100.00
	Total	271	100.00		100.00	

- Calculate the percentages of the events each person or place contributes.
- Cumulate the percentages starting with the most involved person or place.
- Calculate the proportion of the people or places each single person or place represents.
- Compare the cumulative percentage of people or places to the cumulative percentage of outcomes. (Step 19)

Table 11.6 presents an example of this kind of calculation for robberies (victimizations) by addresses (victims) for an entire year. The following list describes each column of the table and how the method was conducted:

- *Column 1:* A rank of the addresses with the most incidents (victimizations). The rankings reflect descending frequency.
- *Column 2:* The list of addresses, which are sorted by descending frequency of robberies. Note that after the first 10 addresses, the specific addresses are not listed. "Addresses with 4 (N = 5)" means that there were five addresses with four robberies each, and so on.

- *Column 3:* The descending frequencies of robbery by address (the number of victimizations).
- *Column 4:* The percentage of the total for the count of robberies at an address.
- *Column 5:* The cumulative percentage of robberies for each address (this is a key field for analysis results).
- *Column 6:* The percentage each address is of all addresses. In this example there are 106 addresses (see column 2: $10 + 5 + 15 + 20 + 56 = 106$), so each address is 1/106 or .94% of the total (victims).
- *Column 7:* The cumulative percentage of addresses (this is a key field for analysis results).
- *Row shaded gray:* Look to columns 5 and 7 to determine that 40.59% of the robberies are occurring at 9.43% of the addresses. Any row can be used to show repeat victimization, depending on the numbers and the purpose of the analysis (e.g., 47.97% of the robberies occur at 14.15% of the addresses, or 64.58% of the robberies occur at 28.30% of the addresses).

To use this method for other types of activity, an analyst would replace counts for *robberies* and their corresponding *addresses*.

Primary Data Collection

Secondary data such as crime reports and information on calls for service and arrests do not always answer important questions about problems. Because of this, crime analysts often have to collect primary data—that is, information collected for specific analysis purposes directly from individuals or locations. Most often, crime analysts conduct **primary data collection** through interviews, either with individuals with groups; surveys of larger groups, such as citizens and police officers; and observation of places (e.g., buildings, blocks, areas). The following are some examples of primary data collection techniques that crime analysts have used or might use:

- In analyzing a crime problem at local motels, analysts interviewed maids at the motels to help determine how the rooms were used by patrons staying in them (e.g., determined by the condition of the room and the garbage left behind) (Schmerler & Velasco, 2002).
- A crime analyst conducts an annual survey of citizens in the local area to determine their rates of victimization, attitudes toward police, quality of life, fear of crime, and crime prevention behaviors. The citizens are selected randomly, and the analyst uses the survey results to help determine problems in need of attention and to contribute to current crime prevention efforts.
- After a safety problem is identified involving crimes occurring around schools and along paths to and from schools used by elementary school children as well as areas where children hang out before and after school, crime analysts conduct observation to determine exactly where the children's pathways before and after school and their hangouts are located. The analysts

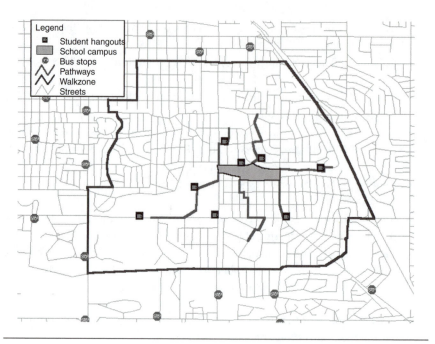

Figure 11.11 Map of Student Pathways to School and Hangouts

then enter the locations of these pathways and hangouts into a geographic information system and analyze them in relation to crime in the area (see Figure 11.11). They also use the information to scan for other problems and to identify intersections that are unsafe for children to cross.

- Crime analysts conduct surveys of burglary victims to find out about any crime prevention methods the victims may have used (Schmerler & Velasco, 2002).
- A crime analyst conducts a focus group interview with construction site building supervisors to gather data on their building practices, current victimizations, and crime reporting methods.
- An analyst interviews repeat victims of auto theft to understand the crime prevention methods they now undertake and their expectations of police response.
- Analysts interview offenders who have been arrested for tagging to learn more about graffiti and tagging practices and the culture of taggers.
- A crime analyst studying the problem of thefts from parking lots conducts observation to determine how many vehicles in particular parking lots are locked, how many have antitheft devices, how many have valuables left in view, and so on.
- To conduct an analysis of crimes per parking space in parking lots in the city, analysts collect information from the lots' owners regarding the lots' boundaries, numbers of parking spaces, and the addresses attributed to them.
- To help determine whether the level of crime in high crime areas of the city is related to lighting, analysts collect information on the amount of lighting along streets, in parking lots, and in commercial areas.

- A crime analyst observes apartment communities to determine whether their environmental design aspects (e.g., access control, natural surveillance, target hardening) are related to high levels of auto theft and theft from autos.

Even though analysts collect primary data directly from individuals and places, before they can use those data to perform systematic analysis and compare them with the data collected subsequently, they must quantify their results by creating coding standards, creating databases, and entering the data. The following example illustrates this process.

Problem: You are a crime analyst who has been asked to help assess a chronic problem of thefts from autos and auto theft at several local apartment communities.

Methodology: In order to understand victim behavior, you decide to gather data about the security habits of the residents who park at one of the affected communities. You create a short survey to guide your observation of cars in the parking lot:

1. Is any door of the vehicle unlocked?	Yes	No
2. Is any window of the vehicle open?	Yes	No
3. Are there any valuables in view within the car (e.g., cash, cell phone, purse)?	Yes	No
4. Is there an antitheft device?	Yes	No
4a. If so, what type?	Steering/alarm lock	No Other

You then code the results of 250 observations and enter them into a database. Table 11.7 shows several cases and some variables that you would include in the database.

Analysis: By examining the data, you learn that although most people lock their car doors and close the windows when they park, 60% of the cars you observed had valuables in view, and few drivers used alarms. The results indicate that the first step in addressing the problem should be to advise community residents not to leave valuables in view in their parked cars and to use their car alarms. After this step is taken, you can conduct subsequent observations to determine whether the residents in fact change their behavior.

Summary Points

This chapter has described the techniques that crime analysts use to gain an understanding of the temporal nature of problems, to study victims and repeat victimization, and to conduct primary data collection. The following are the key points addressed in this chapter:

Table 11.7 Sample Database: Primary Data Collection

Obs. No.	Door	Window	Valuables	Type of Antitheft	Antitheft
1.	Yes	No	Yes	No	
2.	No	No	Yes	Yes	Steering Lock
3.	No	Yes	No	No	
4.	No	No	No	Yes	Alarm
5.	Yes	Yes	No	Yes	Alarm

- In addition to the context and general nature of problems, strategic crime analysis focuses on the temporal nature of problems, on victims and repeat victimization, and on the collection of data specific to particular problems.
- Temporal analysis is important for understanding problems because it establishes baselines of activity and can reveal new trends, such as increases and decreases in activity related to problems. In strategic crime analysis, the time units of interest include year, quarter, month, week, and time of day/day of week.
- A year is the largest time unit used in strategic crime analysis to describe a problem, most frequently to compare local to state and national statistics.
- The time unit most often used in strategic crime analysis is a month, because jurisdictions typically report counts of crime and other types of events by month.
- Strategic crime analysts use the time unit of a week to examine improvement over the course of a month (or 4 weeks) and to compute statistics (mean and standard deviation).
- Strategic crime analysts use time of day/day of week analysis and weighted time span analysis to determine general patterns over longer periods of time.
- Percentage change is the amount of relative increase or decrease between two values over two time periods. That is, it expresses the amount of change as a proportion of the value at the first time period (Time 1), or the difference between a measurement at Time 1 and a measurement at Time 2, divided by the measurement at Time 1, and then multiplied by 100 (to arrive at a percentage).
- To understand the underlying causes of crime or disorder problems, analysts need to understand who and/or what the victims of those problems are. The simplest way of examining the victimization patterns associated with a particular problem is to conduct cross-tabulations of the data.
- Research suggests that "lightning does strike twice"—that is, individuals and targets that are victimized once are likely to be victimized again. In calculating repeat victimization, analysts should use at least 1 year of data (3 years is preferable). Repeat victimizations can be divided into four types: hot dots, hot products, hot spots, and hot targets.

- According to the 80/20 rule, a relatively small proportion of people, products, and places are responsible for or associated with a high proportion of crimes and other negative actions. This suggests that by focusing their efforts on limited groups of people, targets, or products, police can maximize their impact, making their efforts more cost-effective and worthwhile.
- To establish whether or not the 80/20 rule applies to a specific problem, the crime analyst needs to determine the cumulative percentage of the number of incidents and compare that figure to the cumulative percentage of the number of places, victims, or targets associated with those incidents.
- Official data—such as data from crime reports and information on calls for service and arrests—do not always answer important questions about problems, thus analysts may need to collect information (i.e., primary data) directly from individuals or locations in order to fully understand those problems.
- Most often, crime analysts conduct primary data collection through interviews, either with individuals or with groups; surveys of larger groups, such as citizens or police officers; and observation of places.

Exercises

Exercise 11.1

Select a crime or disorder problem and list the various types of primary data that you might collect to understand the problem better. How would you go about collecting these data, and how would they help you understand the problem?

Exercise 11.2

Using the following table, apply the 80/20 rule to robberies by address.

Rank	Address	Number of Robberies	Percentage of Robberies	Cumulative Percentage of Robberies	Percentage of Addresses (N = 59)	Cumulative Percentage of Addresses
1	134 E Main St	25	12.76	12.76	1.69	1.69
2	254 S Clover Av	17	8.67	21.43	1.69	3.39
3	8012 N Grand Blvd	15	7.65	29.08	1.69	5.08
4	8210 N Grand Blvd	10	5.10	34.18	1.69	6.78
5	1430 E Main St	9	4.59	38.78	1.69	8.47
6	365 W Haverty Rd	9	4.59	43.37	1.69	10.17
7	3401 N Staple Dr	8	4.08	47.45	1.69	11.86
8	210 S Daisy Rd	7	3.57	51.02	1.69	13.56
9	4598 N Roan Rd	5	2.55	53.57	1.69	15.25
10	132 E Main St	5	2.55	56.12	1.69	16.95
	Addresses with 4 (N = 2)	8	4.08	60.20	3.39	20.34
	Addresses with 3 (N = 10)	30	15.31	75.51	16.95	37.29
	Addresses with 2 (N = 11)	22	11.22	86.73	18.64	55.93
	Addresses with 1 (N = 26)	26	13.27	100.00	44.07	100.00
	Total	**196**	**100.00**		**100.00**	

12 Analyzing Problems

Spatial Analysis

Crime analysts take two distinct approaches to the spatial analysis of crime and disorder problems. In the first approach, tabular data and statistics are displayed to show the results of analysis using geographic units of analysis. In the second approach, analysts use the exact locations of incidents to determine hot spots or clusters of activity.

Displaying Data and Statistics

Chapter 3 provided a brief discussion of graduated mapping. This section describes the statistical techniques that crime analysts use to produce graduated symbol and color maps, including categorical, statistical, and manual methods. There are many ways to display data geographically, and it is important that analysts select the methods that are most appropriate to the data and the purposes of their analyses. Thus this section also includes a discussion of how each type of map is used in crime analysis.

By Category

Data can be broken down by category and displayed on a map either as different types of symbols or as symbols in different colors or degrees of shading. Crime analysts use this method primarily for categorical variables, because the values of such variables are nominal rather than numeric. Some examples of categorical variables are race, sex, method of entry, point of entry, weapon used, type of location, type of business, and land use. In this method, the values within each of the variables (e.g., male and female for the sex variable) are illustrated differently.

Shading by categorical value is used only with single-symbol maps and primarily with polygon and point features. Categorical mapping cannot be used with graduated size maps because it requires that each point be shaded according to one categorical value. For example, if two robberies have occurred at one location, a graduated size map would represent that location with a larger point than the

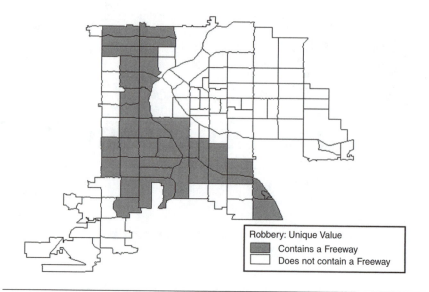

Figure 12.1   Polygon Map Shaded by Whether or Not the Polygon Contains a
Freeway

points used for addresses with one robbery. One cannot then shade that point by
weapon used during the robbery, because different types of weapons may have been
used in the two robberies represented by that single point (e.g., one robbery was
committed with a knife and the other with a gun).

Figure 12.1 is a map that was created for a problem analysis of robbery; the areas
are shaded to indicate whether they contain any interstate highways (i.e., an interstate
provides an offender with a quick way to flee the scene of a robbery). The categorical
variable mapped here is: Is there an interstate in the area? The values that dictate the
different colors are yes (an interstate is present) and no (no interstate is present).
An analyst might use this map with a graduated symbol map of robberies to determine whether more robberies occurred in areas that contain an interstate. The example map in Figure 12.2 uses different symbols (instead of shading) for different types
of businesses. An analyst could use this map in a problem analysis of robbery to help
distinguish among locations regarding their susceptibility to robberies.

By Statistical Classification

A statistical classification used in mapping is a formula that determines the break
points of how the data will be shaded or sized (information about the break points
is displayed in a map's **legend**). The features on a map are distinguished from one
another depending on the classifications into which their values fall. For example,
the colors used to symbolize ranges may be broken down as follows:

- Light gray: 1 to 10 crimes
- Dark gray: 11 to 20 crimes
- Black: 21 to 30 crimes

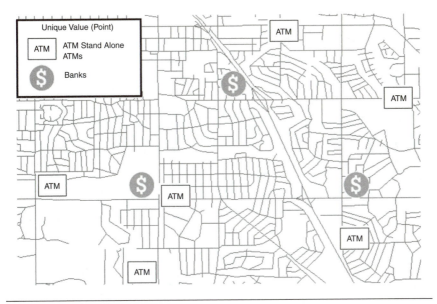

Figure 12.2   Point Map Showing Symbols Indicating Banks or Stand-Alone ATMs

In a map using the above classifications, an area feature, such as a police beat, with 15 crimes would be shaded dark gray. Four statistical classifications are typically used in crime mapping: natural breaks, equal interval, quantile, and standard deviation. Analysts use these classifications for different purposes.

Natural Breaks

An analyst applying the **natural breaks classification** uses geographic information system (GIS) software to identify the natural gaps in the distribution of the data; these gaps are used as the break points for the classifications in the legend. This type of classification is the default in many GIS programs and is one of the types used most frequently in crime analysis. It is most useful for exploratory or descriptive analysis of a snapshot of data (e.g., a general map of a problem) and is not applicable for making comparisons over time.

Figures 12.3, 12.4, and 12.5 are point, line, and polygon maps that illustrate the natural breaks classification. Note that the values of the categories in the legends on these maps seem arbitrary, with intervals that are not equal. That is because the ranges have been decided by a computer program based on break points in the distributions of the variables being mapped.

The graduated point map in Figure 12.3 depicts robberies in an area using three categories. The natural breaks in the data set are between 4–5 and 9–10 robberies at a single address. Table 12.1 displays several of the addresses and their counts of robberies to show the data that were used to create this map.

The graduated line map in Figure 12.4 depicts the number of robberies along the street segments in a specific area with three categories. The natural breaks in these data are between 7–8 and 10–11 robberies per street segment. The graduated

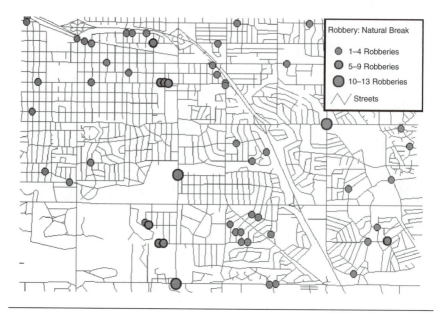

Figure 12.3 Graduated-Size Point Map: Natural Breaks Classification

Table 12.1 Number of Robberies by Address

Address	Number of Robberies
4980 E Main St	3
3920 S Clover Rd	10
930 S Bridge St	9
4500 N River Rd	4
3952 S Thompson St	0
230 S Bridge St	5
4560 N River Rd	1
465 S Bridge St	8
1520 S Bridge St	12

polygon map in Figure 12.5 shows the number of robberies per geographic area. The legends in these two maps are different because the data have been summed differently (e.g., by address, by street segment, and by area) and the gaps in the data distributions are different.

In the following discussions of the remaining types of classifications, only polygon maps are used to illustrate the statistical formulas, but all of these classifications can be used to create graduated point and line maps as well. The following examples

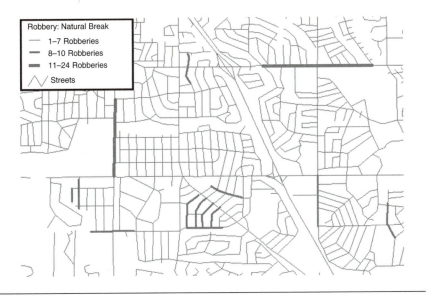

Figure 12.4   Graduated Size Line Map: Natural Breaks Classification

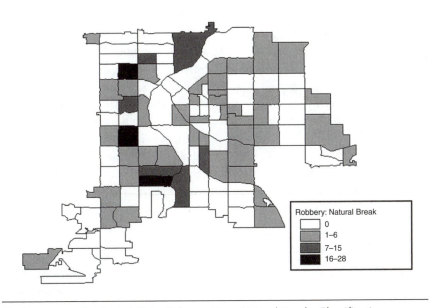

Figure 12.5   Graduated Color Polygon Map: Natural Breaks Classification

use the same data set as that used above to show how the data are displayed differently depending on the classifications employed.

Equal Interval

To arrive at an **equal interval classification**, the analyst uses a GIS to apply a statistical formula that divides the difference between the highest and lowest value

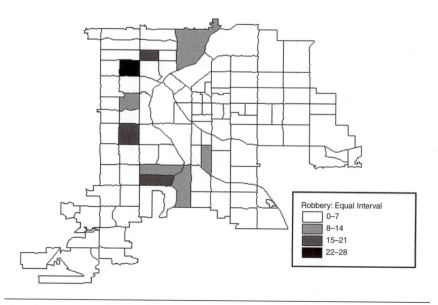

Figure 12.6   Graduated Color Polygon Map: Equal Interval Classification

into equal-sized ranges. In Figure 12.6, the lowest value of robberies per area is 0 and the highest is 28; four categories were selected, thus each range is 7 (e.g., 0–7, 8–14).

The equal interval classification yields different results depending on the values of the data (e.g., values ranging from 0–80 with four categories would be divided into 0–20, 21–40, etc.). This type of map is best suited for data in which there are similar numbers of incidents in all classes. Crime analysts typically use this classification in combination with other maps to get a sense of the nature of the problems they are examining. However, they do not usually disseminate such maps to police because most crime analysis data distributions are skewed (e.g., notice all the white areas in Figure 12.6), and this classification does not typically yield results that are useful for police purposes.

Quantile

An analyst produces a quantile map by dividing the number of records in the database by the number of categories (selected by the user), which results in categories with equal numbers of records. Whereas other classifications are based on values in the selected variable to be mapped, **quantile classification** is first concerned with the number of records in the database, then with the values within the selected variable.

The following example illustrates the quantile classification method for defining the categories. Table 12.2 contains 15 records with areas (polygons) and number of robberies. In a quantile map with three categories created from these data, each range would include 5 cases because there are 15 cases total (15/3 = 5). To determine the break points, the GIS sorts the data by number of robberies (ascending), with the first 5 cases representing the first range and so on, as shown in Table 12.3. The break points for the three categories are 0 to 4 robberies, 5 to 16 robberies, and

Table 12.2   Number of Robberies by Area (Polygon)

Area	Number of Robberies
1	7
2	3
3	16
4	12
5	24
6	0
7	9
8	5
9	19
10	22
11	0
12	4
13	17
14	28
15	0

17 to 28 robberies (shown in the table in boldface italics). Geographic units in the three categories are shaded different colors, with each color representing 33% of the total number of records. Figure 12.7 is a quantile map with four categories, thus the break points come from the values of the first, second, third, and fourth 25% of the cases.

Crime analysts most often use quantile maps to make comparisons between data sets with very different values. For example, an analyst might use two quantile maps to compare robberies and burglaries in 1 year by area. Because there are significantly fewer robberies than burglaries, the values of the categories would be much different in the maps' legends. Using quantile maps enables the analyst to identify and compare areas within the highest 25% (using four ranges) for both types no matter the actual frequencies and allows the analyst to see whether the areas highest in burglaries were also the highest in robberies.

Standard Deviation

When using the **standard deviation classification,** an analyst uses mean and standard deviation of the selected variable to determine the break points of the

Table 12.3 Number of Robberies by Area: Sorted in Ascending Frequency to Determine Quantiles

Area	Number of Robberies
6	0
11	0
15	0
2	3
12	*4*
8	5
1	7
7	9
4	12
3	*16*
13	17
9	19
10	22
5	24
14	*28*

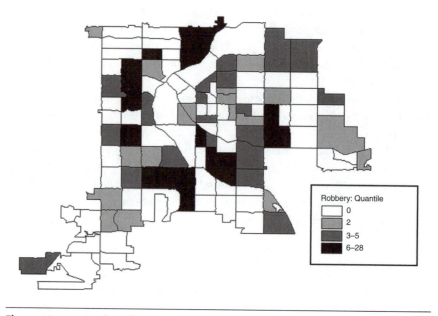

Figure 12.7 Graduated Color Polygon Map: Quantile Classification

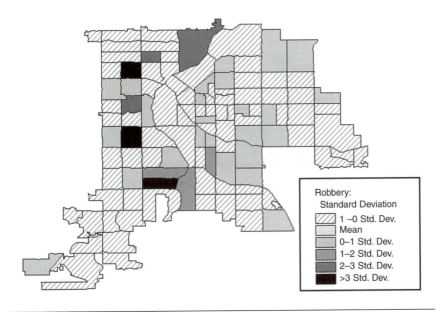

Figure 12.8   Graduated Color Polygon Map: Standard Deviation Classification

categories, which are shown in the legend not as whole numbers but as standard deviations (e.g., +1, –1 standard deviation from the mean). For the map in Figure 12.8, the GIS determines the mean by adding the numbers of robberies in all polygons and dividing the total by the number of polygons. The GIS then computes the standard deviation and adds and subtracts it from the mean to determine the break points of each category. This type of map is most useful for determining polygons, points, or lines that are outliers (plus or minus 3 standard deviations from the mean) and for comparing the outliers of one database to those of another (similar to quantile). That is, for each data set the polygons that have values significantly higher or lower than the mean are shaded a particular color. Because the standard deviation is a standardized measurement and provides the same measures relative to the specific database, the analyst can compare unlike distributions across different maps. Note that in such maps usually no area is shaded the color of the mean, because the mean is not necessarily a value in the data distribution, such as 4.57 robberies in an area.

By Manual Method

The last type of graduated map is a "custom" map; that is, in a map created using **manual method classification**, the ranges displayed in the legend are *not* determined by the values of a variable or a statistical formula, but by the creator of the map. Crime analysts often use custom ranges to compare multiple maps with the same type of data over time, such as to analyze monthly robbery maps in which the same colors represent the same ranges. A comparison of actual values of the

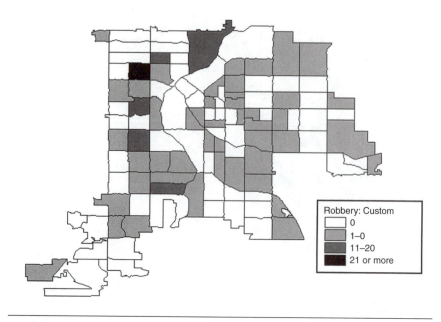

Figure 12.9   Graduated Color Polygon Map: Custom Classification (January 2004)

variable mapped cannot be done using any of the other classifications discussed above because the colors represent different ranges each time the data changed in those classifications. Figures 12.9 and 12.10 are examples of two maps with the same custom legends that allow the analyst to compare differences in robbery by area. Notice that in these maps the label for the fourth category does not have an upper value; instead, it reads "or more." Analysts create such categories when they use the same legend for more than one map, because the upper limit might be different for each data set. In most cases, the break points in custom legends fall on 5s, 10s, 25s, 50s, 100s, and so on.

Setting the break points displayed in the legend is an important element in creating a map, and crime analysts do not set these points haphazardly; rather, they base their decisions on their examination of the data and the planned purposes of the maps. In making these decisions, they often consider local laws, agency policies, and the context of the problem being studied. For example, an analyst who is creating a map to show the number of burglary alarms at specific locations in a city might select as the highest range "5 or more" if the city assesses fines to locations that have five or more alarms in a particular time period.

Classification Guidelines and Summary

All of the maps presented thus far in this chapter have shown frequency of robberies as an example. However, analysts can map many other statistics—such as rates, means, and percentages—using the methods discussed above, and such maps

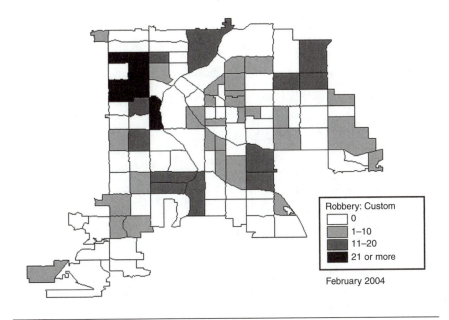

Robbery: Custom
0
1–10
11–20
21 or more

February 2004

Figure 12.10   Graduated Color Polygon Map: Custom Classification (February 2004)

may be more relevant, depending on the analysis. Crime analysts should keep the following guidelines in mind when creating maps to describe data:

- In deciding which classification and how many categories to use, the analyst should first determine the purpose and audience of the map.
- Decisions regarding how a map should be made form the crux of the analysis process; the analyst should not rely on the default settings of a GIS program.
- With the exception of the custom or manual method classification, all of the classification methods are dependent on the data; that is, the values in the ranges will differ from data set to data set, depending on the distributions and values within the data.
- When describing data using these classifications, the analyst should experiment with the classifications and the number of categories; often, comparisons among the different maps can provide insight into and promote understanding of a problem.
- The analyst should be aware that shading an entire area based on the aggregate number of events can give readers of the map the impression that the activity is occurring equally across the area, when in fact it may not be.
- When creating area maps, the analyst should not draw conclusions based on the area about individuals or particular locations within that area (i.e., ecological fallacy).

Table 12.4 provides a summary of mapping classification methods and some examples of their use.

Table 12.4   Summary of Mapping Classifications

	Unique Value	Natural Breaks	Equal Interval	Quantile	Standard Deviation	Custom
Type(s) of variable needed	Categorical	Numeric	Numeric	Numeric	Numeric	Any
Type of feature (point, line, polygon)	All (typically polygon)	All	All	All	All (typically polygon)	All
Ranges dictated by	Values of the variable	Data set	Data set	Data set	Data set	User
How often used in SCA	Often	Very often	Seldom	Seldom	Seldom	Very often
Practical example of use	Shading banks by whether they have drive-up ATMs	Mapping robberies for the past month using graduated symbols	Mapping the number of robberies per area to understand the skewed distribution	Comparing levels of bank robbery to levels of convenience store robbery	Determining areas with unusually high numbers of robberies	Comparing levels of robbery on a monthly basis

Identifying and Categorizing Hot Spots

As noted previously, a hot spot is an "area with high crime intensity" (Ratcliffe, 2004). Crime analysts use the methods described in this section to identify geographic patterns of hot spots and to categorize hot spots in order to understand and communicate the spatial relationships of the data. Analysts identify hot spots in several ways, ranging from simple to complex; these methods are described below, along with the techniques analysts use to categorize hot spots once they are identified.

Identifying Hot Spots

Crime analysis practitioners and scholars engage in ongoing debate concerning the relative advantages and disadvantages of various methods of identifying hot spots. A few of the most common techniques used in crime analysis are described below.

Manual Method

The most straightforward way of determining hot spots is the manual or "eye-ball" method; this is also the most often used method in crime analysis and policing. In Figure 12.11, which depicts robberies as graduated symbols, an analyst has drawn

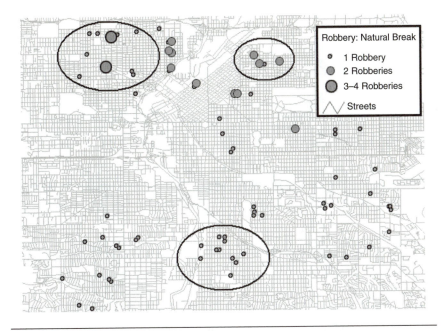

Figure 12.11   Hot Spot Identification: Manual Method

circles around the areas where the concentration of robberies appears to be the greatest.

It is important that analysts use graduated points when identifying hot spots manually, because, as noted in Chapter 4, single-symbol maps place incidents that have occurred at the same location on top of one another, so that a large number of incidents at the same location appear as one. Analysts also need to be aware that the areas appearing to be hot spots will vary depending on the scale of the map and how many data are mapped.

Graduated Color Mapping

For data distributions with large numbers, using points to determine hot spots can be difficult. Graduated color maps of areas allow analysts to examine more incidents summed by larger areas. Graduated color maps also allow analysts to map census information, such as population and income, along with crime analysis data, as census variables are available only by area (e.g., census blocks, census block groups, census tracts). The standard deviation classification is particularly helpful for determining hot spots because it highlights those areas that are more than 3 standard deviations from the mean—that is, areas with frequencies or rates that are well above average. In Figure 12.12, the darkest areas would be identified as hot spots, as their values are more than 3 standard deviations above the mean.

When using graduated color polygon maps, analysts need to be aware that the areas are not of equal size, which makes comparing frequency of incidents among unlike units problematic. Analysts can address this issue by using a normalizing

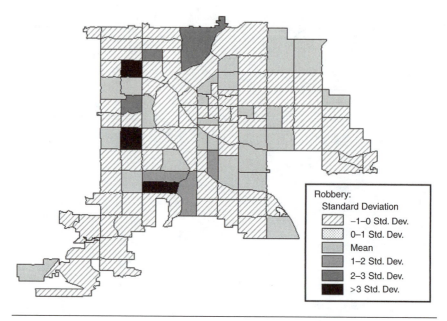

Figure 12.12   Hot Spot Identification: Graduated Color Map Shaded by Standard Deviation

variable, such as population, number of targets, or area of the polygon. Analysts using this method to determine hot spots also need to be aware that incidents within an area could have occurred only along the border of that area, but because the entire area is shaded, the actual data and the resulting hot spot are distorted. Figure 12.13 shows the actual incidents along an area border (probably a major road) and how the shading distorts this concentration of incidents; without the clarification of the incident symbols, it appears that all of the area is equally dense with crime. Sometimes (e.g., when an analyst is faced with a large number of cases and limited software capabilities) analysts have no option but to use this method, but they should do so with caution.

Grid Mapping

Grid mapping is a method for resolving the unequal area in which a standard-sized grid is used for analysis. The analyst begins by placing an artificial grid (generated by the GIS) on top of the area of interest and then uses graduated color shading classifications to show different levels of crime. Figure 12.14 is an example of a grid map showing a standard deviation classification. The shaded areas can be large or small and can follow actual events more closely than in graduated area maps. However, this method has some drawbacks in that it may not depict realistic separation of land areas (e.g., grids may cross over lakes and rivers), and grids along the borders of a jurisdiction have only partial data and so are shaded as lower values.

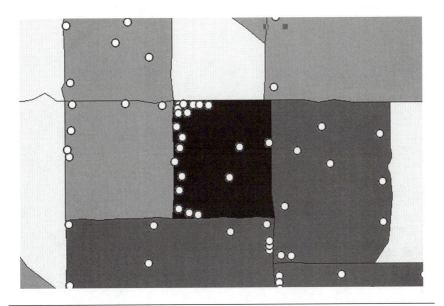

Figure 12.13   Comparison of Actual Crime Locations and Shaded Polygons

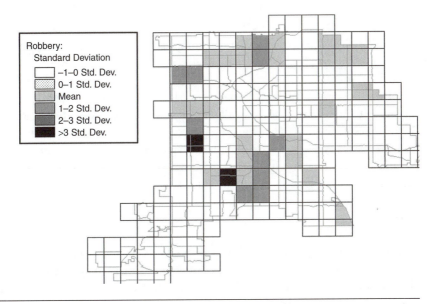

Figure 12.14   Hot Spot Identification: Graduated Color Grid Map Shaded by
Standard Deviation

Ellipses

An **ellipse** is a closed curve that is formed from two foci or points in which the
sum of the distances from any point on the curve to the two foci is a constant.
Unlike a circle, which has an exact center, an ellipse has two foci, allowing it
to accommodate the area of a hot spot both horizontally and vertically. Crime

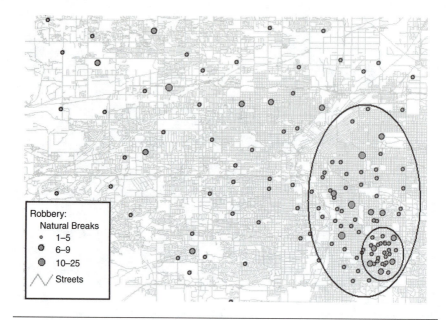

Figure 12.15   Hot Spot Identification: Ellipses

analysts use ellipses to determine hot spots or geographic concentrations of activity in data distributions (i.e., points that are closer to one another than to any other point).[1]

Software designed for spatial analysis, such as STAC (Spatial and Temporal Analysis of Crime), developed by the Illinois Criminal Justice Information Authority (ICJIA), uses a statistical method and user selections (e.g., study area) to determine both first-order and second-order clusters.[2] Figure 12.15 presents a rudimentary example of an ellipse that highlights first-order (larger ellipse) and second-order (smaller ellipse) hot spots of activity within a data distribution.

Density Mapping

In the density mapping method of determining hot spots, analysts identify hot spots by examining graduated color maps that depict concentrations of activity using the exact locations of the incidents. Unlike the graduated symbol and grid mapping methods, density mapping does not limit the analyst to examination of predetermined areas; rather, in density maps "the flow of hotspots mimics the underlying crime patterns and often follows urban geographic features that are known to police officers and other users" (Ratcliffe, 2004, p. 8). Figure 12.16 is an example of a density map.

Crime analysts use standard GIS packages as well as specialized software to create density maps. The process of creating a density map includes the following components:

1. An arbitrary grid is placed over the study area. As in the creation of a grid map, the map creator selects the size of the grid; however, in this type of map

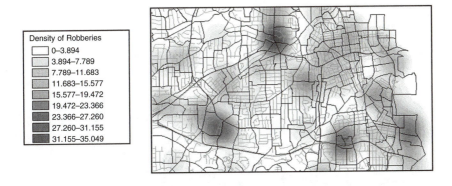

Figure 12.16   Hot Spot Identification: Density Map

the size tends to be very small, to approximate the immediate area of an incident location (i.e., the size used is typically between 50 and 100 feet).

2. A density "score" for each cell is derived as follows: The software searches a predetermined (by the map creator) radius around each cell (the **search radius**), counts the number of incidents within that radius, and divides that count by the size of the search area.

3. The cells are shaded according to their resulting scores. Thus a cell's score does not represent the number of incidents in that cell, but the number of incidents "near" that cell divided by the area "around" that cell, approximating the concentration of activity. In other words, a cell may not contain any incidents at all but have a high score because it is surrounded by areas in which incidents have occurred. This is also how continuous shading is produced.

4. The legend for the map is created. The legend does not illustrate "real" counts of events; rather, it provides a ratio of events in an area by the size of the area (e.g., the number of incidents per square mile).

With changes in cell size and the radius of the search distance, the same data can produce visually different density maps. For example, Figures 12.17 and 12.18 show the same data with a cell size of 50 feet but with search radii of .5 miles and 1.5 miles, respectively. This method is not limited by geographic areas and is suitable for examining large amounts of data. Analysts need to keep the following issues in mind when they use density mapping:

- Changes in cell sizes and search distances can result in very different maps. A general rule is to keep the grid cell size to about 50–100 feet (the approximate size of a land parcel) and adjust the search radius according to the scale of the study area.
- The legends can be confusing to those who are unfamiliar with density maps, and in practice many crime analysts use legends with labels such as "low density," "medium density," and "high density" instead of ranges of numbers.

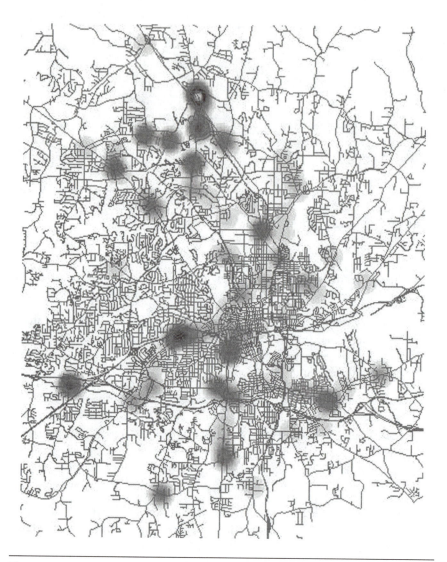

Figure 12.17   Density Map: Search Radius 0.5 miles

Such categories are not useful for comparison of different databases, however (e.g., the same type of data for different time periods or different types of data for the same time period). For example, if a map of 500 simple assaults for 2003 is compared with a map of 50 aggravated assaults for 2003 and the maps have categorical legends, both maps may appear to show the same level of crimes, because the colors and the values are the same. In contrast, if the legends show actual values, it will be clear that simple assault occurs at a much higher rate per square mile. Thus, for purposes of comparing similar data, "custom" legends should be used.

- Because density maps show crime locations as a continuous surface, they may give the impression that crimes have occurred in places where they actually have not occurred (Groff & La Vigne, 2002).

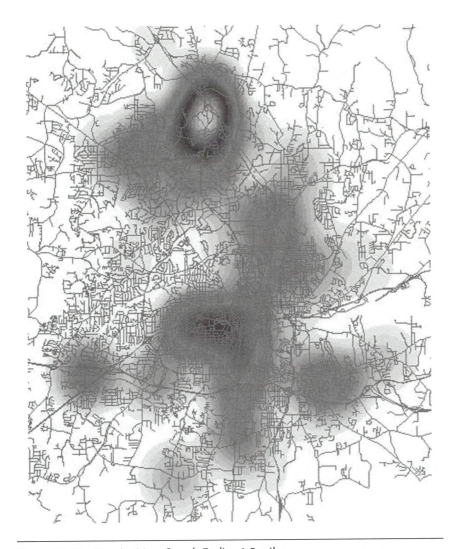

Figure 12.18   Density Map: Search Radius 1.5 miles

- Density maps have an inherent border bias because cells that are close to the edges of the study area may not have the potential for incidents to occur (this problem is similar to one noted regarding grid maps above).

Summary of Hot Spot Identification Methods

Like many of the other analysis techniques discussed throughout this book, each of the hot spot identification methods described above has its own strengths and weaknesses. To understand problems, crime analysts use the simplest and most common of these methods (e.g., manual method and graduated color polygon maps) along with their analyses of the other characteristics discussed in Chapters 10 and 11. Table 12.5 provides a summary of hot spot identification methods and the issues associated with their use.

Table 12.5   Summary of Hot Spot Identification Methods

	Manual Method	Graduated Color Polygon Maps	Grid Maps	Ellipses Maps	Density Maps
Type of feature (point, line polygon)	Graduated points	Polygons	Standardized polygons	Points	Points
Software requirements	Basic GIS	Basic GIS	Basic GIS	Advanced functions or specialized software	Advanced functions or specialized software
Issues	No standardized methodology, dependent on scale	Assumes equal distribution across area	Assumes equal distribution across area; problems with borders	Depends on user selections; erroneously used to predict future crime occurrences	Depends highly on user selections of search radius and cell size; problems with borders; comparison difficult
How often used in SCA	Very often	Often	Seldom[a]	Seldom[a]	Seldom[a]

a. Use of this method is becoming increasingly common.

Categorizing Hot Spots

Hot spots generally fall into one of the following three categories (Ratcliffe, 2004):

- *Dispersed hot spot:* The incident locations within the hot spot are spread throughout the hot spot area but are more concentrated than incidents in other areas. For example, burglary incidents have occurred throughout a residential area in which homes tend to be victimized only once, but the area itself has more burglaries than other areas. Figure 12.19 is a simple illustration of a dispersed hot spot.
- *Clustered hot spot:* The incident locations within the hot spot group together in one or more smaller clusters. For example, in a map of assaults in a downtown entertainment district, there are several clusters of assault incidents at different bars and nightclubs as well as on the street within the downtown area, which itself is the hot spot. Figure 12.20 is a simple illustration of a clustered hot spots.

Figure 12.19   Dispersed Hot Spot

Figure 12.20   Clustered Hot Spot

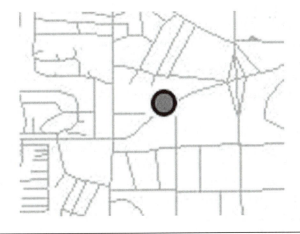

Figure 12.21   Hot Point

- *Hot point:* The incidents occur at one particular place. Unlike the incidents in a clustered hot spot, which form one or more clusters, the incidents in a hot point are centered on one address or place. An example is theft from vehicles at a mall, in that all the incidents happen within the parking lot of the mall, which is separate from other businesses and parking lots. Figure 12.21 is a simple illustration of a hot point.

By categorizing hot spots, crime analysts can identify different types of problems to analyze further using the techniques discussed throughout the chapters in Part IV, including the context of a problem, the temporal nature of a hot spot,[3] patterns of victimization, and other environmental characteristics that they may encounter through primary data collection.

Summary Points

This chapter has described the techniques that crime analysts use to understand the spatial nature of problems. The following are the key points addressed in this chapter:

- Crime analysts take two distinct approaches to the spatial analysis of crime and disorder problems: (a) They use mapping to display tabular data and statistics, and (b) they examine the locations of incidents to determine the spatial relationships of those incidents to one another.
- Crime analysts use categorical, statistical, and manual methods in displaying data and statistics in graduated size and color maps.
- In the categorical method, different shading or different symbols are used to represent features (e.g., points, lines, and polygons) by unique values of a categorical variable.
- In the statistical method, points, lines, and polygons are shaded or graduated according to one of four formulas: natural breaks, equal interval, quantile, and standard deviation.
- In the natural breaks classification, a statistical formula is used to identify the natural break points inherent in the data. Crime analysts often use this classification in their initial examinations of problems.
- In the equal interval classification, a statistical formula is used to divide the difference between the highest and lowest value into equal-sized ranges. This method is best suited to a uniform distribution, where there are similar numbers of incidents in all classes.
- To produce a quantile map, the GIS divides the number of records in the database by the number of categories (selected by the user), which results in categories with equal numbers of records. Whereas other classifications are based on values in the selected variable to be mapped, quantile maps are first concerned with the number of records in the database, and then with the values within the selected variable.

- In the standard deviation classification, mean and standard deviation of the selected variable are used to determine the break points of the categories, which are shown in the legend not as whole numbers but as standard deviations.
- In the manual method, the creator of the map (which is called a custom map) determines the legend. Crime analysts often use custom classifications to compare the same type of data over time, such as analyzing robbery by area each month.
- Crime analysts need to be aware of the following issues when using the methods described in this chapter: (a) For categorical and statistical classifications, break points are determined based on the uniqueness of the database and are not comparable; (b) in mapping, using different numbers of categories can yield different results; (c) analysis should include experimentation with a variety of classifications; (d) decisions about how maps are made should not rely on the default settings of GIS software; (e) a polygon map may give the impression that incidents are occurring equally across the area when in fact they might be clustered or located along a particular street; (f) one cannot draw conclusions about individual incidents based on analysis of incidents by area.
- A hot spot is an area with high crime intensity. Crime analysts use several methods to identify hot spots, including the manual method, the graduated color area method, the grid method, ellipses, and density mapping.
- The method of identifying hot spots that is used most often in crime analysis is the manual or "eyeball" method, in which the analyst studies a graduated size point map and visually locates areas of high activity.
- By using a standard deviation classification in a graduated color map of areas to identify hot spots, an analyst can examine more incidents together as well as examine additional information (e.g., census data).
- Grid mapping improves on graduated color mapping in that it uses standard-sized grids for analysis, thus providing a basis for comparison of areas.
- To determine ellipses, crime analysts use statistical formulas that identify geographic concentrations of activity based on distances of the incidents from one another (i.e., points that are closer to one another than to any other point).
- In the density method, analysts identify hot spots by searching for dense concentrations of activity using the exact locations of the incidents. Unlike graduated symbol and grid mapping, density mapping is not limited to predetermined areas and follows the course of the data.
- Hot spots fall into one of three categories: dispersed, clustered, and hot point. Categorizing a hot spot as one of these can help an analyst determine the nature of the problem under examination.
- In a dispersed hot spot, the incident locations within the hot spot are spread throughout the hot spot area, but they are more concentrated than incidents in other areas.
- In a clustered hot spot, the incident locations within the hot spot group together in one or more smaller clusters.
- A hot point is a hot spot in which the incidents occur at one particular place.

Exercises

Exercise 12.1

As part of an evaluation of a program to reduce commercial burglary, you are asked to prepare two maps to compare the data on commercial burglaries for a set period before the program's implementation with data for the same amount of time after the program's completion. What type(s) of classification(s) would you use in your two maps to enhance the comparison of these time periods? Why?

Exercise 12.2

You are asked to examine the data on aggravated assault in your city to see whether any particular areas have significantly higher rates of aggravated assault than the city average. What type of classification would you use to create a map that would help you complete your task? Why?

Notes

1. Analysts also use ellipses to describe the amounts of data in particular areas (e.g., "95% of the cases fall within the ellipse"). Unfortunately, crime analysts sometimes use ellipses with small numbers of cases to predict the location of the next case in a series; this is not an appropriate use of ellipses.

2. More information about STAC is available on the ICJIA Web site at http://www.icjia.state.il.us.

3. For discussion of the categorization of spatial and temporal hot spots together, see Ratcliffe (2004).

13

Strategic Crime Analysis Products

The three preceding chapters have outlined many different techniques that crime analysts use alone and in combination to understand problems. This chapter focuses on how analysts disseminate the results of their analyses to police personnel. The first section addresses how analysts decide on what information they should disseminate; the chapter then describes specific types of strategic crime analysis reports and provides format guidelines for tables, graphs, and maps.

_____ Choosing Analysis Information to Disseminate

The chapters in Part IV of this volume are not intended as a "recipe book" for crime analysis that provides a step-by-step methodology for analyzing problems, because much of the crime analysis process relies on the analyst's critical thinking skills and the kind of judgment that comes with experience. Crime analysts use different techniques in various combinations to evaluate information about problems, determine the gaps in that information, and collect additional information to fill those gaps. Thus a given problem analysis may produce the equivalent of 50 pages of information, but an efficiently prepared report resulting from that analysis may be comparatively brief. One weakness in current crime analysis practice is that many analysts produce and disseminate to police personnel volumes of reports and information without sifting through their findings to present only the information that is important and interesting for police purposes.

As a general rule, the crime analyst should present the findings of his or her analysis of a problem in a report that follows the order of the discussion in Part IV of this book. Such a report should give specific information about the following:

- The context of the city in which the analysis has taken place in relation to the problem (e.g., the urban and entertainment nature of the city contributes to the high number of robberies)
- The data used in the analysis to understand the current nature of the problem and any limitations of those data (e.g., data on robberies reported to the police

from 2001 through 2003 were used; the data do not account for environmental differences between robbery locations)

- Research findings from other (national or local) studies about the topic (e.g., research shows that other cities of similar type typically have lower rates of robberies; research shows that the presence of two clerks is a significant deterrent to robberies at convenience stores)

- The current trends related to the problem (e.g., average number of robberies per week, types of robberies)

- Temporal patterns of the problem (e.g., robberies increased significantly in the past year; robberies appear to have increased in the spring; robberies have occurred primarily in the evening)

- The types of victims, property, and targets victimized and the rates of repeat victimization (e.g., the most common victimizations involve people being robbed on the street; more than 40% of robberies are occurring at nearly 10% of the victimized addresses)

- Spatial patterns of the problem (e.g., appears to be a clustered hot spot of robberies in and near the entertainment district)

- Conclusions drawn as the result of primary data collection (e.g., interviews of street robbery victims show they were all walking from public transportation areas such as bus stops and train stations)

In addition to this information, the report should include a section (usually headed "Discussion" or "Conclusions") in which the analyst explains how the various finding support or refute the hypotheses that were developed at the beginning of the analysis.

Obviously, a problem analysis report that covers every one of the areas listed above would be quite comprehensive. Often in crime analysis, however, the focus is on one aspect of a problem (with one or two hypotheses), and the resulting analysis statements and reports are also narrowly focused. No rules exist to help crime analysts determine which of their findings are most important and interesting; to make such decisions, they need to consider both the purposes of their analyses (hypotheses) and the audiences for the resulting information. In determining which of their analysis findings they should communicate to others, crime analysts should keep the following guidelines in mind:

- The methods and analysis are only as good as the data used. Analysts need to acknowledge any weaknesses of the data (whether in quality or quantity) in order to provide information about what the results do and do not reveal about the problems analyzed as well as to make recommendations for improving data quality.

- In strategic crime analysis particularly, the amounts of data analyzed must be adequate, in terms of both the total number of cases and amount of time (no fewer than 6 months of data to analyze long-term problems) and the counts of individual categories (e.g., it is difficult to conduct a substantive analysis of homicide with counts of between 0 and 10 per year). If they have conducted their analyses with only small amounts of data, analysts should acknowledge this and interpret their results with caution.

- There are many different ways to show information that can serve different purposes. Adjusting how findings are presented is part of the analysis process; however, analysts should be careful never to make up data or use their data to "lie" for any reason.
- Analysts should keep the audiences for their findings in mind when choosing their analysis methods and deciding on the level of complexity to offer in their reports. For example, if the aim of an analysis is to provide information to line-level officers, the analyst's best choice for communicating the findings effectively may not be to conduct multiple regression.
- When the issues under examination are simple or subjective, analysts need not always use complex methods or statistics. For addressing such issues, critical thinking and simple analysis of thoughtfully collected data can be much more effective than more complicated methods.

The products that result from strategic crime analysts' work vary widely in length and style because the purposes of the analyses and the audiences for their findings also vary. Products can range from a 1-page overview of a problem apartment community to a 50-page in-depth report on auto theft in an entire city. The appendix to this volume presents a sample of a report of a preliminary problem analysis study involving commercial burglary in a fictitious city (adapted from Police Foundation, 2003a). Although the material in that report is presented in an order slightly different from that recommended above, the sample is included here to provide a sense of what an analysis report entails.

Strategic Crime Analysis Products

The results of strategic crime analysis can be presented in a wide array of formats, given the range of analysis techniques available and the many levels on which problems are examined. Although overall formats vary, a number of basic guidelines apply to the general content of analysis reports as well as to the appearance and content of the tables, charts, and maps included in these products.

Types of Products

The types of products that result from strategic crime analysis include the following:

- *Memos:* The results of simple queries or analyses are often presented in the form of memos that include text describing the analyses along with tables, charts, and maps as appropriate.
- *Weekly/monthly/quarterly reports and maps:* These reports are produced regularly and distributed on paper through intradepartmental channels or electronically through e-mail or postings on intranet sites. Typically, they provide descriptive statistics on crime, calls, and/or accidents for particular areas of the city, in addition to explaining notable findings within the results.

- *Annual reports:* These reports, produced yearly, present analysts' conclusions based on descriptive statistics for the entire jurisdiction for the preceding year and comparison of the data with previous years. Most annual reports focus on Uniform Crime Reports Part I crime, arrests, and clearances, but some also include information about calls for service, domestic violence incidents, accidents, hate crimes, and so on, as well as results of citizen surveys. In some cases, rather than standing alone, SCA annual reports are included in general police agency annual reports, which present overall information about agencies.
- *Special reports:* These reports typically present the findings of analyses that were initiated in response to requests for information from particular levels or divisions of a police agency. A special report usually focuses on a specific location or problem activity. Examples include an analysis of the calls for service and crime at the local ValueMart location over the past year, an examination of theft from vehicles in Beat 12 over the past 2 years, and an analysis of false burglary alarm calls for service.
- *Research, evaluation, and problem reports:* These reports tend to be fairly lengthy and complex. They generally include reviews of the literature on the problems or topics analyzed (e.g., construction site burglaries, evaluation of photo radar, staffing analysis), discussion of the analyses of secondary and primary data, presentation of findings, and recommendations based on the findings. Evaluation reports also include descriptions of the programs evaluated and conclusions concerning the programs' effectiveness.

Guidelines for Product Contents

The many different formats that police agencies and individual analysts use in producing various kinds of reports are often dictated by the experience and personal preferences of the people who prepare the reports. The Police Foundation (2003a) recommends that all strategic crime analysis products, no matter the format, include the following elements:

- *Title:* The report title (or, in the case of a memo, the "Re:" line) should include information about (a) the nature of the data, (b) the unit of geography on which the report focuses, and (c) the date range analyzed. For example, "Citizen-Generated Calls for Service in District 3: January 1, 2003, Through December 31, 2003"; "Commercial Burglary in the Downtown Beat: 1999–2004."
- *Tables, graphics, and/or maps:* The tables, graphics, and/or maps that appear in a report reflect the specific analysis techniques used. As noted previously, the final report need not include every map and table produced during analysis; rather, only those that illustrate important and interesting findings or that are useful for helping audiences understand the analysis should appear.
- *Analysis findings:* This narrative summary should provide a synthesis and interpretation of the analysis and highlight important and interesting findings. In some cases, it may include information about tables and statistics that

are not shown in the report but are only written up (e.g., 45% of the addresses account for 95% of the robberies). It is important for a report to provide more than just lists of data and tables of frequencies.

- *Disclaimers:* The report should include clear statements detailing any limitations of the data and analysis techniques. For example: "Conclusions drawn from any report containing crime information are based only on data about crimes known to the police, not all crime"; "Crime-per-population figures may not account for all the differences among areas in the city (e.g., commercial districts, schools)"; "Juvenile arrest statistics do not indicate all the crimes committed by juveniles, only those crimes for which juveniles are arrested."

- *Recommendations:* The report should offer suggestions for improvement of data quality, areas for future analysis, or actions based on the analysis results. For example, "It is recommended that additional information on auto theft recovery be included on the recovery report to enable determination of why the auto theft occurred"; "It is recommended that the department provide crime prevention information to beauty salons and day-care centers, given that such locations have been victimized repeatedly over the past year."

- *File path:* The report should include full information on where the computer files that were produced to write the report are located, so that analysts can locate the files in the future when working on updates or creating similar reports. An example file path: "F:\Part I Crime 2001\Auto Theft\January Report.doc and \JanuaryReport.xls."

- *Credits/date:* The name or division of the individual(s) who created the report and the date it was created should appear on the report so that anyone with questions can direct them to the appropriate person(s). An author credit also encourages recognition for the creator of the report. Examples of credit and date information: "Prepared by Crime Analysis Unit, December 2002"; "Prepared by Jane Doe, 01/06/03."

Guidelines for Table and Chart Contents

The tables and charts that appear in crime analysis reports should be formatted consistently to enable comparisons among them. Also, because reports are often pulled apart, copied, and distributed in pieces, each table and chart in a report needs to be descriptive enough to stand alone. For example, what does Figure 13.1 show? It is a frequency of UCR crime for 1999 and 2000, but what types of crime (e.g., Part I only?), what type of statistic (e.g., frequency or rate?), and where (e.g., the entire city or a particular district?)? Although this chart may have been described in depth in the report it originally appeared in, by itself it is unclear.

Each table and chart in a crime analysis report should include the following elements:

- *Title:* Like the title of a report, the title of a table or chart should include information about the nature of the data, the unit of geography, and the date range of the analysis. This is important because tables and charts often show

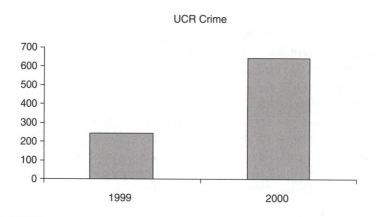

Figure 13.1   Example of a Poorly Labeled Chart

only parts of the analysis (e.g., only residential burglaries in a general report on all burglaries in District 14).

- *Labels:* All rows and columns of a table should be labeled, as should the *x*- and *y*-axes of a chart. Different colors, formatting, or additional text may be used to highlight interesting results or key features, but labels should be used in moderation and only where appropriate and readable within the table or chart.
- *File path:* Because analysts are often asked to update or reprint existing charts and tables, every chart and table in a report should include its own file path information. These types of features are often created in programs other than the ones used to produce reports as a whole (e.g., in spreadsheet programs rather than word processing programs), so anyone who wants to access an individual chart or table will need its specific file path. An example: "G:\District 4 Reports\Part I Crime District 4 2002-2003.xls."
- *Credits/date:* The name or division of the individual(s) who produced the table or graph should appear on the table or graph itself, along with the date the item was created.

Table 13.1 is an example of a properly formatted and labeled table; it shows the frequency and percentage change of Part I crime in District 4. Notice that it includes in a note additional information that may indicate a reason for the significant drop in crime in Beat 40. Figure 13.2, another example of correct formatting and labeling, depicts the data from Table 13.1 but provides additional information on the types of crime that are considered Part I crime and indicates the largest decrease in crime.

In creating tables and charts, analysts must make their decisions about what information to include and highlight based on the audiences for their products. For example, if the audience for a report is police officers and other crime analysts, it would not be necessary to include a definition of Part I crime, whereas such a definition would be useful to an audience of laypersons. Another issue in the formatting of charts is the amount of space available. In the example in Figure 13.2, additional information is contained within the boundaries of the chart; however, if there is room in the report to devote an entire page to this chart, the analyst might

Table 13.1   Example of a Correctly Formatted and Labeled Table

Frequency and Comparison of Part I Crime in District 4: 2002–2003				
	2002	*2003*	*Actual Difference*	*Percentage Change*
Beat 40	253	164	−89	−35.2[a]
Beat 41	261	275	14	5.4
Beat 42	278	210	−68	−24.5
Beat 43	285	301	16	5.6
Beat 44	322	354	32	9.9

*Demolition of the Rivergate Mall occurred in 2003.

Created by Jane Doe, Crime Analysis Unit, February 25, 2004: C:\Crime statistics/percentchange.xls

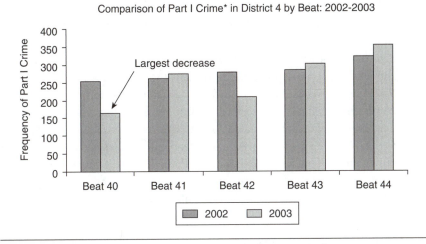

Comparison of Part I Crime* in District 4 by Beat: 2002-2003

Figure 13.2   Example of a Correctly Formatted and Labeled Chart

*Part I crime includes homicide, rape, robbery, aggravated assault, burglary, larceny, auto theft, and arson.

include this type of information on the page but outside the boundaries of the chart, making the chart itself less cluttered.

Guidelines for Map Contents

Because maps differ substantively from other components of strategic crime analysis products, analysts need to follow a different set of guidelines concerning their contents. To be understandable on their own, maps should include the following elements:

- *Title:* Like the title of a full report or a table, the title of a map should include information on the nature of the data, the unit of geography, and the date range of the analysis. This is important because maps within reports often illustrate only subsets of the full data (e.g., only burglaries in Beat 143 in a report on burglaries in all of District 14).
- *Legend:* The legend should list the tabular and geographic data sources displayed in the map in addition to indicating the symbols that are used to represent each data source. In a map that includes graduation by color or size, the legend should also state the classification used, so that the audience knows what technique was used to create the map, which is the heart of that type of analysis. For example: "Classification = Custom"; "Natural Breaks Classification."
- ***Geocoding or address match percentage:*** As with statistics and tables that are presented in social science, the amount of data that have not been geocoded or matched to addresses on the map should be noted (e.g., missing data). This is displayed as a percentage, such as "Geocoded Addresses = 99%" or "5% of Addresses Not Matched."
- *Labels:* Text can be used to label key features of a map, such as streets and landmarks, as well as to highlight interesting findings on the map itself (see Figure 13.3 for an example). However, labels should be used in moderation and only where appropriate and readable within the map.
- *Scale bar:* This element illustrates the distance units used in the map.
- ***North directional:*** This element indicates the geographic orientation of the map. Normally, north is at the top of the page, but that is not always the case.
- *Credits/date:* The name or division of the individual(s) who produced the map should appear on the map itself, along with the date the map was created. This is important because in some cases the maps in a report are created by someone other than the author(s) of the rest of the report.

Templates and Practical Examples

Practical examples of strategic and tactical crime analysis reports as well as examples of bulletins provided by working crime analysts from around the United States are available on the Web site of the International Association of Crime Analysts at http://www.iaca.net. The Police Foundation offers templates and guidelines for creating these types of reports on its Web site at http://www.policefoundation.org. The following is a description of the templates:

Crime analysis and mapping product templates have been designed to serve as models and provide templates for law enforcement analysts who wish to prepare standardized crime analysis reports, bulletins, and maps. The Police Foundation's Crime Mapping Laboratory has collected over 100 examples of

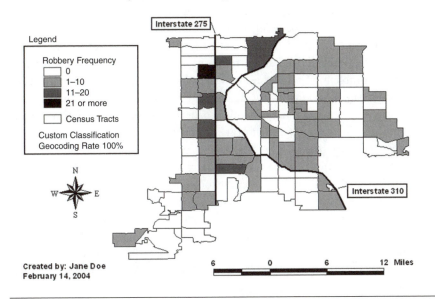

**Robberies in Analysisville
January 1, 2003 Through December 31, 2003**

Figure 13.3   Example of a Correctly Formatted and Labeled Map

crime analysis reports (annual, monthly, weekly, and daily reports of crime and calls for service), memos, crime trend bulletins, and maps submitted by 20 law enforcement agencies across the United States. The products we received range from simple, one-page bulletins or maps to more detailed problem-solving reports that include multiple tables, charts, and maps. After collecting these examples from the field, we categorized and analyzed them to look for commonalities in format, content, relevance, and overall effectiveness in conveying information in a concise manner. With this knowledge, we have created 11 product templates that can be adapted for use by any law enforcement agency. . . . There are six types of templates: (1) bulletin templates, (2) a memo template, (3) an annual report template, (4) a crime analysis and mapping Web page template, (5) regular report templates, and (6) a map template. (Velasco, Griffin, & Boba, 2001, p. 3)

Summary Points

This chapter has discussed how strategic crime analysts select their most important and interesting analysis findings for dissemination as well as the various types of reports they produce. The chapter has also presented guidelines concerning the elements that should be included in reports as a whole and in individual tables, charts, and maps. The following are the key points addressed in this chapter:

- Crime analysts must apply critical thinking and judgment in determining which of their findings are important and interesting enough for dissemination.
- As a general rule, a report on the findings of a problem analysis includes information on the following topics in this order: (a) context of the community/agency; (b) the data used; (c) national trends and academic research about the problem; (d) current trends in the problem; (e) temporal patterns of the problem; (f) the types of victims, property, and targets victimized and repeatedly victimized; (g) spatial patterns of the problem; and (h) conclusions drawn as a result of primary data collection. Such a report generally concludes with a section that explains how the analysis findings support or refute the hypotheses.
- When determining which analysis findings are important enough for dissemination, analysts should consider the following: (a) The methods and analysis are only as good as the data, (b) analysis should be conducted with an adequate amount of data, (c) analysts must never make up data or use the data to "lie" for any reason, (d) analysts should select analysis methods and the formats they use to report findings with the audience for the findings in mind, and (e) analysis of simple or subjective issues does not always require the use of complex methods or statistics.
- Strategic crime analysis products include memos, weekly/monthly/quarterly reports and maps, annual reports, special reports, and research, evaluation, and problem reports.
- Every strategic crime analysis product should include the following basic elements: title; tables, graphics, or maps; analysis findings; disclaimers; recommendations; file path; credits; and date of creation.
- Every table and chart that appears in an SCA product should include the following basic elements: title, labels, file path, credits, and date of creation.
- Every map that appears in an SCA product should include the following basic elements: title, legend, geocoding or address match percentage, labels, scale bar, north directional, credits, and date of creation.

Exercises

Exercise 13.1

Conduct a search of the Internet to find an example of a crime mapping or crime analysis product. Answer the following questions about the product:

- Does it contain all the elements recommended in this chapter for that type of product? If not, what is missing?
- Is the product understandable by itself? If not, is there accompanying text explaining it?
- If there is no accompanying text, what would you suggest adding to the product to help the user understand it better?

Exercise 13.2

Read the sample problem analysis project report that appears in the appendix to this volume. What hypotheses would you develop based on this preliminary analysis? What additional types of data would you collect to understand the problem further? How would you go about analyzing these data?

PART V

Administrative Crime Analysis

As noted in Chapter 2, administrative crime analysis is the presentation of interesting findings of crime research and analysis based on legal, political, and practical concerns to inform audiences within police administration, city government/council, and citizens. Administrative crime analysis is different from other types of crime analysis in that it involves only the presentation of findings rather than pattern identification, statistical analysis, or the examination of problems. Administrative crime analysis is the process of deciding what analysis findings to present and how to present them to specific audiences. *Presentation* in this context refers to all of the different ways in which crime analysis findings are formally reported to different audiences, including in written and electronic form as well as through oral presentations to groups.

The single chapter that makes up Part V is devoted to the subject of the administrative analysis process. The chapter presents a comprehensive example to show how results from one analysis report can be presented to different audiences for different purposes. There is no prescribed step-by-step method for conducting administrative crime analysis, but the example illustrates how various considerations can influence how analysis findings are presented. The chapter ends with a detailed discussion of the use of the Internet for dissemination of analysis findings, as this medium has become increasingly important and influential in recent years.

14

Administrative Crime Analysis

The results of tactical and strategic crime analysis are presented primarily to operational personnel within police agencies. Administrative crime analysis (ACA) is the process of paring down those results for presentation to police and city management, citizens, and any number of other external audiences (i.e., audiences external to police agencies). For instance, a tactical crime analysis bulletin about a residential burglary pattern that is prepared for officers on the street would likely include detailed information about the pattern, such as location, MO, suspects, victims, investigative leads, and vehicles. A bulletin intended to inform citizens about the same pattern, in contrast, would include only information relevant to citizens, so as not to jeopardize the ongoing investigation. Such a bulletin would likely include general information about where and when the pattern is occurring and how the crimes are being committed. The circumstances of individual situations also influence the selection of appropriate information for presentation in administrative crime analysis. For example, if an analyst is preparing to present information to the city council about a project to reduce prescription fraud and will have only 10 to 15 minutes to address the council, the analyst clearly cannot present all of the analysis, response, and evaluation results; rather, he or she must select for presentation only the most important points about the methodology and results.

The type of information that is chosen for presentation in ACA is typically only the "tip of the iceberg" of the research and analysis that were conducted. This chapter offers general guidelines for conducting administrative crime analysis as well as an example that illustrates these guidelines. The chapter closes with a discussion of ACA in relation to the most widely used forum for presentation of crime analysis findings, the Internet.

Guidelines for Conducting Administrative Crime Analysis

The situations for which administrative crime analysis is conducted differ widely, and no two are exactly alike. In some circumstances, a certain type of information may need to be presented to different audiences, whereas in others, different types of information may need to be presented to the same audiences. Analysts must use their experience and judgment in deciding what information to present and how to present it, keeping in mind the audiences for the information, the purposes for which the information is being shared, and the contexts of individual situations.

Audience

The process of administrative crime analysis begins with the analyst's reflection on who the audience for the presentation is—that is, who will use the information provided. The audiences for ACA information are not operational personnel of police agencies; rather, they are people with positions in police and/or city management, citizens, and other groups with various interests (e.g., business owners, neighborhood organizations, news media). Such audiences do not need specific details about analysis methods and findings; instead, they need to be provided with overviews and aggregate information. Different audiences have different needs for, expectations of, and skill levels for understanding and acting on analysis findings.

Purpose

ACA information is presented to audiences for a variety of reasons, most of which fall into the following general categories:

- *Information:* To inform audiences generally about crime and other activities in particular jurisdictions (e.g., information on the number of homicides in the city in the past year)
- *Alerts:* To alert audiences regarding particular events of immediate importance (e.g., a statement regarding the kidnapping of a child outside her home)
- *Community policing:* To give useful information to citizens and other groups working together with the police department to reduce crime and disorder (e.g., crime statistics to a particular neighborhood watch group)
- *Crime prevention:* To inform audiences about specific patterns or problems and make recommendations concerning how potential victims can protect themselves or their property (e.g., a statement that Honda Civics are being stolen and recommendation that drivers use antitheft devices)
- *Decision making:* To provide information to police and city government management, business owners, and developers that may be useful in decision making (e.g., results from an evaluation of red light cameras to inform decision making regarding further adoption or removal of the cameras)

Context

In addition to the audience for and purpose of a presentation, the context of the presentation is also a consideration in ACA. The context of a presentation includes the social and political climates that exist in the community as well as legal and practical concerns related to the information itself.

- *Social climate:* The social climate of a community includes both the general social trends and immediate social concerns specific to that area. For example, a general social trend might be that low interest rates are causing an increase in new housing construction and home purchases, which might contribute to increased numbers of burglaries at residential construction sites. A specific community concern might be that a dramatic influx of immigrants has created housing shortages in particular areas, leading to overcrowding and tensions among different groups.
- *Political climate:* Both the nation's general political climate and the immediate political climate of the community are important contextual considerations in ACA. An example of the general climate might be that immediately after an election year, federal funding is available for crime prevention efforts. An example of immediate political climate might be that the mayor does not approve of the decisions being made by the chief of police and so is working against the chief.
- *Legal concerns:* Both general and specific concerns about the law must be taken into account in ACA. Generally, decisions made by the U.S. Supreme Court influence the everyday practices of police and therefore influence the dissemination of crime information. Specific concerns include the legality of releasing certain kinds of information to different groups (e.g., privacy and confidentiality laws may prevent the sharing of some details).
- *Practical concerns:* A range of concerns regarding the audience, the purpose of the presentation, and the presentation itself may influence ACA decisions. Examples of practical concerns that influence the selection of information for presentation are the length of time for preparation, the desired or required length of the presentation, the complexity of the information, the skill level of the audience, the format of the presentation (e.g., paper, electronic, in person), and the person who will present the information to the audience (e.g., the chief of police is going to present the information to the city council).

Example

As is true of the other types of crime analysis, there is no one formula for conducting administrative crime analysis. In addition, ACA is the most difficult type of crime analysis for undergraduate students to understand, because most of them have not yet worked in government organizations or presented research findings professionally. The following example is provided to illustrate how different aspects of the same crime analysis findings are presented to different audiences for different reasons in different contexts.

Scenario

The police department has identified a construction site residential theft and burglary problem throughout the city. Because the city is currently experiencing a period of dramatic growth that is expected to continue, the problem is a major concern. The department's crime analysis unit has been assigned to conduct an in-depth analysis of the problem for the past 2 years to understand both the overall trends of the crimes and tactical series and patterns. Over the past 6 months, the CAU has notified police officers and detectives of tactical patterns of the problem, and several arrests have been made. The police department's management personnel are now ready to hear the results of the problem analysis so that they can decide on a plan of action for addressing the overall problem and anticipating future levels of the problem. In addition, the CAU will present findings from the analysis to representatives of the city government, to community groups, and to the news media to engage their participation in addressing the problem and to raise public awareness about the problem.

Audience: Police Management

- *Purpose:* To inform management personnel of the overall results of the analysis so they can use the information in deciding how to address the problem.
- *Context:* The meeting on this topic is to be an hour long and will also include a discussion of what to do about the problem, thus the time allotted for the analysis presentation and questions will be 20 minutes. Captains, majors, and the chief will attend the meeting.
- *Information presented:* Because of the brief amount of time available and the nature of the audience, only information from the strategic analysis will be presented by members of the CAU. Some information about patterns and the apprehension of offenders might be discussed, but the focus will be on the overall nature of the problem as informed by crime data and by primary data collection, such as observations of the construction sites and interviews with officers and home builders. Specifics, such as how the different data were obtained (including interviews and observation), will not be discussed. Future projections of construction site crimes based on city building permits will be presented, along with recommendations for addressing the problem. The presentation will take the form of a slide show, and the entire analysis report (including an executive summary) will be handed out to provide audience members with additional information.

Audience: City Council

- *Purpose:* To inform council members about the nature of the problem, future issues, and how the police department is going to address the problem.
- *Context:* The chief of police will present the information at a city council meeting. He will have 15 minutes to present to the council, of which he will have only 5 minutes to summarize the analysis results. The meeting will be televised on a local channel, and members of the news media will be there. (Many times, in a situation like this one, the chief will ask a crime analyst to accompany him or her to the meeting, either to present the analysis information or to answer any questions about the analysis.)

- *Information presented:* The information presented will include only general statistics about the nature of the problem, comparisons of the rates of the problem in other cities and nationally, and general information about what the city can anticipate in the future based on the numbers of city building permits granted. The chief will present the information in a slide show, and one or two general tables of statistics (with explanations) will be handed out to the city council members and others attending the meeting.

Audience: Community Group

- *Purpose:* To provide the citizens in a particular part of the city with information in order to elicit their help in addressing the problem.
- *Context:* The analysis has shown that one particular area in the city has been victimized repeatedly and may be considered a hot spot for this type of theft. Several police officers are going to present information about the problem at a meeting of a community group formed by residents of the area. This part of the city is very new and is not entirely built out yet, so it has the potential to be targeted for many more construction site burglaries. The residents are all new to the area and do not know one another; in addition, their homes are spread out around the community amid houses under construction. Many of the residents' houses have been targets, although before they took residence. The community group is also new, but the members are active and willing to participate. The meeting is to be 90 minutes long, and the crime problem is the only topic on the agenda.
- *Information presented:* The CAU will provide the officers with general information about the burglary problem to present at the meeting, comparing the city as a whole to other cities and this specific community to other communities in the city. In addition, the officers will present information about recent patterns of activity (i.e., tactical crime analysis results), highlighting the MO and time of day of the burglaries. Finally, they will hand out copies of a color map and accompanying information showing the current and future homes under construction to elicit the group members' help, asking them to be alert for suspicious activity at these places and to call the police if they see any such activity.

Audience: News Media

- *Purpose:* To provide the news media with information about the problem and what the police department is doing about it.
- *Context:* The city is a fairly quiet place with very little crime, so the news organizations are looking for any type of information to present. The chief of police would also like to let the community know about the problem and what the police are doing about it.
- *Information presented:* Although the news media organizations can gather information on the problem by visiting the police department's Web site and by attending the chief's presentation to the city council meeting, the police

department's public information officer (media liaison) has decided to provide them with more specific information about all the work the crime analysis unit has done to understand this problem. The liaison, with the help of members of the CAU, will present the media with information about the specific primary data collection methods, such as interviews and observations, along with the results and other research findings from neighboring agencies and crime analysis scholars (collected as part of the initial analysis process). This information will be provided through an in-person presentation and through the dissemination of printed reports. In addition, the liaison may initiate a collaborative effort to design an entire video news feature about the process.

Audience: General

- *Purpose:* To provide citizens with answers to general questions about the problem.
- *Context:* The police department has made a commitment to provide city residents with ongoing information on crime problems in the city.
- *Information presented:* The crime analyst will provide the police department's Web master with general information about the problem, including a historical comparison and comparison to other cities, to post on the Internet. For example, statistics will be provided to allow Web site visitors to compare the city's construction site burglary/theft problem with the same problem in other cities in the area and around the country. In addition, tactical crime patterns and maps will be posted to alert citizens and other police agencies. Details about primary data collection, such as interviews and observation, will probably not be included on the Web site. The police department will also provide the information posted on the Web site to libraries and other community agencies so that it is available to citizens who have no access to the Internet.

As this example shows, the information selected for presentation in administrative crime analysis can vary a great deal depending on the audience, the purpose, and the context of the presentation. Many factors influence analysts' decisions about providing particular information to specific audiences, and analysts must rely on their own judgment and experience in weighing those factors.

The rest of this chapter is devoted to a discussion of ACA's use of a particular medium that has changed the way crime analysis information is being provided to all types of audiences: the Internet.

Administrative Crime Analysis and the Internet

In recent years, as the Internet has become increasingly popular as a medium of communication in general, use of the Internet to disseminate crime analysis information has grown as well.[1] As of 1997, 35% of all police agencies in the United States were using the Internet to allow citizens routine access to crime statistics and maps; for police agencies serving cities with more than 100,000 people, the figure was 80% (Wartell & McEwen, 2001). Police agencies have many reasons to publish crime analysis findings on the Internet, including the following (see Boba, 1999; Wartell & McEwen, 2001):

- To reduce workloads for crime analysts whose duties include responding to citizen requests for crime analysis information
- To avoid having to answer judgment questions such as, "Is the area safe?" by providing statistics and information from which individuals can draw their own conclusions
- To increase awareness of community problems and encourage citizens to get involved in solving those problems
- To keep the public informed so that citizens understand how the police are actively addressing problems
- To share information about common problems with crime analysis scholars and thus enhance their ability to conduct research on those problems
- To share information about patterns and problems with other police agencies in order to address them collectively
- To ensure that citizens have an easily accessible source of accurate information about crime and disorder

Providing analysis information on the Internet can also have some disadvantages for police departments and their communities, such as the following (adapted from Wartell & McEwen, 2001):

- Commercial entities might use the information for profit (e.g., burglar alarm companies might market their services to recently victimized home owners).
- Current and potential criminals may use the information to commit crimes (e.g., to identify areas to be burgled or to avoid areas that police have targeted for DUIs or drugs).
- Information on specific neighborhoods may result in reduced property values or increased insurance rates in those areas (although no studies conducted to date have shown definitively that this has ever occurred).
- The information could be misinterpreted if it is presented in a way that is too complex for the audience to understand (e.g., a graduated color area map can give the impression that incidents are equally distributed across the area when actually they may be concentrated in a single block within that area).

Increasingly, police departments are deciding that the advantages they gain by using the Internet to provide information to various audiences outweigh any disadvantages. The Internet has become an integral part of our society, and its use for ACA is not likely to decrease. In using the Internet to disseminate crime analysis information, police agencies need to understand the specific kinds of audiences they are likely to reach and which types of information are appropriate for sharing through this medium. They must also keep in mind some additional considerations that are related directly to the nature of the Internet.

Audiences

The audience for crime analysis information on the Internet includes essentially everyone who has access to the Internet. Within that large group, smaller audiences exist that are interested in different types of information. In order to provide relevant information to these different audiences, crime analysts must first identify them. Examples of some likely audiences for the information provided by a police agency are as follows (adapted from Boba, 1999):

- Residents (e.g., individuals living within the police jurisdiction's community)
- Potential and new residents (e.g., people who are considering moving into or who have just moved into the community)
- Community groups (e.g., neighborhood watch organizations, home owners' associations)
- Community managers (e.g., YMCA, Girls and Boys Club, religious groups)
- School officials (e.g., school district personnel, teachers, principals)
- Businesses (e.g., store managers, business groups)
- News media organizations (e.g., newspapers, TV stations)
- Crime analysis scholars and students (e.g., high school, college, and graduate-level instructors, researchers, students)
- City and police department personnel (e.g., members of the city government and the police agency)
- Other police professionals (e.g., crime analysts and other police personnel, both in the area and outside it)
- General public (any interested person who does not fall into one of the other categories)

Sometimes police agencies will target the crime analysis information on their Web sites toward one or two particular audiences for specific reasons. For example, if a large agency is trying to eliminate the need to respond to phone calls from media organizations requesting information on crime counts over the past 5 years, it may decided to post this information more quickly than other types of information that are relevant to different groups.

Types of Information

Normally, police department Web sites post information on crime analysis results, calls for service, arrests, and traffic as they receive requests for these types of information from audiences. In most cases, agencies post lists of incidents, frequencies, percentages, and rates per population, and in some cases they also provide information on average crime and other rates (e.g., crime per apartment unit). A small proportion of police agencies provide crime pattern information on the Internet. Much of this information is based on the results of strategic and tactical crime analysis and is presented in a format designed for a general audience.

Because many of the people who visit police agency Web sites are potentially novices when it comes to understanding crime analysis information, most sites that provide such information also provide some or all of the following:

- *Definitions:* Simple definitions of frequently used words and terms (e.g., *clearance rate, call for service*) are often provided; sites may also include explanations of types of crime, types of calls for service, types of geographic areas, and so on.
- *Demographic information:* This information on the population characteristics of the area (e.g., broken down by age, race/ethnicity, income level, and so on) provides some context for the crime and police information. Agencies often make demographic information available on their Web sites through links to city or county resources.
- *Frequently asked questions (FAQs):* Web sites that provide large amounts of crime analysis information may include FAQ sections to help guide users to specific areas that are relevant to their concerns. Questions such as the following are common in these sections: "I'm looking to move my family/business into the city—what is the crime/activity in a certain area?" "What is the crime activity at a certain apartment community/mobile home park/school?" "What is crime analysis?" The sites provide direct links from the answers to relevant areas of the sites, making it easy for visitors to navigate.
- *Description of crime analysis functions:* Because students and police professionals often use the Internet to find examples of crime analysis units that are conducting certain types of analyses, some Web sites provide descriptions of their agencies' crime analysis activities.
- *Publications, presentations, and articles:* Some police agencies post detailed information on crime analysis issues on their Web sites and provide links to articles and other publications on these issues to help further the discipline, stimulate ideas, and provide resources to students, scholars, and police professionals.
- *Requests/contact information:* Many police agency Web sites include information (e.g., phone numbers, e-mail addresses) to allow users to contact agency representatives directly for clarification of any Web site content or to request additional information on the crime analyses conducted.
- *Relevant links:* Because many Web site visitors are likely to be interested in searching for additional information, most police agency sites provide links to sites maintained by other police agencies and city governments in the immediate area, around the state, and even across the country, as well as the sites of federal agencies.

The following are examples of some specific types of information that might be relevant to particular audiences:

- *Residents:* Lists of crime and disorder activity in their neighborhoods; current crime patterns (to protect their homes; to report related activity to the police)

- *Potential and new residents:* Frequency comparisons between neighborhoods and cities over time (to compare potential areas of residence; to be aware of current activity in new areas of residence)
- *Community groups:* Lists of crime and disorder activity in their neighborhoods and surrounding areas; current crime patterns (to alert community and neighborhood members; to take crime prevention measures; to be on the look out for related activity)
- *Community managers:* Demographics and crime rates by neighborhoods; lists of crime and disorder activity around their organization locations (to understand the neighborhoods of their clients; to be alert for activity occurring in and around their locations)
- *School officials:* Frequency comparisons of crime, disorder, and demographics of areas within the school district, directly around school locations, and on school campuses; current crime patterns around school locations (to understand the environments in which students live; to compare crime levels among schools to help determine overall safety; to assist with current crime patterns resolving around schools; to examine safety within and around schools)
- *Businesses:* Lists of crime and disorder activity at their business locations and in business districts; commercial crime patterns (to assist the police in reducing problems and activity at their own locations; to protect themselves from criminal activity; to be on the lookout for related activity)
- *Media:* Frequency, percentage, and crime rate comparisons of multiple years, neighboring jurisdictions as well as state and national levels (to report on general crime trends in the local area compared with others)
- *Crime analysis scholars and students:* Crime and disorder data (i.e., actual databases); comprehensive research reports detailing methodology (to conduct research and analysis of issues related to crime and disorder using police data; to compare research results)
- *City and police department personnel:* Lists of crime and disorder activity by neighborhood (to understand the areas in which they are working or implementing city programs and projects; to present information to community and business groups with which they are working)
- *Other police professionals:* Information about the structure and personnel of the crime analysis unit; frequency, percentage, and crime rate comparisons of multiple years for that jurisdiction (to understand the nature of other crime analysis units; to compare crime figures)
- *General public:* General frequencies and rates of crime by year (to compare crime levels with those in other areas)

Internet-Specific Issues

Police agencies need to be aware that a number of specific social, political, legal, and practical issues are associated with the posting of crime analysis information on the Internet, in part because the audiences for this information are so wide-ranging. The decisions that agencies make about these issues are extremely important and must be made carefully. Currently, no laws are in place dictating how police agencies may or may not post crime analysis information on the Internet, but several documents offer agencies guidelines for doing so (Boba, 1999; Wartell & McEwen, 2001). Two key issues in this area are discussed below.

Privacy and Confidentiality

One of the biggest concerns related to the posting of crime analysis information on the Internet is the protection of the privacy of all persons involved (e.g., officers, victims, suspects, witnesses), the confidentiality of the data, and the security of ongoing investigations. In posting information, police agencies must strike a delicate balance between the public's right to know and the need to protect victims and investigations. Wartell and McEwen (2001) outline this problem as follows:

1. Citizens have a right to know about crime in their communities, but victims have a right to privacy about what happened to them. How can those rights be balanced?

   When a law enforcement agency posts a map of crime incidents on the Internet, it runs the risk of including too much or not enough data. For example, if a sexual assault victim's incident location is provided, then his or her identity can be determined, and his or her privacy has been violated. Yet if a sexual assault is not posted and subsequently an individual falls victim to a sexual assault, has the agency thwarted the public's legitimate interest? That is, in not publishing the risk of sexual assault in an area, is the agency failing to let would-be victims know they are at risk so they can take appropriate precautions?

2. Other interested persons, especially researchers, want access to geocoded data on crime. How can the data be provided without violating victims' privacy?

   Researchers are accustomed to signing agreements to ensure the confidentiality of individuals when analyzing survey data, but such agreements are not prevalent regarding geocoded data. The field has yet to agree on what restrictions should be placed on researchers' use of data that will safeguard confidentiality while enabling researchers to spatially analyze [data using] rigorous methods—methods that ultimately serve the entire criminal justice field.

3. If geocoded data are made available to others, what are the potential negative social outcomes and accompanying liability issues associated with misuse of the data?

   Disseminating crime maps to the public could revitalize informal redlining methods employed by some insurance and banking companies. Whereas a neighborhood identified as a high-crime area could be targeted for various types of positive local interventions, it could also be flagged as undesirable, resulting in residential flight and ultimately causing more damage to an already problematic area. Further, the creation of crime maps or sharing of geocoded data that are inaccurate may result in false perceptions regarding the nature of a crime or public safety problem. Agencies already have published incorrect addresses of released sex offenders under Megan's Law, resulting in serious legal implications.

4. If police departments make crime data available on the Internet, what security measures need to be taken to minimize the risk of intrusion?

It is possible to set up password protection, firewalls, and search-and-query options that block the display of particularly sensitive fields. However, police departments and officers are skeptical about the prospects of ensuring that intelligence information and other restricted data do not end up in the wrong hands. (pp. 2–3)

Most agencies avoid some of these issues by not publishing the names of individuals (an exception is the publication of information on registered sex offenders, which, it should be noted, is not analysis information). Although many agencies seem to be in agreement on this practice, there is inconsistency among agencies in the publication of specific information on the addresses at which crimes or other events have occurred. It is usually difficult for Web site visitors to discern exact addresses from information displayed in maps because the symbols used are much too large. However, the issue of privacy sometimes arises when agencies provide tabular information along with maps. Some agencies publish exact addresses for all crimes and other incidents listed on their sites. Others publish most addresses but make exceptions for sensitive cases such as child abuse, rape, and domestic violence. Most agencies, however, do not provide specific address information at all; instead, they give location information by larger geographic units (e.g., neighborhood, grid, beat), by street names only (e.g., noting just "East Main Street" rather than "123 East Main Street"), or by specific blocks only (e.g., noting "the 100 block of East Main Street" or "1XX East Main Street" rather than 123 East Main Street).

Disclaimers

Although police agencies often include definitions of terms and explanations of the analysis findings posted on their Web sites, this material does not address what the information provided does *not* say. Because audiences unfamiliar with crime analysis may misinterpret the information for various reasons, most agencies also post disclaimers—that is, statements that provide specific warnings to prevent users from misunderstanding the data and analysis results. The following are some examples of such disclaimers:

- Crime data represent crimes reported to or found by the police, not all crime.
- Only 90% of the actual incidents are located (geocoded) on the map.
- An arrest does not mean the individual was found guilty of the crime.
- A call for service does not necessarily indicate the occurrence of a crime.
- Data are susceptible to a degree of error.
- Data are provided by the police department as a courtesy, not an obligation.

- Crime statistics are only one of several criteria that can be used to determine one's safety in an area.
- Crime statistics do not imply that one area is "worse" than another.

Interactive Mapping

Instead of simply posting analysis results, many police agencies are moving toward providing audiences with the ability to conduct analyses themselves through interactive crime mapping systems. Web site visitors use these systems to search databases for the information that interests them and map the results. This type of format gives audiences more flexibility in the information they can obtain and also reduces the amount of work for department personnel.

Currently, most agencies are using single-symbol mapping for this purpose, but a few use graduated color maps of areas. Still other agencies provide interactive features that give Web site visitors the same querying capabilities as mapping systems but provide the resulting information in the form of lists of cases or summary reports instead of maps. The following descriptions of some police agency sites offering interactive crime mapping provide a sense of the variety of applications currently in use:

- *Austin, Texas, Police Department* (http://www.ci.austin.tx.us/police/crimeinformation): Through a feature called the Crime Report Viewer, this site provides crime information aggregated to geographic boundaries, such as neighborhood associations, police sectors or districts, zip codes, census tracts, and custom rectangle search areas determined by users. Site visitors can also search for crime within 500 or 1,000 feet of specific addresses. The site provides a moving 18-month window of data within which users can search (i.e., data are downloaded daily and include 18 months from each day). The crime data selected through users' searches are displayed not as individual cases or as points on maps but in tables of aggregate numbers. Thus, for example, a user interested in auto thefts in a particular area might learn that 45 such crimes have occurred in the area over the preceding 18 months.
- *Chicago, Illinois, Police Department* (http://www.cityofchicago.org/police): This site uses a mapping software program called ICAM (Information Collection for Automated Mapping) to allow visitors to query crime from the preceding 90 days in blocks of 14 days; the results are displayed in single-symbol maps, graphs, and tables. Users can query data by addresses, police beats, interesting streets, and schools.
- *Phoenix, Arizona, Police Department* (http://www.ci.phoenix.az.us/APPINTRO/crimesta.html): This interactive site presents frequencies of crime and other information (traffic collisions, calls for service, gang-involved and domestic violence-related incidents) by city council district, precinct, beat, or grid from 1996 to present. The site provides maps for reference, but all results are presented as tables.

- *City of Port St. Lucie, Florida* (http://pslgis.cityofpsl.com/viewer.htm): As part of a city initiative to provide information to citizens through interactive mapping, this Web site enables visitors to access crime information from the past several years along with property information and water/sewer assessments. The data are displayed in single-symbol maps and tables listing individual crimes and accidents, and users have the option of downloading the data.
- *San Diego, California, Police Department* (http://www.arjis.org/mapping/help/disclaimer.html): As part of a regional effort to share information on crime throughout San Diego County, this site uses single-symbol mapping to provide visitors with information on crime and disorder, vehicles and traffic, and arrests and citations.

In addition to the issues noted earlier in relation to the posting of crime analysis information on the Internet, police agencies' use of interactive software applications raises additional concerns. One of these is the issue of users' levels of knowledge of crime data and mapping. As this book makes clear, crime analysis and crime mapping are complex fields of study, and the possibility exists that novice users of systems such as those described here might misuse or misinterpret the data they find. In addition, some practical issues of concern to police agencies offering such sites include the technological skills of the users (e.g., if the software is too complex, site visitors will be less likely to use it) and the speed of the Internet connection users need to run such programs adequately (e.g., slow connections make complex applications very difficult and cumbersome to use).

Finding Crime Analysis Examples on the Internet

Because Web sites devoted to general crime analysis are constantly being established, updated, and improved, no specific site addresses are offered here. To find a wealth of current sites, use an Internet search engine such as Google, entering (within quotation marks) the key phrases "crime analysis," "crime statistics," and "crime mapping." In addition, a particularly useful online source for links to local, state, federal, academic, and international agencies with crime analysis and crime mapping information is maintained by the U.S. government's Mapping and Analysis for Public Safety program at http://www.ojp.usdoj.gov/nij/maps/related.html.

Summary Points

This chapter has presented guidelines for conducting administrative crime analysis and discussion of the use of the Internet in ACA. The following are the key points addressed in this chapter:

- The results of tactical and strategic crime analysis results are presented primarily to operational personnel within police agencies. Administrative crime analysis is the process of paring down those results for presentation to nonoperational personnel such as police and city management, citizens, and any number of other audiences external to police agencies.

- Administrative crime analysis information is presented for several reasons, including the following: (a) to inform the public generally about crime and other activities in particular jurisdictions, (b) to alert audiences to particular events of immediate importance, (c) to inform citizens and other groups working together with the police department to reduce crime and disorder, (d) to inform potential victims about specific patterns and to make recommendations concerning how they can protect themselves or their property, and (e) to give police management, city government, business owners, developers, and others information they need to make decisions.

- The information presented in ACA, and how it is presented, depends on the audiences for the information, the purposes for which the information is being shared, and the contexts of individual situations.

- Audiences for ACA information include people with positions in police and/or city management, citizens, and other groups with various interests (e.g., business owners, neighborhood organizations, news media).

- The elements of context that can affect the presentation of ACA information include the current social and political climates as well as legal concerns and practical concerns.

- In recent years, the Internet has become the most widely used medium for the dissemination of administrative crime analysis information.

- By using the Internet to publish crime analysis findings, police agencies can (a) reduce the workload for crime analysts, (b) avoid answering crime-related judgment questions, (c) increase awareness of community problems and encourage citizens to get involved with solving them, (d) inform the public, (e) share information with crime analysis scholars, (f) share information with other police agencies, and (g) ensure that audiences have a source of accurate information about crime and disorder.

- The disadvantages of police agencies' use of the Internet to publish crime analysis findings include the following: (a) Commercial entities might use the information for profit, (b) current and potential criminals might use the information to commit crimes, (c) information about crime in specific neighborhoods might negatively affect those areas, and (d) audiences might misinterpret the information provided.

- Audiences for the crime analysis information available on a police agency Web site include local residents, potential and new residents of the local area, community groups, community managers, school officials, businesses, news media organizations, crime analysis scholars and students, city and police department personnel, other police professionals, and the general public.

- Most police agency Web sites provide lists of crime incidents showing frequencies, percentages, and rates per population; some also provide average crime rates and other rates (e.g., crime per apartment unit). In addition, these sites frequently provide definitions, demographic information, frequently asked questions, descriptions of crime analysis functions, crime analysis publications, contact information, and links to related sites.

- Among the issues that police agencies need to address in posting crime analysis information on the Internet are the need to maintain privacy and confidentiality (e.g., of victims, ongoing investigations) and the need to include disclaimers (e.g., to inform users of limitations of the data).
- Police agency Web sites are increasingly disseminating crime analysis information through simple interactive mapping systems that allow users to search databases and map the results.

Exercises

Exercise 14.1

Find a local-level police department Web site that contains crime analysis information. (If the amount of information available on the site is significant, select one section to focus on for this exercise, such as historical statistics, maps, or current neighborhood counts of crime.) Assess the site by answering the following questions:

- What type of data is used (e.g., crime, calls for service, arrests)?
- What time period is included (e.g., 5 years, last several months)?
- What is the statistical nature of the information provided (e.g., frequencies, rates, means)?
- What seems to be the purpose of the information? Is it helpful for that purpose?
- How might the agency improve the information?

Exercise 14.2

Using the information in the sample problem analysis report that appears in the appendix to this volume, create a 10-minute PowerPoint presentation for one of the following audiences: police officials, city council members, news media, school officials, citizens, business owners.

Note

1. This discussion is concerned only with police agency dissemination of information on the Internet, which is an electronic forum available to the general public; this should not be confused with police agency use of intranets, which are closed networks accessible only to selected individuals.

Appendix _____

Sample Problem Analysis Project

T he following sample project is adapted from an example created by the Police Foundation (2003a) for a course titled Advanced Problem Analysis, Crime Analysis, and Crime Mapping Training. This sample represents a crime analyst's first attempt at analyzing a commercial burglary problem in the fictitious city of Los Analysis, thus what follows can and should be improved in many ways.

_____ Commercial Burglary in Los Analysis

Introduction

The Los Analysis Police Department is a midsize agency with 420 sworn and 185 civilian personnel serving approximately 164,000 citizens over 48 square miles. Los Analysis is a suburb to a major metropolitan city; however, Los Analysis has its own downtown area in addition to several commercial and industrial areas. Generally, the industrial areas are located on the west side and the commercial areas are in the northwest section of the city. The northeast, east, and south sides of the city are predominantly residential. The downtown area is in the center of the city. Because Los Analysis is landlocked, population growth has leveled off in recent years.

Over the past 5 years, Part I crime has declined in Los Analysis; however, over the past 2 years, the city has experienced a dramatic increase in burglary activity in its commercial and industrial areas. In addition, the news media have recently begun to cover this problem because the downtown business association has brought it to their attention. Thus it has become a high priority for the mayor and, consequently, the police chief.

The Problem

The increase in commercial burglary activity over the past 2 years has prompted the police department to partner with local business owners to better understand and respond to the problem. The Crime Analysis Unit was recently asked to attend

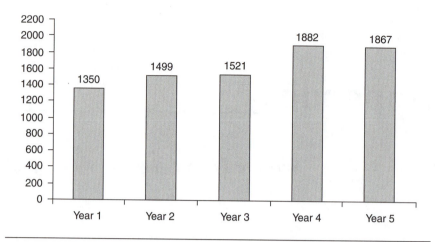

Figure A.1   Commercial Burglary Frequency in Los Analysis: Past 5 Years

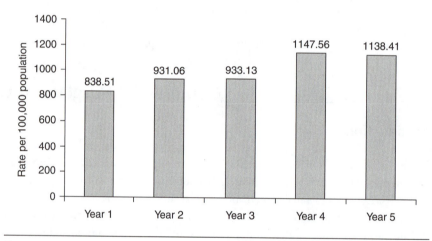

Figure A.2   Commercial Burglary Rate per 100,000 Persons in Los Analysis: Past 5 Years

the partnership meetings and provide data on the city's commercial burglary problem. Figure A.1 depicts the annual frequency of commercial burglary in Los Analysis over the past 5 years. Note that the increase in activity has occurred primarily over the past 2 years.

The increase in activity is further illustrated in Figure A.2, which depicts the rate of commercial burglary by population. The increase in population has been relatively small and consistent (161,000 in Year 1 with an increase to 164,000 in Year 5, a 1.9% increase over 5 years). Note how the rate jumped from 933.13 in Year 3 to 1147.56 in Year 4 and remained steady at 1138.41 in Year 5. The commercial burglary rate in Los Analysis is much higher than the statewide rate of 714.45 per 100,000 persons and the national burglary rate of 740.85 per 100,000.

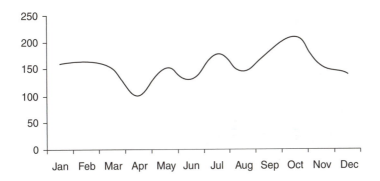

Figure A.3   Commercial Burglary Frequency in Los Analysis: Year 5

The clearance rate for commercial burglary in Los Analysis is 7.69%, lower than the national burglary clearance rate of 12.7%. In addition, it appears that a small number of repeat offenders are responsible for multiple crimes, as approximately 20% of the offenders account for 45% of the arrests. However, these numbers should be interpreted with caution, as less than 8% of commercial burglaries are cleared by arrest.

Temporal Analysis

A temporal analysis was conducted to determine if any recent, seasonal, monthly, day of week, or time of day patterns emerged. Figure A.3 illustrates the frequency of commercial burglary in the most recent full year. This chart shows that commercial burglary activity tends to be greater in the last 6 months of the year, with 54% of the reports occurring between July and December. Last year, the number of reports reached a low of 99 in April and peaked at 210 in October. The high number of incidents occurring during the month of October can partly be attributed to ongoing office and industrial/construction site crime trends discussed in the following sections.

To determine seasonal variation to the crime, Figure A.4 depicts 2 years of commercial burglary data by month. Interestingly, commercial burglary trends for the past 2 years have been similar between the months of January and July. Overall, the crime tends to increase in the early part of the year, decrease in April and June, and increase in May and July. However, trends in the latter part of last year were different from the preceding year. For example, commercial burglary activity spiked in October of last year, with 210 crimes reported, an increase of 36 from the previous October. The month of December is also different from the preceding year. Last December, only 142 commercial burglaries were reported, down from 189 the previous December. Generally, Figure A.4 indicates that commercial burglary activity is greater in the last 6 months of the year and is substantially lower during the months of April and June. Also, the trend line shows that, despite monthly variation, commercial burglary has gradually increased over the past 2 years.

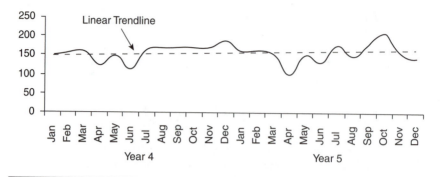

Figure A.4   Commercial Burglary Frequency in Los Analysis: Years 4 and 5

Weighted Method

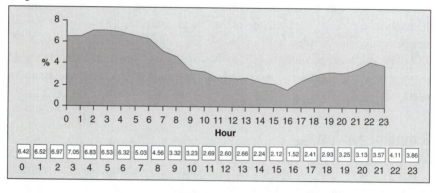

Figure A.5   Commercial Burglary Weighted Time Span Analysis

A temporal analysis was conducted to determine if any time of day patterns emerge. Figure A.5 depicts the time of day based on the time span recorded on incident reports taken in the past year. The chart depicts temporal analysis using the weighted method. For example, if a commercial burglary occurred sometime between the hours of 0100 and 0500, each hour in the 4-hour time span is given a weight of 0.25. Rather than relying on the time the crime was reported or the first time in the time span, every hour is accounted for by using the weighted method of analysis. This method of temporal analysis can be hand calculated or automatically generated using the Automated Tactical Analysis of Crime (ATAC) software from Bair Software Inc.

As one might expect, Figure A.5 reveals that most commercial burglary activity takes place overnight, when businesses are unoccupied. Activity declines during the daytime hours and then begins to increase again at 1700, when many businesses close for the day. The numbers at the bottom of the chart, automatically generated by the ATAC software, indicate the percentage of activity that occurs during each hour. Thus we can see that a large percentage (46.6%) of the time spans overlap the hours of midnight and 0600.

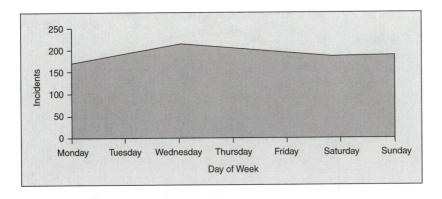

Figure A.6   Commercial Burglary Day of Week Analysis

To determine variation in commercial burglary by day of week, Figure A.6 depicts the day of week based on the first possible date the crime could have occurred from reports taken in the last year. Ideally, given that commercial burglary tends to occur over a time span, a day of week analysis should take every day in the time span into account, weighting each day in the time span equally. However, a majority of the cases occur within 1 or 2 days. This chart, created using ATAC software, illustrates that a slightly higher number of commercial burglaries occur or have a time span beginning on Wednesday. For the most part, however, the crime seems to be fairly evenly spread over all days of the week. However, this chart should be interpreted carefully, because it accounts only for the first day of the time span.

Spatial Analysis

The maps presented in Figures A.7, A.8, and A.9 reveal that much of the commercial burglary activity is concentrated in the west/northwest sections of Los Analysis, which is where the city's industrial and commercial areas are located. The density map in Figure A.7 illustrates commercial burglary hot spots for the past year. The densest concentration of activity is in the northwest section of the city. This area includes commercial locations such as office buildings, strip malls, and gas stations. In the latter part of the year, burglary of office buildings increased substantially as the result of an ongoing crime pattern. Of the 22 incidents in this crime pattern, 7 occurred in the grey area on the density map, and the remaining incidents occurred in the surrounding area. The hot spot in the center of the density map represents the downtown area, where commercial burglaries tend to occur at restaurants, retail stores, and office buildings. The smaller hot spot on the lower west side of the map is in the city's industrial area. Burglaries in this area tend to occur at commercial yards, storage facilities, and construction sites. Over the past 6 months, 18 incidents have occurred as part of an ongoing crime pattern in this area. Note that the east side of Los Analysis, which is primarily residential, experiences very little commercial burglary activity.

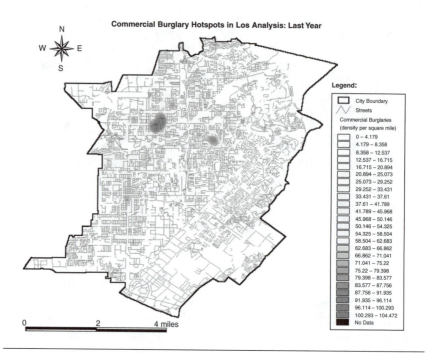

Figure A.7   Commercial Burglary Hot Spots in Los Analysis: Past Year

To further illustrate commercial burglary hot spots, the graduated map in Figure A.8 was created. The map depicts the last year of commercial burglary data by police grid. The standard deviation classification is used to illustrate outliers— that is, those grids that have more or fewer commercial burglaries than average. In this map, the slash (marks) areas signify areas with fewer commercial burglaries than the mean, or the average number of burglaries per grid. The gray areas represent grids that have higher-than-average numbers of commercial burglaries. The areas that are shaded dark gray are three or more standard deviations from the mean, meaning that they have a substantially higher number of commercial burglaries than the grids in the rest of the city. Note that the dark grey grids are concentrated downtown and in the commercial area in the northwest section of the city.

The map in Figure A.9 depicts the top 10 addresses for commercial burglary in Los Analysis. The map is also based on the past year of commercial burglary data. The top address for commercial burglary in Los Analysis is the Parkside Office Complex at 1310 N. Main St. Last year, 29 commercial burglaries were reported from office suites at this location. The remaining top addresses consist of office buildings, commercial yards, storage facilities, and strip malls. Many of the top addresses are along main thoroughfares, and 8 of the top 10 locations do not have alarms or security guards.

Victims

As Figure A.9 illustrates, certain types of locations are repeatedly victimized. Table A.1 shows the most frequently victimized location types in Los Analysis, and

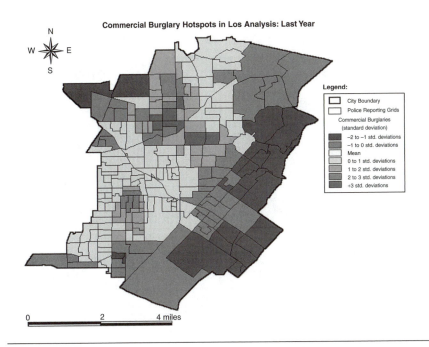

Figure A.8   Commercial Burglary Hot Spots in Los Analysis: Past Year

Figure A.9   Top 10 Addresses for Commercial Burglary in Los Analysis: Past Year

the pie chart in Figure A.10 illustrates the top five types of locations. Almost 20% of commercial burglaries occur at office buildings, most of which are concentrated in the northwest and downtown areas of the city. Office buildings are likely targeted because they tend to be unoccupied between the hours of 1700 and 0800 and

Table A.1   Types of Locations Repeatedly Victimized

Location Type	Frequency	Percentage
Office building	352	18.9
Storage fenced	205	11.0
Commercial yard	160	8.6
Construction site	127	6.8
Restaurant	83	4.4
School	69	3.7
Apartment	65	3.5
Clothing/retail/thrift	59	3.2
Medical/dental/hospital	59	3.2
Auto parts/repair	49	2.6
Electronics/appliance	47	2.5
Warehouse	45	2.4
Church	43	2.3
Hotel/motel	43	2.3
Bar	41	2.2
Beauty salon	34	1.8
Other	386	20.7
Total	1,867	100.0

because, in many instances, several office suites can be burglarized once entry is made to the exterior building. Offices are a reliable source of valuable property, such as computer equipment, office supplies, and cash. The next three types of locations—storage facilities, commercial yards, and construction sites—tend to be concentrated on the west side of the city. All of these sites contain similar types of property, such as construction equipment, hardware/tools, auto parts, and industrial machinery. The last type of location, which accounted for 4% of commercial burglaries last year, is restaurants. Although restaurants are located throughout Los Analysis, those in the downtown area are burglarized most often. The most common property taken from restaurants is cash. The location types collapsed into the "other" category include schools (3.7%), apartment buildings (3.5%), retail stores (3.2%), and medical offices (3.2%).

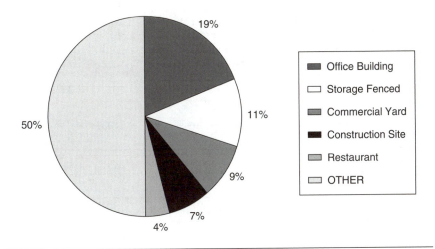

Figure A.10   Top Five Types of Locations Victimized, Commercial Burglary in Los Analysis: Year 5

Repeat Victimization

The term *repeat victimization* refers to the recurrence of crime against the same people and/or places. The maps in the "Spatial Analysis" section above illustrate that commercial burglary in Los Analysis does tend to concentrate at specific locations and in certain areas. For example, 5 of the city's 20 reporting grids (those encompassing the commercial area in the northwest section of the city) account for 790, or 42.3%, of last year's commercial burglaries. In addition, the top 10 addresses account for 191, or 10.2%, of last year's crimes. By focusing prevention strategies on repeatedly victimized areas and/or places, the police department can likely bring about a dramatic reduction in the commercial burglary problem.

Modus Operandi

Although the modus operandi largely depends on the unique opportunities available at each crime scene, some commonalities do emerge. Tables A.2, A.3, and A.4 depict the point and method of entry as well as the property taken for commercial burglaries occurring in the past year.

Generally, the front door is the most common point of entry (18.2%) in Los Analysis commercial burglaries. The "other" category also accounts for 18.2% of last year's burglaries. This category covers entry points such as garage doors, air vents, and roofs. Because this category is collapsed at the time data are entered, one would have to read the original incident reports to learn more about the point of entry in these 340 incidents. The remaining top five points of entry include windows (14.4%), storage doors (11.2%), and fences/walls (11.1%).

The top method of entry is a window break (19.9%), commonly perpetrated with an item, such as landscaping rocks, that the offender finds at the scene. Interestingly,

Table A.2   Commercial Burglaries Point of Entry

Point of Entry	Frequency	Percentage
Door: front	340	18.2
Window	268	14.4
Door: storage	209	11.2
Fence/wall	207	11.1
Door: rear	132	7.1
Door: window	118	6.3
Door: side	63	3.4
Other	**340**	**18.2**
Unknown	190	10.2
Total	1,337	71.6

entry with no sign of force is the next most common category, accounting for 16.3% of the past year's incidents. Although this finding indicates that some businesses are left unsecured, it should be noted that no sign of force is often found at construction sites and commercial yards, where gaps in perimeter fencing make it easy for offender(s) to enter the property. The remaining top methods of entry are door or window pries (15.0%), remove/cut lock (8.1%), forced but undetermined (5.8%), and cut (4.5%). Once again, the "other" category represents a limitation in the modus operandi data.

Table A.4 shows the most common types of property taken during commercial burglaries occurring in the past year. As one would expect, cash is the most common type of property taken because it can be readily used and is nearly impossible to trace. The "unknown" category refers to burglaries where property is taken, but the owner or responsible party cannot identify every item that is missing. Other hot products include hardware/tools (11.2%), computer equipment (11.1%), and construction equipment (5.1%). These are the primary types of property that are being taken in the two ongoing commercial burglary patterns described below.

The problem-solving partnership between the police department and the business community was formed 2 months ago as the result of the notable increase in activity. Over the past 6 months, two separate crime patterns have occurred in the west and northwest sections of the city. The pattern occurring in the commercial area on the city's northwest side involved overnight entries to office buildings, where office and computer equipment has been taken. In two separate incidents, the offender(s) burglarized multiple suites in the same office building. The primary methods of entry in these incidents have been through prying open the front door and breaking a window. Overall, approximately $32,000 in property has been stolen from offices in this area over the past 6 months. In one incident, a suspicious white

Table A.3   Commercial Burglaries Method of Entry

Method of Entry	Frequency	Percentage
Break	372	19.9
Pry tool	280	15.0
Remove/cut lock	152	8.1
Forced	109	5.8
Cut	84	4.5
Rock	76	4.1
Remove	36	1.9
Foot impact/impact tool	33	1.8
Bolt cutters	17	0.9
Channel locks/vice grips	2	0.1
Lift off track	2	0.1
Other	**244**	**13.1**
Unknown	156	8.4
No sign forced	304	16.3
Total	1,163	62.3

Honda Accord was seen in the area immediately after the burglary, but no license plate number was obtained.

The pattern occurring on the west side of town involves overnight burglaries at unguarded commercial yards and construction sites. In 4 of the 18 total cases, the offenders have cut or driven a vehicle over a perimeter fence; however, in most of the remaining incidents, there was no sign of forced entry to the property. Property taken in these incidents includes approximately $23,000 worth of hardware/tools, construction equipment, and auto parts. In one incident, a surveillance camera recorded two white males loading property into a dark blue or black pickup truck; however, because the recording quality is poor, no additional information was obtained from the tape. Two weeks ago, the police Special Enforcement Team used a bulletin prepared by the Crime Analysis Unit to set up an overnight surveillance in an area with a high amount of activity; however, the surveillance effort failed to generate any leads.

Analysis

Over the past 2 years, Los Analysis has experienced a dramatic increase in burglary activity in its commercial and industrial areas, and this activity has become a focus of both the mayor and the police chief. The activity peaked in October of last

Table A.4   Property Taken in Commercial Burglaries

Property Taken	Frequency	Percentage
Cash/notes	258	13.8
Hardware/tools	210	11.2
Computer equipment	207	11.1
Construction equipment	95	5.1
Stereo equipment	62	3.3
TV	62	3.3
Office equipment	57	3.1
Clothes	53	2.8
Bike	44	2.4
Auto parts	43	2.3
Consumables	42	2.2
Appliances	30	1.6
Sporting goods	23	1.2
Alcohol	21	1.1
Phones	20	1.1
Furniture	17	0.9
Jewelry/precious metal	16	0.9
VCRs	16	0.9
Credit cards/checks	15	0.8
Purses/wallets	15	0.8
Yard equipment	14	0.7
Coins/collections	13	0.7
Cell phones	12	0.6
Firearms	11	0.6
Other	264	14.1
Unknown	242	13.0
No property taken	5	0.3
Total	1,867	100.0

year, largely driven by two ongoing crime trends—the first is a pattern of burglaries occurring overnight at office buildings in the northwest section of the city, and the second involves overnight burglaries at commercial yards and construction sites on the west side of town. The commercial burglary rate in Los Analysis is higher than both state and national levels, and the clearance rate is very low but also much lower than the national level.

More specifically, the commercial burglary problem is generally during evening and night hours, when businesses are closed, but there does not appear to be any pattern of occurrence by day of the week. Much of the commercial burglary activity is concentrated in the west/northwest sections of Los Analysis, which is where the city's industrial and commercial areas are located. In fact, almost 20% of commercial burglaries occur at office buildings, which are located primarily in the northwest and downtown areas of the city. Also, 20% of the city's reporting grids (those encompassing the commercial area in the northwest section of the city) account for 42.3% of the past year's commercial burglaries, and the 10 most frequently victimized addresses account for 10.2% of the past year's commercial burglaries. Finally, the front door is the most common point of entry (18.2%) in Los Analysis commercial burglaries, and breaking a window is the most common method of entry. Interestingly, entry with no sign of force is also frequent, accounting for 16.3% of incidents in the past year. Although this finding indicates that some businesses are left unsecured, it should be noted that no sign of force is often found at construction sites and commercial yards, where gaps in perimeter fencing make it easy for offender(s) to enter the property. As one would expect, cash is the most common type of property taken because it can be readily used and is nearly impossible to trace.

In sum, this report has provided preliminary information about the commercial burglary problem in Los Analysis over the past several years, focusing on the most recent year's activity. Additional analysis is recommended before a response to this problem is developed.

Glossary _____

Administrative crime analysis: The presentation of interesting findings of crime research and analysis based on legal, political, and practical concerns to inform audiences within police administration, city government/council, and citizens.

Buffer: An area around a feature on a map that represents a specified distance from that feature in all directions.

Call for service: A call about activity (criminal or noncriminal) to which an officer responds.

Call for service, citizen-generated: A call for service initiated by a citizen request for police response.

Call for service, officer-generated: A call for service initiated by a police officer, such as a traffic or subject stop.

Chart mapping: A method of mapping that allows the visualization of several values within a particular variable at the same time (e.g., variable = crime, values = robbery, assault, and rape).

Chart mapping, bar chart: A type of mapping in which the relative frequencies (represented by bars) of values within a variable are displayed.

Chart mapping, pie chart: A type of mapping in which the relative percentages (represented by slices of a pie) of values within a variable are displayed.

Classification, equal interval: A mapping classification for graduation that uses a statistical formula to divide the difference between the highest and lowest value into equal-sized ranges.

Classification, manual method: A mapping classification in which the ranges displayed in the legend are not determined by the values of a variable or a statistical formula but by the creator of the map. Also known as *custom* mapping.

Classification, natural breaks: A mapping classification for graduation that uses a statistical formula to identify the natural gaps in the distribution of the data.

Classification, quantile: A mapping classification for graduation in which the GIS produces categories by dividing the number of records in the database by the number of categories (selected by the user), which results in categories with equal numbers of records.

Classification, standard deviation: A mapping classification for graduation that uses mean and standard deviation of the selected variable to determine the break points of the categories, which are shown in the legend not as whole numbers but as standard deviations (e.g., +1, −1 standard deviation from the mean).

Clearance rate: The number of crimes cleared divided by the number of crimes reported. The Uniform Crime Report program acknowledges two ways in which crimes are cleared: by arrest and by exceptional means.

Clearing cases: The process of linking unsolved cases to a recently solved case in order to close them and link them to enhance the prosecution of an individual suspect.

Commission on Accreditation for Law Enforcement Agencies (CALEA): An independent accrediting authority whose purpose is to improve delivery of police service by offering a body of standards, developed by police practitioners, covering a wide range of up-to-date police topics.

Compstat: A data- and mapping-driven police management strategy implemented by the New York City Police Department in 1994. A core component of the program is the use of crime mapping software and analysis in weekly meetings of police officials to improve understanding of local crime and disorder incidents.

Computer-aided dispatch (CAD) system: A highly specialized system that uses telecommunications and geographic display to support police dispatch and response functions (as well as those of public safety agencies, such as fire and ambulance services).

Crime analysis: The systematic study of crime and disorder problems as well as other police-related issues—including sociodemographic, spatial, and temporal factors—to assist the police in criminal apprehension, crime and disorder reduction, crime prevention, and evaluation.

Crime analysis assistant/technician: An administrative support person who answers the phone, conducts data entry, makes copies, keeps files, produces simple standardized reports, and does anything else that arises administratively in a crime analysis unit.

Crime analysis process: The general way crime analysis is practiced, including data collection, data collation, analysis, dissemination of results, and incorporation of feedback from users of the information.

Crime analysis supervisor: A person with substantial crime analysis knowledge and experience who supervises a crime analysis unit.

Crime analysis unit (CAU): A police agency unit responsible for conducting crime analysis.

Crime analyst, entry-level: A person who conducts relatively routine crime analysis duties; this person is likely to be new to the field and to have had limited crime analysis experience.

Crime analyst, experienced: A person who (compared with an entry-level crime analyst) holds more responsibility and is expected to conduct more advanced crime analysis.

Crime analyst, specialty: An analyst who is hired to conduct a particular type of crime analysis. Types of specialty crime analysts include tactical crime analysts, problem analysts, sex crime analysts, school safety analysts, and GIS analysts.

Crime mapping: The process of using a geographic information system to conduct spatial analysis of crime problems and other police-related issues.

Crime pattern theory: A theory that addresses the nature of the immediate situations in which crimes occur. According to this theory, criminal events are most likely to occur in areas where the activity space of offenders overlaps with the activity space of potential victims/targets.

Crime prevention through environmental design (CPTED): A set of principles based on the theory that the physical environment can be designed in such a way as to reduce or eliminate opportunities for crime.

Crime triangle: The concept at the core of environmental criminological theory, which asserts that a crime occurs only when a motivated offender and a victim/target come together at a particular place, with the likelihood of occurrence affected by several controls (known as handlers, guardians, and managers).

Criminal investigative analysis: A type of analysis that entails the process of constructing "profiles" of offenders who have committed serious crimes. Analysts use the elements of the crimes to infer certain things about the offenders, including characteristics such as personality type, social habits, and work habits. (This kind of analysis was formerly known as *criminal profiling.*)

Cross-tabulation: A process in which frequencies are computed for one variable separated into categories of the other and vice versa.

Data modification subcycle: A subprocess within the crime analysis process in which the analyst makes changes in data collection and collation procedures based on insights gained during the analysis. The subcycle illustrates that crime analysis is not linear; rather, it moves from collection to collation to analysis, but each of these steps informs the next.

Database: A collection of data that have been organized for the purposes of retrieval, searching, and analysis through a computer.

Database, accidents/crashes: A database containing police report information about vehicle accidents, or crashes.

Database, arrests: A database containing information about arrests gleaned from arrest reports.

Database, calls for service: A database containing information about officer- and citizen-generated calls for service obtained from a computer-aided dispatch system.

Database, crime incidents: A database containing information about crime incidents (including how, when, and where the incidents occurred) gleaned from crime reports taken by police officers or other police personnel.

Database, field information: A database containing information collected by patrol officers about suspicious behavior and unique features of individuals.

Database, known offender: A database containing information on individuals arrested and convicted in a particular jurisdiction.

Database, registered sex offender: A database containing information on individuals who have been convicted of sex crimes and have registered with authorities as sex offenders.

Database, vehicle: A database (maintained by the police agency) containing information on vehicles (e.g., registration information, vehicle identification numbers, license plate numbers, make/model information) that have been stolen, recovered, or used in the commission of crimes.

Deduction: The process of examining a phenomenon by starting with general ideas about it and moving to specific facts supporting those general ideas.

Density mapping: A type of mapping in which analysts use point data to shade surfaces that are not limited to area boundaries (as is the case in graduated color mapping).

Diffusion of benefits: A phenomenon in which the elimination of a targeted problem results in the reduction of other types of problems in the area as well.

Displacement: A phenomenon in which crime problems change by shifting to other forms, times, and/or locales instead of being eliminated.

Displacement, spatial: Displacement that consists of a shift from targets in one area to those in another area.

Displacement, tactical: Displacement that consists of a shift in the tactics of the offender.

Displacement, target: Displacement that consists of shift from one victim/target to a more vulnerable one.

Displacement, temporal: Displacement that consists of a shift of activity from one time to another.

80/20 rule: A concept that comes from the common observation that 80% of some kinds of outcomes are the results of only 20% of the related causes.

Ellipse: A closed curve that is formed from two foci or points in which the sum of the distances from any point on the curve to the two foci is a constant. Crime analysts use ellipses to determine hot spots or geographic concentrations of activity in data distributions (i.e., points that are closer to one another than to any other point).

Environmental criminology: A perspective in criminology, encompassing several theories, that is different from other perspectives in that it focuses on offenders' patterns of motivation, opportunities that exist for crime, levels of protection for victims within the criminal events, and the environments in which criminal events occur.

Exact time series analysis: The examination of incidents that have exact times of occurrence, such as robbery and sexual assault.

Feature, image: In crime mapping, a vertical photograph taken from a satellite or an airplane that is digitized and placed within the appropriate coordinates in a geographic information system.

Feature, line: A real-world element that can be represented on a map by a line or set of lines.

Feature, point: A discrete location that is usually depicted on a map by a symbol or label.

Feature, polygon: A geographic area represented on a map by a multisided figure with a closed set of lines.

FI card: A small card completed by an officer in the field; designed for the collection of information on noncriminal incidents. (FI stands for *field information* or *field interview.*)

Field information: Information collected by a patrol officer when there is not enough probable cause to take a police report, but some information about the incident, the person, or a vehicle is worth collecting.

Frequency: The number (count) of all categories of a variable.

Geocoding: The process of linking an address with its map coordinates so that (a) the address can be displayed on a map and (b) the geographic information system can recognize that address in the future.

Geocoding or address match percentage: The number of addresses in the database that have been successfully geocoded or matched to the geographic data.

Geographic data system: A system that creates, maintains, and stores geographic data.

Geographic information system (GIS): A set of computer-based tools that allows the user to modify, visualize, query, and analyze geographic and tabular data.

Geographic profiling: A subset of criminal investigative analysis in which the analyst uses the geographic locations of an offender's crimes (e.g., body dump sites, encounter sites) to identify and prioritize areas the offender is likely to live.

Graduated maps: Maps in which different sizes or colors of features represent particular values of variables.

Grid mapping: A method for resolving the unequal area in which a standard-sized grid is used for analysis. The analyst begins by placing an artificial grid (generated by the GIS) on top of the area of interest and then uses graduated color shading classifications to show different levels of crime.

Hot dot: An individual associated with an unusual amount of criminal activity, either as an offender or as a victim.

Hot point: A type of hot spot in which the incidents occur at one particular place.

Hot product: A specific type of property that is repeatedly victimized or a consumer item that is particularly attractive to thieves.

Hot spot: A specific location or small area that suffers a large amount of crime.

Hot spot, clustered: A hot spot in which the incident locations group together in one or more smaller clusters.

Hot spot, dispersed: A hot spot in which the incident locations are spread throughout the hot spot area but are more concentrated than incidents in other areas.

Hot spot, tactical crime analysis: A specific location or small area where an unusual amount of criminal activity occurs that is committed by one or more offenders.

Hot target: A type of place that is frequently victimized; common hot targets include beauty salons, schools, and convenience stores.

Incident: One crime event that occurs over minutes, hours, or, in rare cases, days.

Index crime rate: The official number of index crimes in an area divided by the number of people living in the area, multiplied by 100,000.

Index crimes: The crimes tracked by the Uniform Crime Reports program: homicide, rape, robbery, aggravated assault, burglary, larceny, motor vehicle theft, and arson. Also known as *Part I crimes.*

Induction: The process of examining a phenomenon by beginning with individual facts or specific ideas about it and relating them back to general concepts.

Intelligence analysis: A type of crime analysis that supports the identification and investigation of organized crime, gangs, drug networks, prostitution rings, financial networks, or combinations of these criminal enterprises using surveillance, wire taps, informants, and participant observation (i.e., undercover work) to collect data.

Interactive crime mapping: Crime mapping conducted using simplified geographic information systems made available to novice users over the Internet.

Intern: An undergraduate or graduate student who works in a police department to obtain practical work experience and college credit.

International Association of Crime Analysts (IACA): A nonprofit member organization formed in 1990 to help crime analysts around the world improve their skills and make valuable contacts, to help law enforcement agencies make the best use of crime analysis, and to advocate for standards of performance and technique within the profession of crime analysis.

Internet: A global network that connects millions of computers. (The terms *Internet* and *World Wide Web* are generally used interchangeably, although technically not everything on the Internet is also on the Web.) Independent computers connect to the Internet through a wide range of software applications (e.g., Netscape, Explorer).

Intranet: A network that functions much like the Internet but connects only a limited number of users, usually people associated with a particular organization.

Investigative lead: A person who is a potential suspect for a crime.

Known offender: A person who has been convicted, *not just arrested,* of any crime other than a sex offense.

Legend: An element of a map in which the map's tabular and geographic data sources are displayed and the symbols used to represent each data source are indicated.

Matrix: A set of rows and columns containing data that can be manipulated for analysis.

Median: The value within a data distribution at which 50% of the data are higher and 50% are lower.

Mention: A person mentioned in a police report who might be a possible investigative lead or suspect in the crime.

Mode: The most frequent value within a data distribution.

Modus operandi (MO): The method of the crime; that is, the key elements of the crime incident itself, such as what the crime entailed and how, where, and when the crime was committed. (*Modus operandi* is a Latin term meaning literally "method of procedure.")

North directional: The element on a map that indicates the geographic orientation of the map.

Operational analysis: The examination of such police procedures as deployment and staffing or redistricting of beats or precincts.

Pattern: A group of crime events that are similar in nature and occur over several days, weeks, or months.

Pattern finalization: The process of refining the list of cases thought to be related by determining which cases have key characteristics in common.

Pattern identification, ad hoc linking: The linking of cases by memory in the course of the analyst's everyday work.

Pattern identification, query method: The linking of cases through an iterative process in which the analyst manipulates, searches, and sorts characteristics of crimes using a database matrix.

Pattern identification, Trend Hunter method: The linking of cases through a process in which various characteristics of crimes are weighted and the weights summed up for each case. This process highlights cases that meet a particular threshold indicating they have similar characteristics.

Percentage: The proportion of the count of one category by the count of all categories of a variable, multiplied by 100.

Percentage change: The amount of relative increase or decrease between two values over two time periods; expressed as a proportion of the value at the first time period (Time 1), or the difference between a measurement at Time 1 and a measurement at Time 2, divided by the measurement at Time 1, and then multiplied by 100 (to arrive at a percentage).

Percentile: A value above and below which a certain percentage of cases lie.

Persons crime: Crime in which a person is the target, such as robbery, sexual assault, indecent exposure, public sexual indecency, and kidnapping.

Primary data: Data collected specifically for the purposes of the analysis at hand.

Primary data collection: The collection of information directly from individuals or locations for purposes of the analysis at hand through methods such as interviews, surveys (individual and focus group), and observation.

Principal case: The case within a pattern that best represents the characteristics of the pattern and is used to determine the other key cases in the pattern.

Problem: A set of related crime activities or other harmful events that occur over several months, seasons, or years and that the public expects the police to address.

Problem analysis: The process through which a police agency employs formal criminal justice theory, research methods, and comprehensive data collection and analysis procedures in a systematic way to conduct in-depth examination of crime and disorder problems and develop informed responses to those problems.

Problem-oriented policing: A systematic approach to crime reduction in which problems are identified, analyzed, and addressed, and the resulting efforts evaluated.

Property crime: Crime in which property is the target, such as residential and commercial burglary, criminal trespass, and criminal damage.

Qualitative data and methods: Nonnumerical data and the methods used to examine them (e.g., field research, content analysis). Crime analysts use qualitative data and methods to discover the underlying meanings and patterns of relationships.

Quantitative data and methods: Numerical or categorical data and the methods used to examine them (e.g., statistical analysis).

Rate: A statistic that uses one variable (the denominator) to determine the relative difference between values of another variable (the numerator).

Rational choice theory: A theory that asserts that all people (e.g., offenders) make choices about the actions they take (e.g., committing crimes) based on the opportunities and rewards they anticipate receiving as a result. This theory suggests that, if given a chance, or the right "opportunity," any person will commit a crime.

Records management system (RMS): A data entry and storage system designed especially for police records.

Recovery rate: The percentage of vehicles that have been stolen in a jurisdiction and subsequently recovered.

Repeat victimization: The recurrence of crime in the same places and/or against the same people.

Routine activities theory: A theory that focuses on how opportunities for crime change based on changes in behavior on a societal level.

Scale bar: An element in a map that illustrates the distance units used in the map.

Search radius: In density mapping, the distance set by the user that determines the breadth of the calculations of concentration of incidents.

Secondary data: Data that have been collected previously; such data are typically housed in electronic databases.

Series: A run of similar crimes committed by the same individual(s) against one or various victims or targets.

Sex offender: A person who has been convicted, *not just arrested,* of a sex offense.

Single-symbol maps: Maps in which individual, uniform symbols represent features such as the locations of stores, streets or roads, or states.

Situational crime prevention: A practice initiated in England in the 1980s based on the concepts of environmental criminology, which addresses why crime occurs in specific settings and seeks solutions that reflect the nature of those settings.

Sociodemographic information: Information on the personal characteristics of individuals and groups, such as sex, race, income, age, and education.

Software, database management (DBMS): Software that allows the user to enter and store data in a database and to modify and extract information from a database.

Software, geographic information system (GIS): Software that allows the user to modify, visualize, query, and analyze geographic and tabular data.

Software, graphics: Software that allows the user to create and manipulate pictures and images.

Software, presentation: Software that allows the user to create slide shows to enhance the presentation of information.

Software, publishing: Software that allows the user to create professional-looking printed or electronic products such as reports, brochures, and newsletters.

Software, spreadsheet: Software that allows the user to create and change spreadsheets easily.

Software, statistical: Software that accesses databases obtained from spreadsheets and DBMS and facilitates data entry. The core purposes of statistical software are statistical computation and data manipulation, and these applications are designed to handle large numbers of records.

Software, word processing: Software that primarily supports the creation and manipulation of text, but may also include functionality for incorporating tables, charts, and pictures in a document.

Spreadsheet: A table that displays information in rows and columns of cells.

Spree: A run of crime activity characterized by such high frequency that the activity appears almost continuous.

Standard deviation: In simple terms, the standardized average variation of the values from the mean. The standard deviation indicates the shape of a data distribution.

Strategic crime analysis: The study of crime problems and other police-related issues to determine long-term patterns of activity as well as to evaluate police responses and organizational procedures.

Suspect: A person who was seen committing a crime or about whom there is enough evidence to "suspect" he or she committed the crime.

Tabular data: Data that describe events that are not inherently geographic but that may contain geographic variables.

Tactical crime analysis: The study of recent criminal incidents and potential criminal activity through the examination of characteristics such as how, when, and where the activity has occurred to assist in pattern development, investigative lead and suspect identification, and case clearance.

Temporal analysis: The analysis of data in relation to units of time. Also known as *time series analysis.*

Volunteer: A person who works for a police department without pay. Many volunteers are students or retired persons.

Weighted time span analysis: Analysis of time span data in which each time span is assigned a value of 1 and each hour within the time span is a proportion of the time span.

References _____

Austin, R., Cooper, G., Gagnon, D., Hodges, J., Martensen, K., & O'Neal, M. (1973). *Police crime analysis unit handbook.* Washington, DC: U.S. Department of Justice, National Institute of Law Enforcement and Criminal Justice.

Bair, S., Boba, R., Fritz, N., Helms, D., & Hick, S. (Eds.). (2002). *Advanced crime mapping topics: Results of the First Invitational Advanced Crime Mapping Topics Symposium.* Denver, CO: National Law Enforcement Corrections Technology Center.

Bair Software. (1999). *ATAC for analysts: Series breaking.* Highlands Ranch, CO: Author.

Bair Software. (2004). *ATAC workbook.* Highlands Ranch, CO: Author.

Bender, C. F., Cox, L. A., & Chappell, G. A. (1976). *Application of pattern recognition techniques to crime analysis.* Washington, DC: U.S. Energy Research and Development Administration.

Block, R. C., Dabdoub, M., & Fregly, S. (Eds.). (1995). *Crime analysis through computer mapping.* Washington, DC: Police Executive Research Forum.

Boba, R. (1999). Using the Internet to disseminate crime information. *Law Enforcement Bulletin, 68*(10), 6–9.

Boba, R. (2001). *Introductory guide to crime analysis and mapping.* Washington, DC: U.S. Department of Justice, Office of Community Oriented Policing Services.

Boba, R. (2003). *Problem analysis in policing.* Washington, DC: Police Foundation.

Boba, R., & Price, J. (2002). Integrating systematic research and analysis into police practice. In S. Bair, R. Boba, N. Fritz, D. Helms, & S. Hick (Eds.), *Advanced crime mapping topics: Results of the First Invitational Advanced Crime Mapping Topics Symposium* (pp. 79–82). Denver, CO: National Law Enforcement Corrections Technology Center.

Booth, W. L. (1979). Management function of a crime analysis unit. *Law and Order, 27*(5), 28, 30–33.

Brantingham, P. J., & Brantingham, P. L. (1981). *Environmental criminology.* Beverly Hills, CA: Sage.

Brantingham, P. L., & Brantingham, P. J. (1990). Situational crime prevention in practice. *Canadian Journal of Criminology, 32,* 17–40.

Center for Problem-Oriented Policing. (2004). *Mission of the Center for Problem-Oriented Policing.* Retrieved September 30, 2004, from http://www.popcenter.org/aboutCPOP.html

Chang, S. K., Simms, W. H., Makres, C. M., & Bodnar, A. (1979). *Crime analysis system support: Descriptive report of manual and automated crime analysis functions.* Washington, DC: National Criminal Justice Information and Statistics Service.

Clarke, R. V. (1980). "Situational" crime prevention: Theory and practice. *British Journal of Criminology, 20,* 136–147.

Clarke, R. V. (1983). Situational crime prevention: Its theoretical basis and practical scope. In M. Tonry & N. Morris (Eds.), *Crime and justice: An annual review of research* (Vol. 4, pp. 225–256). Chicago: University of Chicago Press.

Clarke, R. V. (Ed.). (1992). *Situational crime prevention: Successful case studies.* Albany, NY: Harrow & Heston.

Clarke, R. V. (1999). *Hot products: Understanding, anticipating, and reducing demand for stolen goods* (Police Research Series Paper 112). London: Home Office, Research, Development and Statistics Directorate, Policing and Reducing Crime Unit.

Clarke, R. V., & Eck, J. (2003). *Become a problem-solving crime analyst in 55 small steps.* London: Jill Dando Institute of Crime Science.

Clarke, R. V., & Weisburd, D. (1994). Diffusion of crime control benefits: Observations on the reverse of displacement. In R. V. Clarke (Ed.), *Crime prevention studies* (Vol. 2, pp. 165–183). Monsey, NY: Criminal Justice Press.

Cohen, M., & Felson, M. (1979). Social change and crime rate trends: A routine activities approach. *American Sociological Review, 44,* 588–608.

Commission on Accreditation for Law Enforcement Agencies. (2004). *About CALEA.* Retrieved March 2, 2005, from http://www.calea.org/newweb/AboutUs/Aboutus.htm

Cornish, D. B., & Clarke, R. V. (1986). *The reasoning criminal.* New York: Springer-Verlag.

Cornish, D. B., & Clarke, R. V. (2003). Opportunities, precipitators, and criminal decisions: A reply to Wortley's critique of situational crime prevention. In M. J. Smith & D. B. Cornish (Eds.), *Theory for practice in situational crime prevention* (pp. 41–96). Monsey, NY: Criminal Justice Press.

Cox, L. A., Kolender, W. B., Bender, C. F., & McQueeney, J. A. (1977). Crime analysis and manpower allocation through computer pattern recognition. *Police Chief, 44*(10), 40–42, 44–46.

Crime Mapping and Analysis Program. (2003). *Tactical crime analysis: Trend and pattern detection (Matrix analysis-trend sifting).* Paper presented at the National Law Enforcement and Corrections Technology Center, Denver.

Crime Mapping and Analysis Program. (2004). [Statement]. Retrieved October 1, 2004, from http://www.nlectc.org/cmap

Emig, M., Heck, R., & Kravitz, M. (1980). *Crime analysis: A selected bibliography.* Washington, DC: U.S. National Criminal Justice Reference Service.

Farrell, G., & Pease, K. (1993). *Once bitten, twice bitten: Repeat victimisation and its implications for crime prevention* (Crime Prevention Unit Series Paper 46). London: Home Office, Police Research Group.

Farrell, G., Sousa, W., & Weisel, D. (2002). The time-window effect in the measurement of repeat victimization: A methodology for its examination, and an empirical study. In N. Tilley (Ed.), *Analysis for crime prevention* (pp. 15–27). Monsey, NY: Criminal Justice Press.

Federal Bureau of Investigation. (2003). *Crime in the United States 2002.* Washington, DC: U.S. Department of Justice.

Felson, M., & Clarke, R. V. (1998). *Opportunity makes the thief: Practical theory for crime prevention* (Police Research Series Paper 98). London: Home Office, Research, Development and Statistics Directorate, Policing and Reducing Crime Unit.

Goldstein, H. (1979). Improving policing: A problem oriented approach. *Crime & Delinquency, 24,* 236–258.

Goldstein, H. (1990). *Problem-oriented policing.* New York: McGraw-Hill.

Gottlieb, S., Arenberg, S., & Singh, R. (1994). *Crime analysis: From first report to final arrest.* Montclair, CA: Alpha.

Grassie, R. P., Waymire, R. V., Burrows, J. W., Anderson, C. L. R., & Wallace, W. D. (1977). *Integrated Criminal Apprehension Program: Crime analysis—executive manual.* Washington, DC: U.S. Department of Justice, Law Enforcement Assistance Administration.

Groff, E. R., & La Vigne, N. G. (2002). Forecasting the future of predictive crime mapping. In N. Tilley (Ed.), *Analysis for crime prevention* (pp. 29–58). Monsey, NY: Criminal Justice Press.

Harries, K. D. (1980). *Crime and the environment.* Springfield, IL: Charles C Thomas.

Hesseling, R. (1994). Displacement: A review of the empirical literature. In R. V. Clarke (Ed.), *Crime prevention studies* (Vol. 3, pp. 197–230). Monsey, NY: Criminal Justice Press.

LeBeau, J. L. (1987). The methods and measures of centrography and the spatial dynamics of rape. *Journal of Quantitative Criminology, 3,* 125–141.

Mamalian, C. A., & La Vigne, N. G. (1999). *Research preview: The use of computerized crime mapping by law enforcement: Survey results.* Washington, DC: U.S. Department of Justice, National Institute of Justice.

Mapping and Analysis for Public Safety. (2004). *About MAPS.* Retrieved October 1, 2004, from http://www.ojp.usdoj.gov/nij/maps

Marshall, C. W. (1977). *Application of time series methodology to crime analysis.* Washington, DC: U.S. Department of Justice, Law Enforcement Assistance Administration.

Metropolitan Police Service. (2004). *Metropolitan Police Service: Timeline 1829–1849.* Retrieved September 30, 2004, from http://www.met.police.uk/history/timeline1829-1849.htm

National Criminal Intelligence Service. (2000). *The national intelligence model.* London: Author.

Office of Community Oriented Policing Services. (2004). [Statement]. Retrieved October 8, 2004, from http://www.cops.usdoj.gov

O'Shea, T., & Nicholls, K. (2003). *Crime analysis in America: Findings and recommendations.* Washington, DC: U.S. Department of Justice, Office of Community Oriented Policing Services.

Pease, K. (1998). *Repeat victimisation: Taking stock* (Crime Detection and Prevention Series Paper 90). London: Home Office, Police Research Group.

Pease, K., & Laycock, G. (1996). *Revictimization: Reducing the heat on hot victims.* Washington, DC: U.S. Department of Justice, National Institute of Justice.

Petersen, M. (1994). *Applications in criminal analysis.* Westport, CT: Praeger.

Police Foundation. (2003a). *Advanced problem analysis, crime analysis, and crime mapping training.* Washington, DC: Author.

Police Foundation. (2003b). *User's guide to crime mapping software.* Washington, DC: Author.

Police Foundation crime mapping laboratory: An overview. (2003). *Crime Mapping News, 5*(4), 1.

Pomrenke, N. E. (1969). *Police selection, training and education action grant programs in 1969: State law enforcement plans submitted under Title I, Omnibus Crime Control and Safe Streets Act of 1968–1969 state plan analysis.* Washington, DC: National Sheriffs' Association.

Practitioner recommendations for the role of analysts in the advancement of problem analysis. (2003). *Crime Mapping News, 5*(4), 8–9.

Ratcliffe, J. H. (2002). Aoristic signatures and the spatio-temporal analysis of high-volume crime patterns. *Journal of Quantitative Criminology, 18,* 23–43.

Ratcliffe, J. H. (2004). The hotspot matrix: A framework for the spatio-temporal targeting of crime reduction. *Police Practice and Research, 5*(1), 5–23.

Rengert, G., & Wasilchick, J. (1985). *Suburban burglary: A time and a place for everything.* Springfield, IL: Charles C Thomas.

Rossmo, D. K. (2000). *Geographic profiling.* Boca Raton, FL: CRC.

Sampson, R. (2003). *Crime analysis in the United States: What it's accomplished, where it's going.* Paper presented at the annual training meeting of the International Association of Crime Analysts, Kansas City, MO.

Schmerler, K., & Velasco, M. (2002). Primary data collection: A problem-solving necessity. *Crime Mapping News, 4*(2), 4–8.

Scott, M. (2000). *Problem-oriented policing: Reflections on the first 20 years.* Washington, DC: U.S. Department of Justice, Office of Community Oriented Policing Services.

Sherman, L. W., Gartin, P. R., & Buerger, M. E. (1989). Hot spots of predatory crime: Routine activities and the criminology of place. *Criminology, 27,* 27–55.

Taxman, F. S., & McEwen, T. (1997). Using geographical tools with interagency work groups to develop and implement crime control strategies. In D. Weisburd & T. McEwen (Eds.), *Crime mapping and crime prevention* (pp. 83–111). Monsey, NY: Criminal Justice Press.

Tempe Police Department, Crime Analysis Unit. (2003). *Tactical analysis procedures.* Tempe, AZ: Author.

Theodore, J. (2001). Crime mapping goes Hollywood: CBS's *The District* demonstrates crime mapping to millions of TV viewers. *Crime Mapping News, 3*(3), 7.

U.S. Bureau of Justice Statistics. (1999). *Law enforcement management and administrative statistics, 1997.* Washington, DC: U.S. Department of Justice.

U.S. Congress. (1990). *Omnibus Crime Control and Safe Streets Act of 1968 and Amendments to 1990.* Washington, DC: Author.

Velasco, M., & Boba, R. (2000). Tactical crime analysis and geographic information systems: Concepts and examples. *Crime Mapping News, 2*(2), 1–4.

Velasco, M., Griffin, J., & Boba, R. (2001). *Crime analysis and mapping product templates.* Washington, DC: U.S. Department of Justice, Office of Community Oriented Policing Services.

Vellani, K. H., Nahoun, J. (2001). *Applied crime analysis.* Boston: Butterworth-Heinemann.

Wartell, J., & McEwen, T. (2001). *Privacy in the information age: A guide for sharing crime maps and spatial data.* Washington, DC: U.S. Department of Justice, National Institute of Justice.

Weisburd, D., & Lum, C. (2001). *Translating research into practice: Reflections on the diffusion of crime mapping innovation.* Keynote address (delivered by D. Weisburd) at the Fifth Annual International Crime Mapping Research Conference, Dallas, TX.

Weisburd, D., Mastrofski, S. D., McNally, A. M., Greenspan, R., & Willis, J. J. (2003). Reforming to preserve: Compstat and strategic problem solving in American policing. *Criminology and Public Policy, 2,* 421–456.

Weisburd, D., & McEwen, T. (1997). Crime mapping and crime prevention. In D. Weisburd & T. McEwen (Eds.), *Crime mapping and crime prevention* (pp. 1–26). Monsey, NY: Criminal Justice Press.

Wilson O. W. (1957). *Police planning* (2nd ed.). Springfield, IL: Charles C Thomas.

Wilson, O. W., & McLaren, R. C. (1977). *Police administration* (4th ed.). New York: McGraw-Hill.

Index

Page references followed by *fig* indicates an illustrated figure; followed by *t* indicates a table.

About the Author _____

Rachel Boba received her Ph.D. in sociology from Arizona State University in 1996. She is currently Assistant Professor in the Criminology and Criminal Justice Program at Florida Atlantic University. She formerly served as the Director of the Crime Mapping Laboratory at the Police Foundation and as a Faculty Associate at the University of Maryland at College Park. She has also taught sociology at Arizona State University and has worked as a Crime Analyst for the Tempe (Arizona) Police Department.